Jan Smuts

Jan Smuts: portrait by JK de Vries, 1947. Museum Africa, Johannesburg

Jan Smuts

Unafraid of Greatness

Richard Steyn

Jonathan Ball Publishers

Johannesburg & Cape Town

Originally published in South Africa in 2015 by
JONATHAN BALL PUBLISHERS
A division of Media24 Limited
P O Box 33977
Jeppestown
2043

Reprinted once in 2015

This limited edition printed twice in 2015 and once in 2016

ISBN 978-1-86842-694-2
Ebook 978-1-86842-695-9

*Every effort has been made to trace copyright holders and to obtain their permission for the use of
copyright material. The publishers apologise for any errors or omissions and would be grateful to
be notified of any corrections that should be incorporated in future editions of this book.*

Twitter: http://www.twitter.com/JonathanBallPub
Facebook: http://www.facebook.com/pages/Jonathan-Ball-Publishers/298034457992
Blog: http://jonathanball.bookslive.co.za/

Cover design by publicide
Design and typesetting by Triple M Design, Johannesburg
Set in 10,5pt/15pt ITC Berkeley Oldstyle Std

Printed by *paarlmedia*, a division of Novus Holdings

... be not afraid of greatness.
Some are born great, some achieve greatness,
and some have greatness thrust upon 'em.

Twelfth Night
William Shakespeare

To Elizabeth,
and our children,
and their children.

Contents

PREFACE

When I let slip to a friend, an academic of renown, that I had always been fascinated by Jan Smuts and was contemplating a new study of him because so few young people seem aware of his influence on the country we live in, he replied that I could bury myself in research for the next few years and produce a thick tome that would gather dust on shelves, or write a shorter and less daunting book that busy people like himself might be tempted to read. I have tried to follow his advice.

For a relatively young nation, remote from the centres of world affairs, South Africa has thrown up a remarkable assortment of exceptional, larger-than-life characters – some admirable, others much less so. They are the products of a turbulent history of some 350 years of wars, both tribal and ethnic, racial confrontations, fights over resources, cultural clashes, ideological arguments, political accommodations and spectacular reconciliations. Two of them – Smuts and Nelson Mandela – added lustre, in the eyes of the world, to the country they led. Two other outstanding figures of the twentieth century – Winston Churchill and Mahatma Gandhi – also left their imprint here.

If I let my imagination run away with me, I sometimes picture these four men gathered together at a celestial dinner-table, looking down on South Africa and discussing their contributions to its history. On the menu, besides ambrosia and nectar – and champagne for Churchill – there would have to be slices of humble pie, for some of their expectations turned out much differently from what they had expected and so confidently predicted. In most cases, the world stubbornly refused to be re-shaped in ways that they had hoped. The dinner would have ended early, no doubt. Churchill might have wished to ramble on into the early hours of next morning but the more self-denying Smuts, Gandhi and Mandela would have been in bed by ten.

In reviewing a recent book by Doris Kearns Goodwin, author of *Lincoln*, the American critic Nicholas Lemann wrote that Goodwin's kind of history was different from that produced by most academic scholars. He described it as popular history – 'a sort of journalism about the past' in which the story and characters are the key elements and the argument is secondary. That is precisely the kind of book I have tried to write.

So, a work of journalism which recounts and re-examines the life and times of the phenomenally gifted, tenacious and always controversial Jan Christian Smuts. In writing it, I have stood on the shoulders of many people who either knew Smuts personally or wrote books about him. From these many and varied sources, I have attempted to distil, for a new audience, the essence of an extraordinary individual, in his time more famous than his country, whose influence may still be felt for good or ill in modern post-colonial, post-apartheid South Africa. My debt to historians such as Sir Keith Hancock, Kenneth Ingham, FS Crafford, Piet Beukes, Piet Meiring and others is immense, and I have acknowledged their works at the end of the book as fully as I can.

◆

What, you may well ask, is the relevance of Jan Smuts' life and example to South Africans today? First and foremost, I would suggest, is his lifelong – indeed overlong – dedication to public service. Throughout his life, he deployed his talents not to amuse or enrich himself – though he was not poor – but in the service of his countrymen and women. As a politician, he worked harder than anyone else and, unlike many modern leaders, never shied away from taking tough decisions. As a young government official he was prepared to court unpopularity in his drive to combat cronyism and corruption. Unlike some of those before and after him, he let it be understood that public resources were not there to be plundered by politicians or civil servants. In his private life, he was frugal in his habits, faithful to his spiritual beliefs, and always extremely fit. He grew up in, and stood out in, a society much tougher and in many ways more demanding than the one we live in today.

William Hazlitt could have been describing Smuts when he wrote that man is an intellectual animal and an everlasting contradiction to himself: 'His senses centre in himself, his ideas reach to the ends of the universe; so that he is torn in pieces between the two, without a possibility of its ever being otherwise.'[1] There were indeed many contradictions in the character of Smuts, most notably his simultaneous belief in racial segregation and human rights, the two most conflicting moral causes in the twentieth century.

This book has been written in two parts. The first is a straightforward account of Smuts's long and eventful life; the second is an attempt to portray him in all his many dimensions – his personality, his home and family, relationships with women, his spiritual life and the philosophy of holism, his interest in matters ecological, the matter of the black franchise, and his experiences as a world statesman. I have assumed little or no knowledge of Smuts on the part of new readers, and have striven to make his intellectual ideas and philosophising understandable to those who might have been intimidated by some earlier books about him. My hope is to rekindle an awareness of the role played by this remarkable Afrikaner in the history of our and other countries.

Johannesburg, 2015

Author's Note

As has often been said, South Africa is a terminological minefield. In Smuts's time, the law and custom distinguished between Europeans (or Whites), Coloureds (mixed race), Asiatics (or Indians) and Natives. The term 'native' – as in the South African Native National Congress – did not have the pejorative meaning it has acquired today. In this book, I have used the racial descriptions applicable at the time: so the words 'native', 'black' and 'African' are used interchangeably.

Prologue

In Parliament Square in London, there are eleven statues. Four of them are of non-Britons, and two of those – Jan Smuts and Nelson Mandela – are South African. The third is America's Abraham Lincoln and the recently added fourth, Mahatma Gandhi. While Mandela, Lincoln and Gandhi have been the subjects of many contemporary articles, books and films, Smuts, by contrast, has been allowed to drift into obscurity. Yet in his time, South Africa's warrior-leader and international statesman was a figure of comparable stature and renown.

'In his time' is the key phrase, because Smuts's views on empire and race, forged in the nineteenth century and typical of most of his contemporaries, have put him beyond the pale in modern, majority-ruled South Africa. As a founding father and the architect of a new country more than a century ago, his preoccupation was the welding of white Afrikaners and English-speakers into a united nation, under the shelter of an imperial umbrella. Smuts and his fellow whites, settled in precarious isolation at the foot of Africa, were confronted by a 'native problem' that seemed insoluble. While insistent that South Africa was a unitary country, full of promise, in which black and white people had no option but to work out their future together, he thought – mistakenly – that the 'native question' could be kept separate from politics. Smuts was a firm believer in the inevitability of gradual change in biological, social and political evolution. South Africans, he asserted repeatedly, should resolve their political, economic and cultural differences in an atmosphere of hope rather than fear. Political solutions would come only in the fullness of time.

If there is one trait common to the four figures in Parliament Square which has won them the affection and respect of the British people, it is that highest of political virtues – magnanimity. Lincoln's generosity of spirit towards his political rivals, and America's slaves, was the key to his greatness as a human being and president. Gandhi's humanity is legendary, while Mandela's great-heartedness in reaching out to his captors and political foes after 27 years of incarceration will forever be held up as an example to mankind. And Smuts too, once a fiery opponent of the British, was so inspired by the generosity of spirit displayed by Henry Campbell-Bannerman in granting self-government to the defeated Boers that he devoted the rest of his life to spreading 'the contagion of magnanimity' among South Africans and Britons, Afrikaners and English-speakers, and warring nations the world over.

Jan Smuts was an Afrikaner of extraordinary intellect, versatility and resilience. A scholar, lawyer, guerrilla leader, military commander, philosopher, scientist, politician and international statesman, his uniqueness as a human being lay in his deep spirituality, his physical bravery, his love of nature, the spartan quality of his personal life, and the pleasure he derived from simple things. Above all, he was a seeker: a lifelong searcher after religious truth and those eternal values that could be applied to politics and other spheres of human endeavour. Like Job, his faith was sorely tested throughout a tumultuous, 80-year-long life marred by personal tragedy, inner struggle and despair, and the bitter enmity of many Afrikaners who had once revered him.

In a recent tribute in a British legal journal, Sir Louis Blom-Cooper QC wrote that any proper understanding of Jan Smuts's approach to the political and human rights of black people has to be contrasted with the position which faced Nelson Mandela in the latter years of the last century.[2] Smuts chose to sidestep the problem, while Mandela, in different circumstances, confronted it head on and was not distracted by other issues. In his inspiring leadership of the ANC, Mandela 'focused starkly on the home front'. Smuts, on the other hand, although caught up initially in his country's politics, found himself drawn ever more deeply into international affairs, where his counsel was sought by kings and commoners alike.

While serving as South Africa's minister of defence during World War I, Smuts became a member of Britain's war cabinet and helped found the Royal Air Force; he drafted the outlines of British policy at the Peace Conference at Versailles and played a key part in setting up the League of Nations; he also proposed the establishment of the British Commonwealth and laid the foundation for the Statute of Westminster which brought political emancipation to the Dominions of Canada, Australia, New Zealand and South Africa. During the course of World War II, he paid nine visits to Europe and the Middle East to confer with Allied leaders and military commanders. Winston Churchill, a like-minded warrior, wanted to appoint him as acting prime minister during his (Churchill's) absence from Britain in 1943, declaring 'my faith in Smuts is unbreakable'.[3] He was the only man to attend the Peace Conferences that ended both World Wars, and after World War II he drew up the Preamble to the Charter of the United Nations. As Alan Paton, who understood him better than most, reflected, 'Even the great thought that he was great.'[4]

Smuts was not without flaws and weaknesses. He lacked the patience and warmth of his great comrade Louis Botha, and mostly kept aloof from the common man, for whom a contemporary noted he had no deep affection and probably little real sympathy, even though he felt deeply for humanity as a whole.[5] He also had such confidence in his own judgement that once his brilliant mind had come up with a rational answer to any problem, he could not always understand why others didn't see matters in the same way. Over time, he allowed too much distance to grow between himself and his fellow Afrikaans-speakers. He had an authoritarian streak, and could be ruthless when he decided that circumstances required it.

But if Smuts lacked the compassion and forbearance of a Lincoln or a Mandela, his other spiritual, intellectual, and moral qualities made him an exceptional human being. As Paton wrote, 'he had the fearlessness which comes from nature as a rare and splendid gift'.[6] His courage, together with his intellect and energy, made him one of the pioneering figures of the twentieth century, while his personal dynamism and idealism inspired an uncommon degree of loyalty among those who followed him, or admired him from afar.

This then is the man whom the current generation of South Africans has chosen to ignore or forget. Yet if Ralph Waldo Emerson is correct in saying 'there is properly no history; only biography',[7] it is time to revisit our history through the life and times of one of this country's finest sons, of whom Churchill said: 'He did not belong to any single state or nation. He *fought* for his own country, he *thought* for the whole world.'[8]

PART ONE

Life and Times

Virtue is like a rich stone, best plain set.
Francis Bacon

The gun carriage bearing Smuts's coffin passes through downtown Johannesburg. INPRA

CHAPTER 1

'Totsiens, Oubaas'

A light has gone out in the world of free men.
Clement Atlee

September 11 (or 9/11) is a day of the year etched indelibly into the history of modern times. Back in 1950, it was the day on which General Smuts, the warrior-politician and statesman at the heart of South Africa's affairs for as long as anyone could remember, died of a heart attack at his home in Irene, near Pretoria. He was 80 years old and his passing was, as one newspaper put it, 'the toppling of an oak tree under which we have sheltered for generations'.[1]

Less than 20 kilometres from Irene, Smuts's political nemesis – South Africa's prime minister, Dr DF Malan – had come to the end of a 90-minute address to his National Party congress in the Pretoria City Hall. According to the *Rand Daily Mail*'s parliamentary correspondent, after the Prime Minister had read a note handed to him, he sat with his head in his hands for almost a minute. Manifestly upset, he had to be helped to the microphone, where he told his 1 000-strong audience that General Smuts, 'a great figure of his time'[2] had just died. He asked delegates to stand in silence as a mark of respect, and then to adjourn. A cabinet minister told the reporter that he had never seen Malan so affected.

As the news flashed around the country, South Africans of all races began, in their own ways, to absorb the knowledge that the 'Oubaas', the man who had single-handedly dominated the country's political life for almost half a century, was no more. Radio programmes were interrupted and in cities and towns across South Africa meetings, public shows and private entertainments were cut short. A day later, leading the country in paying homage to a man with whom he had grown up as a small boy and been friends with as a student, but who had since become a bitter political enemy, Malan went on national radio to deliver an awkwardly worded and carefully nuanced tribute: 'General Smuts was undoubtedly one of South Africa's greatest and most renowned sons,' the Prime Minister intoned. 'In his own person he combined the most outstanding gifts of intellectual power, capability of expression, strength of will and energy, coupled with a remarkable physical endurance, even in old age – features which in their entirety constituted that strong personality which never failed to impress.'[3]

'Both in the public life of our own country and in the wider field of international relations,' the Prime Minister continued, 'his departure will leave an emptiness which it will not be possible to fill.' South Africa's wealth did not lie in gold and diamonds, he added, but in the production of men and women who by their personal qualities and deeds were able to leave deep footprints in the sands of time, and on their country's history. One of those was Smuts – a 'great South African'.

Over in Britain, where Smuts had enjoyed heroic status because of his wartime activities, the praise was more heartfelt. Prime Minister Clement Attlee described him as having the 'true simplicity of heart which marks great men for what they are'.[4] A visibly emotional Sir Winston Churchill, leader of the opposition, told Parliament that 'in all the numerous fields in which he shone – warrior, statesman, philosopher, philanthropist – Jan Smuts commands in his majestic career the admiration of all. There is no personal tragedy,' Churchill continued, 'in the close of so long and complete a life as this. But his friends who are left behind to face the unending problems and perils of human existence feel an overpowering sense of impoverishment and irreparable loss. This sense is also the measure of the gratitude with which we and lovers of freedom and civilisation in every land salute his memory.'[5]

Not all South Africans remembered the 'Oubaas' with as much affection. *Die Transvaler*, a mouthpiece of Afrikaner nationalism, after noting that Smuts's spirit had been so restless, his energy so consuming, his body so nervously strung with impetuosity that he never knew old age or arrived at the outspan of rest and quiet contemplation, described his life in terms of a tragic failure: 'The outstanding tragedy was that he stood entirely apart from the struggle and emergence of his own people.' The newspaper felt obliged to concede, however, that even if their fellow-Afrikaner had not served his own people, he had served the world 'with distinction'.[6]

◆

As was usual in the racially divided South Africa of the mid-twentieth century, opinions of Smuts differed from race to race and even within racial groups. Spokesmen for the 'coloured' and Asian communities paid public tribute to the departed statesman. Many coloured people, especially those who had served in the armed forces, looked upon him with reverence. Yet there were many more who either kept their opinions to themselves or were not asked to express them. Dr JS Moroka, president-general of the African National Congress, said that 'in South Africa we did not always see eye to eye on those issues which we felt affected our interests and many were the bitter struggles we had. But we have been irresistibly and continuously conscious of the giant stature of his mind and soul.'[7] In Natal, Pika Zulu, grandson of Shaka's brother Mpande, rose from a sick-bed to express his regret at the great loss suffered by 'the white people of South Africa' in the death of General Smuts, a man 'our people regarded as a true and honoured friend'.[8]

None of the leading newspapers invited any African leaders to comment on Smuts's passing. The *Rand Daily Mail* commented editorially that in all the tributes to Smuts on national radio, no one had been invited to speak on behalf of South Africa's 8 million 'natives'. The obvious person to have spoken, the newspaper suggested tentatively, would have been a member of the Native Representative Council, such as Mrs Margaret Ballinger.[9]

◆

The Malan government offered the Smuts family a state funeral, but the offer was declined in favour of a military ceremony. On Friday, 15 September – a day of national mourning – crowds stood in respectful silence along the streets of Pretoria as Smuts's cortege slowly made its way to the Groote Kerk, where Ds Johan Reyneke and the Revd JB Webb conducted the bilingual funeral service. A reporter noted that nearly every other person in the crowd seemed to have a camera with them.

Smuts's coffin, lashed to an open gun carriage, was followed by a lone charger, draped in black, with riding boots and spurs reversed in the stirrups. Atop the casket was a wreath of Cape heather from an ailing Isie Smuts – not well enough to attend the funeral – which carried the simple inscription 'Totsiens, Pappa.'

Ds Reyneke used the solemn occasion to plead with the people of 'our beloved fatherland' for a new spirit of peacefulness and tolerance among all races. The relationship between white and black is getting worse, he observed, and that between whites becoming bitterer. If we are united in mourning in death, does God not wish us to feel like this in life, he asked. 'Jan Christiaan Smuts,' he concluded, 'you had a place among the greatest of the world; you had a place among the humblest of individuals … We bid you farewell, "Oubaas".'[10]

From the Groote Kerk, the funeral procession led by bands of the Defence Force and Air Force passed by the statue of Paul Kruger on its way to the railway station, where a 19-gun salute reverberated from a hillside nearby. As the gunfire and strains of the Last Post died away, eight Air Force Spitfires swooped low over the building and the special funeral train slid slowly out of the station on its way to Johannesburg.

At Irene, hundreds of people had laid blossoms and wildflowers along the station's platform. As the train stopped briefly, a lone bugler sounded the Last Post once again, and an African choir sang 'Nkosi Sikelel' iAfrika'. Along the route to Johannesburg, people of all races stood hatless and silent, some in the open veld, as the train went slowly by; at Olifantsfontein, 2 000 African workers lined the embankment to pay their respects.

In Johannesburg, a crowd of about 400 000 people of all races, spilling over from every conceivable vantage point, bowed their heads as the cortege passed through streets lined with ex-servicemen and soldiers, military and railway policemen, to the Braamfontein Crematorium. It was the biggest procession that Johannesburg had ever witnessed. The behaviour of the huge crowd, according to a senior policeman, was the most exemplary he had seen in his 32-year experience.[11] The cremation service was restricted to members of the family; a few days later Smuts's ashes were strewn on the koppie above Doornkloof, his family homestead, where an obelisk in his memory stands today.

Throughout the week, newspapers in South Africa and around the world carried lengthy assessments of Smuts's life and legacy. In London, *The Times* wrote that the old warrior statesman had enjoyed a span of active public life that, for staying power, raised him to the lonely pinnacle scaled only by a few historic figures such as Palmerston, Gladstone and Clemenceau. The paper ascribed his rare vitality to his long and stable marriage and his mental curiosity. It is impossible to believe, *The Times* asserted, that Smuts was ever in his life bored, 'and the absence of boredom, surely makes for perpetual youth'.[12]

In Johannesburg, the *Rand Daily Mail* wrote of Smuts that he was one of those men whom small countries produce from time to time, but whose proper place is on the stage of world affairs.[13] However, it was *The Star* which encapsulated what made him such an exceptional individual: 'To say that he was beloved is trite and inadequate. Smuts had the quality of greatness that attracted to itself not only a passionate loyalty from his followers but a kind of awed reverence alike from those who supported him and those who opposed him. It was impossible to be in his company without falling under his spell. Few understood him fully, yet he commanded the devotion of many to whom his philosophy had not even a name. In war and peace, men were prepared to follow him to unseen goals. No other man of comparable stature has appeared on the South African scene for 300 years. Many nations have had to wait much longer.'[14]

South Africa has been blessed, of course, with at least two men who have left deep footprints on the sands of time, not only in their own country but in the wider world as well. In the age-old argument over whether history is shaped by great men, or whether great men are the products of their social environments, Jan Smuts and Nelson Mandela are powerful examples of the former – though the devout Smuts would probably have agreed with Tolstoy that such men are merely instruments of a Divine Providence. Mandela has rightly been canonised for seizing the opportunity to bring South Africans of all races together for the first time in his country's history. But Jan Smuts, of an earlier time and in different circumstances, also deserves an honoured place in our pantheon of heroes.

CHAPTER 2

A Queer Fellow

EARLY DAYS

Riebeek West is a pretty village lying below the imposing Kasteelberg in the well-to-do wheat- and wine-growing Swartland region of the Western Cape. It was there that Jan Christiaan[1] Smuts was born on the family farm Bovenplaats on 24 May 1870. His father, Jacobus Abraham Smuts, a sixth-generation descendant of the first Smuts who came to the Cape from Holland in 1692, was a pillar of the Dutch Reformed Church and a member of the Cape colonial legislature. His mother, Catherina (Cato) Petronella (née De Vries) was a seventh-generation descendant of Jacob Cloete, who had come to the Cape with Jan van Riebeeck in 1652. She hailed from the Worcester area and had studied French and music in Cape Town before she was married.

The world the infant Smuts was born into was one ruled by empires – of Britain, France, Spain, the Netherlands and Belgium, among others. At the time, the colonisation of the globe had been underway for 400 years and colonialism was regarded as natural, legitimate and, by and large, in the interests of both rulers and the ruled. Of the colonial empires, Britain's was comfortably the largest, most powerful, and – in her own estimation – by far the most benign. As citizens of the Cape Colony, the Smuts family though of Dutch origin were the subjects of Queen Victoria.

Jan was a frail, sickly child who grew up tending cattle and sheep on the farm and was given no formal schooling until he was twelve. His lively, public-spirited father did not know what to make of him, describing him as 'a queer fellow without much intelligence'.[2] When Jan was six, the family left Bovenplaats and moved to the farm Klipfontein, some 16 km from Riebeek West. Here, long before he could read or write, Jan's intense passion for the landscape and its flora and fauna was nurtured. Years later he would recall:

'Month after month I had spent there in lonely occupation – alone with the cattle, myself and God. The veld had grown part of me, not only in the sense that my bones were part of it, but in that more vital sense which identifies nature with man.'[3]

When their eldest son, Michiel, destined for the ministry, died from typhoid, Jan's parents decided that he should be educated in order to become a pastor in the Dutch Reformed Church. He was despatched to the boarding house, Die Ark, at Mr TC Stoffberg's school at Riebeek Kasteel, where his insatiable thirst for knowledge began immediately to manifest itself. His memory was quite phenomenal and it was not long before he had caught up with, and left behind, fellow pupils who had been at school for several years. Stoffberg would say of Jan that he was among the most brilliant of his pupils and the hardest-working boy he had ever met.[4]

The youngster was also deeply religious, having been influenced from an early age by his parents, his uncle, the *predikant* Boudewyn de Vries, and the local dominee, AJ Louw, whose assistant he became at Sunday school. As his official biographer notes, without his religious beliefs, Jan could well have become an animist, discovering a spirit in every rock and tree; or a pantheist, believing that God is in everything.[5] At various times throughout his long life, he was apt to lapse into pantheist heresy.

In the Riebeek West farmhouses in which Jan spent his early childhood, Afrikaans was the only language spoken. He encountered English for the first time when he went to school, and mastered the language quickly. At school and at home, he read everything he could lay his hands on in both Dutch and English. Four years later, he was able to write fluently in both, though still conversing most of the time in his home language. A solitary, contemplative soul who much preferred reading his books to playing games with his fellows, when he went home for the holidays, his parents often found him wandering around the farm, lost in contemplation.

ALOOF AND BOOKISH

Having spent only four years at school in Riebeek West instead of the usual seven, Jan passed out second in the Colony's standard eight examinations. In 1886, at the age of 16, he was sent to nearby Stellenbosch to matriculate and

thereafter to study for a degree at the town's Victoria College. Deeply serious, self-conscious about his physical deficiencies and painfully shy, he kept
always from other students who thought him aloof and bookish, and did not
like him much.

As an adolescent, Jan must have been an awful prig. Before going to Victoria College, fearful of being led astray by his fellow students, he wrote these
remarkable words in a letter to Professor Charles Murray, a Scottish don in the
English faculty: 'I intend coming to Stellenbosch in July next … and I trust
you will favour me by keeping your eye upon me and helping me with your
kindly advice. Moreover, … I shall be a perfect stranger there, and as you
know, such a place, where a large puerile element exists, affords fair scope for
moral, and what is more important, religious temptation, which, if yielded
to, will eclipse alike the expectations of my parents and the attentions of
myself…'.[6] If the College had had anything as frivolous as a 'rag' procession
in those days, it goes without saying that Jan would not have been among the
float-builders.

During his first year at Stellenbosch, Smuts lived a life 'altogether exemplary both in diligence and piety'.[7] While his roots were in the Afrikaans *taal*
and the language of his church was Dutch, his language of study and debate
was predominantly English, which he spoke with the distinctive accent of the
Swartland known as a Malmesbury 'brei'. In his boarding house, he worked
hard at mathematics, science, and Latin, besides reading and writing poetry.

One of the subjects he had to pass – as he found out belatedly – was Greek,
which he had never come across before. During the six-day holiday before his
final term, he locked himself away in his room to master the language and was
so successful that he passed out top of the Cape Colony in the subject, a feat
of memory he regarded as the most remarkable of his life.[8] At the end of the
year, he matriculated with distinction, coming third in the order of merit. In
ninth place was the book-loving young girl he had recently begun courting,
and was eventually to marry.

◆

Sybella Margaretha Krige (better known as Isie – pronounced 'Icy'), daughter of a wine farmer of Huguenot descent, was six months younger than Jan

and of a similarly serious disposition. The two met while walking along the oak-lined Dorp Street to school each day. She was, by all accounts, a slender, pretty girl, 'with wide-awake intelligent eyes', bursting with mental and physical energy.[9] The teenaged couple were reserved and undemonstrative but their friendship grew as they studied botany and poetry together. Though fluent in Dutch and by now in English, they always spoke to each other in Afrikaans.[10] Isie was particularly fond of the German poets, Goethe and Schiller, while Jan had discovered Milton, Shakespeare, Shelley and Keats. Shelley's *Prometheus Unbound* was a particular favourite. Even though the poet was an atheist, 'I have never read a poet who re-echoes so deeply the spirit of the Bible and who infuses such an ethereal spirit in me,' Jan enthused to Isie.[11]

Smuts expressed his feelings for Isie in a long, lyrical letter to her on her seventeenth birthday. In part it read: 'Some wishes I have expressed in verse – some aspirations which I know accord with your own. May I add one more? It is that we may be faithful to each other, that our mutual love may be pure and unselfish, that in whatever relation and circumstance we may be, it may grow from more to more and, if possible, never be dissolved; that we may be bound together in soul and spirit by a holy and true love.'[12]

The cerebral young couple took little part in the social life of the College and neither ever dated anyone else. But Isie gave Jan the confidence to change his mind about studying theology and switch to majoring in physical science and literature instead. Now 5 feet 9 inches (1.75 metres) tall, fair-haired and stronger in stature, with piercing blue eyes, he began also to shed some of his shyness and take more notice of the 'puerile element' on the campus, though showing no interest whatsoever in sport. He became a leading light in the student debating society, however, which made him its secretary. In 1889, he brought into the society an admiring former Sunday school pupil of his from Riebeek West, none other than his eventual political foe, DF ('Danie') Malan.

He also started to show an interest in politics, and in the cause of Afrikaner unity. At meetings of the Union Debating Society, one of two debating forums on the campus, he would plead for Afrikaans to be given a similar status to the more widely used English. In 1888, when the premier of the Cape, Cecil John Rhodes, visited the College, Smuts was chosen to respond to his address on behalf of the students. He commended himself to Rhodes by echoing the latter's views on the need for a unified Africa.[13]

At Christ's College, Cambridge, 1892. Western Cape Archives and Records Service

At this time, the young Smuts was as fervently nationalistic as his friend from Riebeek West, Danie Malan. Although professing to be an enlightened Cape liberal, his conservative political views were actually much closer to those of the Boers in the Transvaal Republic. 'Perhaps, at first glance, the Transvaal character may seem crude,' he wrote, 'but it does contain the greatest promise and the most excellent potential for all that is good in people and nations.'[14]

CAMBRIDGE

In his finals, Smuts took a double first in science and literature and was awarded the Ebden scholarship to Cambridge to study law. His absence from Isie for the next four years was the first of many long separations she had to endure. On arriving in Cambridge after a voyage marred by sea-sickness, he entered Christ's College and settled down to work immediately. Lonely, home-sick and short of money, he endured a miserable first year. As at Stellenbosch, he had little time for anything but study, and took his exercise in long, solitary walks in the countryside. His social alienation was compounded by a lack of money, which prevented him from reciprocating the hospitality of the few students who tried to befriend him.[15]

Shivering through his first English winter because he could not afford warm underwear – the Ebden scholarship being worth only half what he had been led to expect – he was forced to borrow money from his mentor and friend at Stellenbosch, Professor JI Marais of the Theological Faculty. Though disappointed at Smuts's decision to turn his back on theology in favour of law, which he described as 'classified humbug', Marais wrote regularly to his young protégé, reminding him that the Afrikaner owed everything to the providence of God and warning him against the evils of irreligion and 'Anglomania'. He and Smuts – who was already inclining towards a theoretical synthesis of 'nature, conduct and religion'[16] – wrote regularly to each other on subjects ranging from philosophy and literature to science and theology.

Smuts's second year at Cambridge was much more enjoyable than his first, mainly because a number of other Afrikaners from Victoria College, including NJ (Klaasie) de Wet, a future Chief Justice of South Africa, as well as his later political colleague FS Malan, had arrived at the university. On one occasion he travelled to London with them to watch the Oxford-Cambridge boat race but lost his companions en route. It later transpired that he had found his way to the British Museum, where he had spent the afternoon doing research instead. He also became friendly with a fellow walking enthusiast, Ethel Brown, with whom he carried on a friendly and entirely chaste relationship that was to endure for years. To her, he was always 'Mr Smuts' whenever she wrote to him.[17]

Walking in the hills of Derbyshire with Ethel as his guide, Smuts would pour out his thoughts on philosophy, science and politics; although not really understanding many of his ideas, Ethel would listen attentively and give him moral support and encouragement. It was at her mother's simple abode in Belper, Derbyshire that he first began to feel at home in England.

A KINDRED SPIRIT

While taking a break in the picture-perfect Lake District in the north of England, Smuts became absorbed by the writings of the American poet, Walt Whitman, whose ideas on religion and the evolution of personality were to free him (Smuts) from some of the constraints imposed by his excessively pious upbringing with its heavy emphasis on sin. He was to write his first book on Whitman, a kindred spirit[18] in whom he discovered his own passion for synthesis, which later found expression in the philosophy of holism, the idea that the particular only acquired meaning as part of a greater whole.[19]

While the ultra-serious Smuts found most of the younger Cambridge undergraduates too light-hearted, he became friendly with some older and more mature law tutors and with two dons in particular. One was EW Hobson, a Fellow of Christ's and Professor of Pure Mathematics and member of a radical Quaker family whose political ideas and moral attitudes were to influence Smuts deeply in later life.[20] The other was the reclusive HJ Wolstenholme, who had once intended to become a Congregational minister but had subsequently lost his faith. The latter was an unlikely friendship: the younger man so full of idealism and religious zeal; the older sceptical about the meaning and purpose of life in a morally indifferent universe.[21] The pair continued to correspond regularly from 1892 until Wolstenholme's lonely death in 1917.

It was probably while at Cambridge that Smuts became inspired by the notion of an Afrikaner-led empire in southern Africa, stretching from Table Bay to the Zambezi.[22] In an article for the college magazine, he wrote of the common destiny of Englishmen and Afrikaners in his homeland, the only dividing line between them being religion. He looked forward to the future amalgamation of the two white groups, which he believed was profoundly important because of the racial struggle that inevitably lay ahead in Africa.[23]

The diligent young Smuts's achievements in his law finals were spectacular. He became the first person at Cambridge to take both parts of the Law Tripos in the same year, and was placed first in each with distinction. He was awarded a special merit prize in Roman law and Jurisprudence and granted an extra year of study under the Ebden scholarship. His tutor FW Maitland, a distinguished scholar himself, regarded him as the best student he had ever taught. After spending a month reading and studying in Germany, Smuts was admitted as a barrister of the Middle Temple and offered a professorship at his Cambridge college. Yet he chose to spend his days in the British Museum, reading everything he could find about Whitman, in order to complete the manuscript of 'Walt Whitman: A Study in the Evolution of Personality', for which he was unable to find a publisher.[24]

Tempting though a career in England must have been, home in South Africa beckoned. In June 1895, Smuts arrived by ship in Cape Town to find a faithful and welcoming Isie on the quayside to meet him. Life had not gone well for her in the intervening four years. Her parents had been unable to pay for medical studies at college, so she had taken a poorly paid job as a country school teacher. It was to be some time before her impecunious husband-to-be was earning enough money to enable them to marry.

CHAPTER 3

Bursting with Idealism

BETRAYED BY RHODES

Settling in Cape Town, a self-assured Smuts set up in practice as a barrister. However, although his stellar academic reputation had preceded him,
despite some early successes he found briefs harder and harder to come by.
The reason, according to his fellow-Afrikaner biographer, FS Crafford, was
his austere personality. Having never really mixed with ordinary people, he
found it difficult to rub along with the common man and his aloof tactlessness
antagonised colleagues in the Cape's clubby legal fraternity. His awkwardness
was not altogether surprising, for most of his experience up to then had been
of 'a world of books and dreams and unsubstantial things'.[1]

To bolster his meagre earnings, he took to writing articles on a wide variety
of topics for Cape newspapers, in both English and Dutch. He also rekindled
his interest in Cape politics and became an enthusiastic member of his father's
party, the Afrikaner Bond, whose guiding spirit was JH Hofmeyr ('Onze Jan').
Hofmeyr was a staunch ally of the Cape premier, Cecil John Rhodes, who
he believed held the key to Afrikaner-English unity. Smuts was inspired by a
similar ideal. Confident of his intellectual powers and bursting with idealism,
he foresaw a promising future for himself in the unified South Africa propounded by Hofmeyr and Rhodes.[2]

Though sympathetic to the ideals of the Transvaalers, Smuts regarded their
leader Paul Kruger as narrow-minded and inward-looking, and too disposed
to employ 'Hollanders' instead of Afrikaners. Rhodes, by contrast, offered an
inspiring vision of a greater, united nation of Afrikaners and Englishmen in
which the former would not have to sacrifice their language and traditions.
Sent by Hofmeyr in October 1895 in response to a request by Rhodes, to
address a meeting in Kimberley, the home of De Beers Consolidated, Smuts

seized the opportunity to defend the mining magnate and enthusiastically endorse his actions and policies. Under the leadership of 'Mr Rhodes', he asserted confidently, the Colony's native policy, as enshrined in the Glen Grey Act, as well as the question of the (deliberately highly qualified) franchise were headed in the right direction. Well received though his speech might have been, not everyone in his audience was convinced. Two prominent Kimberley citizens, Samuel Cronwright and his wife, the author Olive Schreiner, were deeply sceptical about Rhodes's true intentions. In an article aimed directly at Smuts's fellow-Afrikaners in the Cape, they warned that Rhodes was not to be trusted: he was an imperialist at heart, who wished to promote British and not Afrikaner interests.[3]

Great was Smuts's mortification and anger, therefore, when a few months later the infamous Jameson Raid laid bare Rhodes's machinations. Having been acclaimed as a rising political talent after his Kimberley speech, the neo-phyte politician had been made to look utterly foolish by the Cape premier. For some days, Smuts 'found himself to be in the quicksands',[4] not knowing what to say or think. Yet he recovered quickly to join John X Merriman a fort-night later on an anti-Rhodes political platform near Malmesbury, where the pair denounced the Englishman's duplicity.

For some months thereafter, Smuts remained mired in despair. He had counted on Rhodes to give him a start in Cape politics, but that avenue was now closed. Yet although he felt betrayed and humiliated, he did not join enthusiastically in the general vilification of the Cape's prime minister. Was it because he recognised what his critics would later claim, that in the Victo-rian empire-builder he saw a kindred spirit, whose idealism and expansionist ideas matched his own?

After this blow to his self-esteem, Smuts could no longer foresee a role for himself in the British-run Cape Colony. As he was later to write ruefully, 'In the course of 1896, it became so clear to me that the British connection was harmful to South Africa, that I feared my further position as a Cape politician would be a false one. I therefore left the old colony for good and settled in the Transvaal.'[5] Renouncing his British citizenship, he turned his back on the Cape – leaving Isie behind – and threw in his lot with his fellow-Afrikaners to the north.

BECOMING A TRANSVAALER

The dusty, unattractive mining camp of Johannesburg, with its lawless, fortune-seeking inhabitants, both white and black, was an unfortunate choice of domicile for the strait-laced Smuts. His law practice, from chambers in Commissioner Street, was no more successful than it had been in the Cape and he felt ill at ease in the get-rich-quick atmosphere that prevailed among other men of his age. He pined for the natural beauty of the Cape – and of course he missed Isie. To supplement his income, he gave lectures in jurisprudence at night and continued to write for newspapers.

In April 1897, he paid a hurried return to the Cape on business, and while there – at a mere day's notice to their families – he and Isie were married. The nuptials were conducted by his friend Professor JI Marais and the next day the young couple took the train to Johannesburg. Settling in a simple and unpretentious house in Twist Street, they received as their first visitor none other than Danie Malan.[6] In 1898, Isie gave birth to premature twins, neither of whom survived for longer than a few weeks.

After a difficult few months, at Isie's urging, Smuts resolved to return to politics. Taken to meet Paul Kruger for the first time, his youthfulness and keen intelligence made an immediate impression on the old Boer leader. For his part, Smuts felt a deep sympathy for Kruger and his difficulties with British. Never one to split his loyalties, when the President dismissed his pro-British Chief Justice, JG Kotze – an act which outraged the legal profession in the Transvaal Republic – the now fervently anti-British lawyer issued a cleverly argued statement of support for the Kruger government. His reward was not long in coming: in 1898, at the tender age of 28 – two years below the minimum prescribed for the post – he was appointed as the Transvaal's State Attorney, responsible for upholding law and order and advising the government on legal matters. Later that year, he and Isie moved permanently to Pretoria, where less than a year later their son Jacobus 'Koosie' was born.

Smuts took to his new role with enthusiasm and the zeal of an avenging angel. The Transvaal administration was notoriously inefficient and corrupt, so he gave priority to purging the police force and bringing an end to illicit trading in liquor and gold. He fired the chief of police, whom he described as 'a specially smart man, singularly unsuccessful at getting at criminals'[7] and had legislation passed to put the detective force under the personal control of the State Attorney. Determined to crack down on pimping and prostitution as well, he appointed a Second Public Prosecutor in Johannesburg, reporting to him, whose responsibility it was to implement 'morals legislation'.[8] In so doing, he made many enemies. As Crafford writes, he was met with opposition and resentment from officials who disliked and feared 'the gaunt young man with the coldly staring, steely eyes, inexhaustible working power and amazing efficiency'.[9]

In his new post, Smuts drew extremely close to Kruger. Writing to his Quaker friend Emily Hobhouse after Kruger's death, he likened their relationship to one between father and son. Until his own death, he was to speak of the late president as 'the greatest Afrikaner of all'.[10] Yet the two men could hardly have been more different in character: the elderly patriarch was stolid, dignified and ready to talk patiently to everyone who came to see him; the younger man, by contrast, was quick-thinking, impatient and often rude.[11] Although Kruger was sometimes irritated by Smuts's youthful impetuosity, he developed a high regard for his law officer's intellect and administrative ability, while his knowledge of England made him most useful in dealings with the British High Commissioner, Sir Alfred Milner.

AT KRUGER'S RIGHT HAND

Milner had been sent to South Africa in 1897 in the aftermath of the Jameson Raid. A legal scholar and born administrator, his brief from the Colonial Secretary Joseph Chamberlain, was to reduce tensions between the Transvaal government and the *uitlanders* (immigrants) who had settled on the Rand to make a living on the mines. Yet Milner was an avowed imperialist at heart, who made no secret of his belief that Afrikanerdom had to be crushed if British rule was to be upheld in South Africa. His detractors at home described him as having the qualities of 'a natural dictator',[12] while even admirers thought 'his genius was of the autocratic kind'.[13]

Though obedient to Chamberlain's instructions at first, Milner became convinced that South Africa was the weakest link in the Imperial chain and did not believe that 'a mediaeval race oligarchy and a modern industrial state recognising no difference of status between various white races'[14] could live side by side. He was outspokenly critical of the Transvaal government's inefficiencies

Smuts, Isie and daughter Santa, 1904. Smuts House Museum

and its unwillingness to grant franchise rights to *uitlanders*. Intent on provoking a *casus belli*, he wrote to Chamberlain in 1898 to say that the way forward in South Africa should be either 'reform in the Transvaal or war'.[15]

Neither Kruger nor Smuts wanted war, but they were under no illusions about Milner's intentions. At the urging of President Steyn of the Free State, Kruger and Milner met in Bloemfontein to try to settle their differences and avoid armed conflict, the former showing his faith in Smuts by letting him effectively lead the Transvaal delegation. In the determined young State Attorney, the patrician and uncompromising Milner found his match in arrogance.[16] The personal animosity that grew between the two undoubtedly helped take South Africa to the war that the Englishman so clearly wanted.

The sticking point at the week-long Bloemfontein conference was the franchise. Milner demanded the vote for the *uitlanders,* a requirement that Kruger deemed quite unreasonable because his 'burghers' would be outvoted by two to one. Behind the scenes, Smuts advised Kruger to compromise, but Milner indicated that he was not prepared to negotiate – an attitude that infuriated Smuts, who had to hold himself in check at Milner's dismissive treatment of the old president.[17]

Returning to Pretoria after the failure of the conference, Smuts said to Kruger's secretary, Piet Grobler, 'It is absolutely clear to me that Milner is planning to make war'.[18] At Smuts's urging, Kruger offered the British government a five-year residential franchise for *uitlanders*, but on Milner's advice, Chamberlain rejected the proposal. On 2 September, the Colonial Secretary broke off diplomatic relations with the Kruger government. Left with no alternative, Smuts drafted an ultimatum to the British government on Kruger's behalf which the intransigent Milner rejected.

Smuts made one last-ditch attempt to avert war by quietly offering the British agent in the Transvaal, Conyngham Green, some further concessions on the franchise, but the discussions went nowhere. And so, on 11 October 1899 – to universal astonishment – war broke out between the two Boer Republics and the all-powerful British Empire. The unequal military struggle was to last three years. Though ending in defeat for the Boers, it was to capture the imagination of the watching world and inflict lasting damage on British imperial prestige and self-confidence.

CHAPTER 4

Boer Strategist

PREPARING FOR WAR

Both sides in the Anglo-Boer War[1] were spoiling for a fight. Although public opinion in Britain was against going to war and there were doubts about its desirability in some government circles, Joseph Chamberlain had been persuaded by Milner that the time had come to teach Kruger and the Boers a lesson. Decision-making took time, however, and British military commanders in the field in South Africa were fretting at the delay.[2] The Brits were confident, however, that if war were eventually to come, it would be no more than a short conflict of a few months before the professionalism of their soldiers overcame any Boer resistance.

In the Volksraad, Kruger had first to face down his colleagues Piet Joubert, Koos de la Rey and Louis Botha, who were wary of taking on the might of the British Empire. After a thunderous clash of wills, the President, with the support of Smuts and State Secretary FW Reitz, won the vote in favour of going to war as soon as the opportunity arose. Kruger had already been persuaded by Smuts that since war was inevitable, the sooner it began the better. The latter hoped that a quick strike by Boer forces before British troops arrived in numbers might be enough to persuade the Imperial government that peace was preferable to a protracted struggle.

At the tender age of 29, Smuts found himself alongside Reitz at the helm of the Transvaal government, responsible for running the administration in Pretoria while the generals readied for war. Despite having had no military training whatsoever, he had drafted – and without being asked – an 18-page memorandum setting out the measures needed to support Boer units in the field: all agricultural and manufacturing production had to be geared towards the war effort; gold output was to be increased, armaments manufactured, and a war tax imposed. As usual, Smuts worked himself to the bone, shouldering the heaviest burden of anyone in government, issuing proclamations and dispatches, and laying the logistical groundwork for war.

His plan called for a surprise assault by Boer forces, as well as simultaneous preparation for a long and costly struggle. Having done his best to ward off conflict, he must have had mixed feelings about the wisdom of going to war. His head would have told him that the fighting could be drawn-out and bloody, and result in untold Boer suffering. His heart led him to believe (wishfully, it must be said) that Boer successes might incite Britain's many enemies in Europe to mobilise and help bring down the Empire. Moreover, he surmised to himself, if Afrikaners in the Cape were to come to the aid of their compatriots and declare a third Afrikaner republic, Afrikanerdom might inherit Britain's hegemony over territory from the Cape to the banks of the Zambezi.

To rally support for the war among his fellow Afrikaners – and in the wider world – the impulsive young Smuts took a step he would later regret. He produced an emotive 30 000-word tract, *Eene Eeuw van Onrecht (A Century of Wrong)*, written in Dutch and translated into English by Isie, which excoriated British governments for their behaviour in southern Africa over the preceding century and ended with the stirring cry: 'We now lay our whole case with full confidence before the world. Whether we conquer or whether we die: freedom shall rise in South Africa as the sun arises from the morning clouds … Then shall it be from the Zambesi to Simon's Bay: "Africa for the Africander".'[3]

FS Crafford observed that there must have been few things in life that Smuts was to regret more than his authorship of *A Century of Wrong*: 'As a piece of Boer propaganda before and during the war, the purpose it served was negligible and afterwards it was invariably cast in his teeth by his countrymen.'[4] British historian Kenneth Ingham observes tartly that Smuts's 'adolescent rhetoric' contrasted sharply with the good sense displayed in his military plans.[5]

BATTLE JOINED

The war began in earnest with the invasion of British-held Natal by two Boer columns, led by Generals Piet Joubert and Lukas Meyer. At the time, there were no more than 25 000 British troops in the whole of South Africa. Having to fight on unfamiliar terrain, the 'khakis' were no match at first for the better-equipped and more numerous Boers. Well-armed with their heavy artillery pieces and newly acquired Mauser rifles, the latter were survivalists, used to living off the land, with an inborn talent for fighting. What they lacked, as Smuts came to realise, was discipline and staying power – hardly surprising in an army consisting mainly of volunteers.

Knowing that their best hope lay in quick victories, the Boers routed the British at Talana Hill and Nicholson's Nek in Natal, forcing the enemy to retreat to Ladysmith, where the town was surrounded and the vital rail link to Durban cut. On the Western front, a Boer force had already laid siege to Mafeking, which was defended by Lt Col Baden Powell and a few hundred colonial troops, and also to Kimberley in the Cape, where Rhodes himself, though at odds with the military, marshalled the engineers of the De Beers Company to construct a 'Long Cecil' gun. In the Free State, Lord Methuen's troops were trounced by General de la Rey's men, who then dug in at Magersfontein, where they inflicted heavy losses on the Scottish Highland Brigade, led by the Black Watch. In the Tugela Valley, Sir Redvers Buller's attempts to fight back at Colenso and Spioenkop ended in stalemate. In Britain, public opinion was stunned by the scale of British casualties: not even the Indian Mutiny or the Crimean War had posed such a threat to the future of Empire.[6]

At home in Pretoria, the hyperactive Smuts was chafing at his enforced inaction. He may have had no military experience, but if a war had to be fought, he wanted to be at the heart of it, implementing his own strategy. As he was to demonstrate, merely to command his own men in the field was never enough; his true bent was strategic.[7] His repeated requests to be allowed to take up arms himself fell on deaf ears, however; he was far more valuable away from the front, keeping the administration ticking over. Kept from the action, he took it upon himself to make frequent trips to the battlefront, from where he was able to report back on the progress of the war as well as agitate the rear of any Boer general unaware of the need for hurry.[8]

In November 1899, Louis Botha and his men captured an armoured train near Chievely in the Tugela Valley and took 60 prisoners, among them the young correspondent of Britain's *Morning Post*, Winston Spencer Churchill. Brought before Smuts in Pretoria to be interrogated, the 'defiant young man', as Smuts described him, looking 'dishevelled and indignant', claimed immunity as a non-combatant until it was pointed out to him that he had been carrying a pistol, which was why he had been detained. Recounting the incident to Churchill at Chequers 45 years later, Smuts confessed to having persuaded General Joubert that there was no point in detaining a foreign newspaper reporter on a technicality. Before Churchill could be released, however, he had escaped from custody and was on his way to Lourenço Marques, and to international attention and celebrity as a war correspondent.[9] Smuts immediately issued a warrant for Churchill's arrest, which read as follows: 'Englishman, twenty-five years old, about five foot eight inches high, walks with a bend forward, pale appearance, red-brownish hair, small moustache hardly perceptible, talks through his nose and cannot pronounce the letter "S" properly.'[10]

At this stage of the conflict, both Boers and the British were suffering from the tardiness and decrepitude of their commanders-in-chief. General Piet Joubert – who was soon to die at the age of 70 and be replaced on Smuts's recommendation by Louis Botha – was well past his prime, as was the old warhorse on the British side, Sir Redvers Buller, who had won his VC back in the Anglo-Zulu War. In London, British setbacks had finally stung the government into action. Lords Roberts and Kitchener, commander-in-chief and chief-of-staff respectively of the British army, as well as some 110 000 troops, were sent post haste to South Africa with orders to stem the Boer tide. Force numbers on the Boer side, boosted by volunteers from around the world, were no more than 70 000 fighting men, supported by 10 000 often unwilling African auxiliaries.[11]

THE TIDE TURNS

The arrival of Field Marshal Roberts and his huge troop contingent gradually turned the tide of the war in Britain's favour. The Boers made the strategic mistake of concentrating too large a proportion of their forces on the three besieged towns of Kimberley, Ladysmith and Mafeking, instead of thrusting more deeply into British-held territory.[12] After the three towns had been relieved and General Cronje heavily defeated at Paardeberg, the way lay open for Roberts to capture Bloemfontein – which he duly did on 13 March 1900 – and to annex the Orange Free State. On Queen Victoria's birthday, the former Boer republic became the Orange River Colony.

By now, the outgunned Boers, plagued by low morale and desertion, were in flight, not only in the Free State but in Natal too, from where Generals Botha and De la Rey were being driven steadily back into the Transvaal. It began to dawn on the Boer leadership that the opportunity to inflict a significant defeat on the British had come and gone. From now on, the war was to become one long dispiriting retreat in the face of superior weaponry and greater numbers.[13]

On 31 May, Johannesburg fell to the advancing British, and Boer forces in the Transvaal – now only 7 000 in number – retreated to the hills and valleys of the Magaliesberg, north of Pretoria. At a meeting of the Boer high command, it was decided that Kruger and senior officials should flee the capital by train and relocate the seat of government in the eastern Transvaal, along the Delagoa Railway. A few generals even tried to persuade Kruger to surrender. 'I shall never forget the bitter humiliation and despondency of that awful moment,' Smuts wrote later, 'when the stoutest hearts and strongest wills in the Transvaal army, were, albeit for a moment, to sink beneath the tide of our misfortune.'[14]

Dismayed at the collapse in morale of his troops, Kruger raised the question of surrender with President Steyn of the Free State, by telegraph. Steyn was vehemently opposed to making peace with Britain, and virtually accused the Transvaalers of selfishness and cowardice. The Free State, he declared, would fight on to the bitter end. After further councils of war, by which stage Kruger had set up government offices in his special train at a railway siding at Machadodorp, the Transvaalers decided there could be no more talk of surrender; the war had to continue.

The departing Kruger had left Acting-President Schalk Burger and Smuts behind in Pretoria to run the administration and maintain law and order as retreating commandos poured into the demoralised capital. Burger left almost immediately, leaving it to Smuts to ship the Republic's remaining coin and gold reserves (of under £500 000) as well as munitions down to Machadodorp, as shells began to rain on the last train out of Pretoria.

On the evening of 4 June, as British forces advanced on the capital, Smuts himself slipped away to join Louis Botha in the Magaliesberg, where the latter had managed to rally some 6 000 men for a last desperate defence of the Republic. Smuts had no option but to leave Isie and little Koosie at home.

Knowing full well that the house would be searched, Isie was prepared for the British soldiers who arrived on her doorstep soon after Pretoria had fallen. She had rolled up secret telegrams between Kruger and Smuts into wads and stuffed them into hollow curtain rods.[15] The 200 gold sovereigns left to her by her husband were sewn into a money belt, which she dropped into the kitchen boiler. Yet despite her bitter hostility to all things British, kind-hearted Isie could not be inhospitable to the hungry young British soldiers, who had survived for weeks on bully beef and biscuits. They were given warm bread from her oven.

GUERRILLA WARFARE

The British attack on the Boers at Donkerhoek (or Diamond Hill) marked what Smuts later described as the last defensive battle of the war. Though it ended in defeat for the Boers, the battle served to embolden the leadership and reawaken the fighting spirit of the rank and file. The success of daring raids by Christiaan de Wet and Koos de la Rey on enemy supply lines in the Free State and Western Transvaal was instrumental in persuading Boer leaders to resume the offensive, which they did by rounding up deserters, rebuilding commandos and directing the latter into unorthodox hit-and-run operations. Anger at Roberts's new 'scorched earth' policy also helped drive many burghers back into Boer ranks.

The new Boer strategy embraced the cutting of enemy supply lines and sabotaging of railway tracks, bridges and telegraph wires. It was decided that, in order to implement these tactics effectively, the Boer army would be split into three units, each operating independently of one another: Botha took charge of operations in the Eastern Transvaal, De Wet and Hertzog in the Free State, and De la Rey and Smuts in the Western Transvaal.[16] However, the adoption of guerrilla tactics posed a formidable moral problem for Boer leaders: was it right, they asked each other, to draw women and children, all alone on their farms, into what might become a more savage kind of warfare?[17]

In late August 1900, while Smuts was away in the field, he and Isie suffered a devastating personal loss when their little son Koosie died after a week-long illness. Isie, who had already lost two infant children, telegraphed the awful news to her absent husband, who never received her message. Her anguish at having to bear her hurt alone was conveyed in a heart-wrenching letter she wrote ten months later, after receiving a letter from Smuts sent on by an English officer. (Because of military censorship, both letters had to be written in English.) Not long after Koosie's death, Isie was forced by the British to leave Pretoria and go and live with her sister in a small cottage in British-held Pietermaritzburg.

A tactical meeting with Kruger at Waterval Boven was the last time he and Smuts were to meet. The British victory at Donkerhoek had opened the way for the 'khakis' to advance along the railway line to Kruger's makeshift head-quarters. The embattled President was forced to retreat even further eastwards to Nelspruit, before he slipped across the border to Delagoa Bay, where a ship took him into a lonely exile in Europe, from which he was never to return.

On 25 October 1900, Lord Roberts announced Britain's formal annexure of the Transvaal. Shortly afterwards, he departed South Africa, declaring the war to be 'practically' over and appointing Lord Kitchener in his stead as commander-in-chief. But, as Kitchener was soon to learn, the war was far from over: about 30 000 Boers were still at large in the Free State and Western Transvaal. Because of the ill-treatment of Boer women and children, a new and more bitter stage of the conflict was about to begin.[18]

WAR INTENSIFIES

Unable to counter the Boers' mobile hit-and-run tactics effectively, the British began to deal brutally with any civilians in the rural areas found to be supporting the commandos. Kitchener's 'search and scour' strategy, aimed at depriving the commandos in the rural areas of food, shelter and horses, and the construction of blockhouses and barbed-wire entanglements across the countryside were designed as a response to guerrilla tactics. These measures changed the nature of the conflict entirely, and forced the Boers to come up with a counter-strategy.

At a meeting of Boer leaders from the Transvaal and Free State at Cyferfontein in the Magaliesberg in October 1900, a two-pronged plan was formulated: Boer forces would attack mines on the Rand in the hope of reducing the mine-owners' support for the British; this would be followed by an invasion of the Cape Colony. The former never materialised, but Smuts, who had always

Smuts (seated) and his brother-in-law 'Tottie' Krige during the
Anglo-Boer War, 1901. Smuts House Museum

attached more importance to the Colony than his colleagues, pleaded to be
allowed to lead a Boer commando into the Cape. Determined to display his
leadership skills in the field, he still nurtured a hope of inspiring a revolt of
fellow-Afrikaners in the Colony.[19] While waiting for permission to take the
fight into the Cape, he absorbed some hands-on lessons in guerrilla warfare
from his friend and hero, 'Oom Koos' de la Rey, as the pair led raids on British
encampments in the Rustenburg and Potchefstroom areas.[20]

29

In early 1901, the fortunes of war began to worsen for the Boers. Kitchener's blockhouses were restricting the mobility of commandos, while the herding of women and children into concentration camps was having a severe impact on morale. Confident that victory was not far off, and ignoring his differences with Milner – whom he considered intransigent and vindictive – the British commander invited Botha for peace talks at Middelburg. But Milner's insistence on unconditional surrender resulted in the failure of the negotiations over the issue of independence.

Over the next few months, separate Boer commandos from the Free State led by De Wet, Hertzog and Kritzinger embarked on incursions into the Colony, only to find the hoped-for support of Cape Afrikaners not forthcoming. Anticipating these raids, the Cape government had declared martial law in most parts of the Colony, recruited loyalists into the military to round up any commandos and set up special courts to try colonists assisting the 'rebel' cause.[21]

At a meeting of senior Boer leaders near Standerton in June 1901, Smuts argued for a bolder incursion into the Cape Colony, the only 'unscorched' territory in which Boer guerrillas could move relatively freely. He proposed joining forces with Kritzinger in the Free State and together trying to unite the various commandos roaming in the Cape mountains. He himself would lead a band of men into the Eastern Cape and then the Western Cape, to pave the way for a larger-scale invasion from the Transvaal, led by De la Rey. Like his fellows, Smuts was sickened at the devastation wreaked on Boer farms and outraged at conditions in the concentration camps. He itched to carry the fight to the enemy.

At last, while making plans to recapture Johannesburg from the British, he was given the go-ahead to infiltrate the Cape – in order to foment rebellion in the Colony and relieve the pressure on the Boer republics. Louis Botha, for his part, would mount a similar operation in Natal.

CHAPTER 5

Fighting the British

ON COMMANDO

Smuts embarked on his foray into the Cape Colony with vigour and enthusiasm renewed. At the age of 31, he was experiencing for the first time in his life the joys of intense physical activity, as well as the pleasures of comradeship. His body had become stronger and more sturdy and his complexion ruddier from its constant exposure to the elements. A beard made him look much older than he was. In his saddlebag, he carried Kant's *Critique of Pure Reason* and a well-thumbed copy of the New Testament in Greek.[1]

On 1 August 1901, he and some 340 hand-picked but raggedly dressed volunteers, whose ranks included the young Deneys Reitz, crossed into the Colony at a remote point on the Orange River, between Zastron and Aliwal North, where the borders of the Free State, Basutoland (now Lesotho) and the Cape meet. It was the beginning of an epic journey that would traverse 2 000 miles and tie up some 35 000 British troops in pursuit of the invaders.[2] Highly motivated though it was, the commando was short of ammunition, medical supplies and forage.

Smuts's reputation in the Cape had preceded him; the British received news of his expedition with some misgiving. They feared that under bold and clear-sighted leadership, potential Boer fighters scattered around the Colony might become a magnet for the many Afrikaners with anti-colonial sympathies. The Brits thus redoubled their efforts to clear the Free State and Northern Cape of insurgents, and Kitchener charged General French specifically with cornering Smuts and his men. As a result, the infiltrators were constantly on the run, evading enemy patrols and barely avoiding capture.[3]

In *Commando*, his classic account of Boer exploits in the field, Reitz describes how Smuts and his men entered the Cape by making a hazardous crossing of the Orange River, in single file at three o'clock in the morning, in order to evade British troops guarding approaches to the river. Once in the Colony, they had to do battle with armed and mounted Basutos – on the side of the British – in a skirmish that cost the lives of six Boers and 30 horses. Eventually, the commando reached the safety of an Afrikaner farm, where Reitz enjoyed the first bread and butter and coffee he had tasted in a year.[4]

Two days later, Smuts himself had the narrowest of escapes from death. At Moordenaar's Poort, a narrow gorge in the mountains near Dordrecht, he and three men went out to reconnoitre and ran into a British ambush. Smuts's horse was shot from under him, but he managed to escape by running down a donga. His companions were not so fortunate: all three lost their lives.

For six weeks, the Smuts commando picked its way carefully through the mountains of the Eastern Cape, coming into frequent contact with British troops and losing men and horses on the way. The spring rains had begun, and the icy conditions and biting wind gave the drenched Boers and their horses no respite from the elements, while the omnipresence of British patrols meant no rest. One evening, on a plateau near Dordrecht in the Stormberg Mountains, General French's troops closed in on the exhausted company, which had holed up in a hollow. French and his men pitched camp to await the Boers' surrender in daylight next morning. Miraculously, later that night a little hunchback, one Hans Kleynhans, emerged from a farmhouse nearby and led the 250 men and more than 500 horses in silence down an almost vertical mountain path to safety. So close were the Boers to the British camp that the khakis' voices could be heard clearly.

Soon after this narrow escape, on coming upon a railway station where an empty goods train stood, the commando was amused to find a Cape newspaper carrying a report that Smuts had invaded the Colony 'with the riff-raff of the Boer armies'.[5] At this stage, mid-September 1901, he and his men did not know that Kitchener had decreed it to be a capital crime for any Boer to fight in captured khaki. In due course, the Boers were distressed to learn that one of their number caught wearing a British uniform had been summarily tried and executed.[6] Smuts found it hard to accept that the enemy could shoot captured soldiers.

◆

As Reitz recounts graphically, it was the appalling weather rather than their British pursuers which almost defeated Smuts's commando. After one terrible night, he recorded, 'Our guide lost his way; we went floundering ankle-deep in mud and water; our poor weakened horses stumbling and slipping at every turn; the rain beat down on us and the cold was awful. Towards midnight it began to sleet. The grain-bag which I wore froze solid on my body, like a coat of mail, and I believe if we had not kept moving every one of us would have died. We had known two years of war, but we became closer to despair that night that I care to remember.'[7] Fourteen men and a large number of horses perished from the cold in the 'Night of the Great Rain'.

The abject condition of Smuts's men and animals inevitably gave rise to muttering in the ranks about his leadership. What was his strategy, his men wondered. Where was he leading them? Where was the Afrikaner support they had been promised? And even if they broke through the British defences, how could they survive in such conditions without food, water, ammunition, and horses?[8] The answer came two days later.

In this depressed frame of mind, the bedraggled commando had made its way through the Elandsrivierpoort, where it ran into a 200-strong force from the 17th Lancers. A bloody clash ensued, in which the Boers' deadly accuracy with the rifle accounted for 29 of the enemy killed and 49 wounded, against one dead and six wounded in their own ranks. With new rifles, fresh supplies, clothing, saddlery and boots to carry away from the British camp, morale soared once more. As Reitz recorded, 'we had renewed confidence in our leader and in ourselves, a factor of considerable importance to a body of men in a hostile country'.[9]

Colonel Douglas Haig, OC of the Lancers and directly responsible to General French for the Eland's River area, was only 14 miles away at Tarkastad when he learned with horror of his regiment's losses. For the next four weeks, according to Thomas Pakenham, the guerrilla war in the mountains of the Eastern Cape became a personal duel between Haig and Smuts, two well-matched, intensely professional and relentless drivers of men.[10] The pair, as well as General French, were to meet again in World War I, but this time on the same side.

WELDING A FIGHTING FORCE

By now Smuts had been forced to acknowledge that progress in recruiting colonial Afrikaners to the Boer cause had been unsatisfactory, largely because their horses had been taken from them by the British. More disappointingly, reinforcements from the Free State and Transvaal had not materialised.[11] Abandoning the idea of establishing an Afrikaner republic in the Cape, Smuts took upon himself the powers of Boer commander-in-chief in the Colony and set about re-organising his forces so as to maintain his harassment of the British and ease the pressure on the two Boer republics.

He welded the 17 commandos dotted around the Colony into four fighting groups under generals who reported directly to him.[12] One unit, under Malan, was sent eastwards; a second, under Maritz, was dispatched in the direction of German South West Africa; a third, under his close confidant, Van Deventer, was sent southwards to Worcester, and a fourth, under Lategan, along the Orange River. A command structure, order and discipline were imposed upon every commando: there was to be no unseemly behaviour, no scrambling for booty, no looting and no ill-treatment of civilians or prisoners. Every suspect had to be brought for trial before a military court.

As a leader, Smuts always had his men's interests at heart. In the forefront of any action by day, he would withdraw into his tent at night to read his New Testament or books on philosophy. If he had to share a blanket, it would be with his brother-in-law, 'Tottie' Krige. Though uncommunicative at times – or 'moody and curt, as was his custom when displeased', in the words of Deneys Reitz[13] – he was respected and trusted by his men, and the comradeship which grew up between them was to survive some of the political differences that emerged many years later.[14]

In October 1901, Smuts's men broke through Haig's cordon and marauded south towards Port Elizabeth, evading British patrols and commandeering supplies from Afrikaner- and English-speaking farmers along the route. Reitz recounts an incident that revealed Smuts's remarkable toughness. At the foot of the Zuurberge, with Algoa Bay in sight, the hungry commando fell with alacrity upon a wild, pineapple-like fruit which, unbeknown to them, was highly poisonous. Within a short while, half of the party had collapsed on the ground in agony. Smuts himself lay comatose.[15] To make matters worse, a strong enemy force had spotted the commando and was

Smuts and his commando at Concordia, Namaqualand, 1901. Parliament

descending a nearby slope to attack. With dusk approaching, the stricken Boers managed to fight off the British soldiers with rifle fire. They realised, however, that they had to get away before daylight, even though it was apparent from the groans of pain that many of the party were not fit to travel.

The night was dark and chilly and the embattled Boers dared not light a fire to keep warm. Those men who were not ill were starving. By early morning, most of the party had recovered but some 20 were still very sick, including Smuts himself, who lay prostrate on the ground. Only just able to take stock of the situation, he gave orders that those, like himself, who could not help themselves should be tied to their horses' saddles. By so doing, the entire group managed once again to evade capture by slipping away via a narrow gorge through the mountains.

Smuts was as tough mentally as he was physically. By enforcing military discipline, sometimes cold-heartedly, he instilled respect and even fear in his men. On one celebrated occasion, he was told that a Boer traitor named Lambert Colyn had gone over to the British side for money. Colyn had led a detachment of British soldiers into a Boer camp one night, where they killed or wounded 17 Boers before disappearing into the darkness. Within a week, Smuts's men had his men storm the British camp in which Colyn was hiding, taking him prisoner. Brought before a court-martial presided over by Smuts, Colyn was found guilty and sentenced to death. Upon his knees, he begged for mercy, but Smuts refused to listen, saying 'No, Colyn, for you there can be no mercy. You have done the dirty work of the English.'[16] The turncoat was taken away and shot.

In October 1901, Smuts split his troops in two, sending Van Deventer in the direction of the Western Cape while proceeding himself across the Little Karoo towards the Olifants River and Namaqualand. Now able to roam freely across a vast and mostly empty territory, he occupied himself at night by reading books confiscated from plundered British camps and studying philosophy. With large swathes of the Colony now under his control, he felt bold enough to issue a proclamation forbidding the inhabitants of districts held by the Boers from obeying British laws and supplying provisions to the enemy.[17]

He also wrote a long and optimistic letter to De la Rey to report on his reorganisation of Boer forces and the progress made in the Colony. While admitting that the recruitment of rebels had not gone as well as expected, he looked forward to victory within a year if reinforcements were forthcoming from the Transvaal. He believed from reports reaching him via German South West Africa that in Britain the government was coming under severe pressure because of the awful conditions in the concentration camps. 'Perhaps God's will is that through our ill-treated women and children a decisive end should be made to this war,' he mused to De la Rey.[18]

To add to the psychological pressure on Britain, while in the Cape Smuts compiled another powerful propagandist tract, highlighting the Boers' progress in the field and excoriating the British for their cruelty and inhumanity. The document was published by pro-Boer forces in Paris and, as intended, attracted much attention in Britain, where Smuts had become known not only as a skilful soldier and strategist, but as an implacable foe of King and country.[19]

PEACE NEGOTIATIONS

Elsewhere in South Africa, however, the Boer leaders – De Wet in the Free State, De la Rey in the Transvaal and Botha in Natal – were on their uppers. Outnumbered by the British, their forces were hemmed in by Kitchener's blockhouses and confined to areas devastated by his scorched-earth tactics. Entire farming villages had been destroyed, thousands of farmsteads burned to the ground, cattle and sheep slaughtered, and lands laid waste. It was only the hardliners in Boer ranks, the *bittereinders*, who were determined to carry on fighting.[20] Sensing the division in the opposing ranks, the more forward-looking Kitchener – always keener than Milner on ending the war – once more invited the Boer leaders for talks.

Having only just captured the towns of Springbok and Concordia in Namaqualand, Smuts was in the throes of attacking the copper-producing town of O'kiep when two British officers rode up to his camp in a cart, carrying a white flag. He was informed that as state attorney of the Transvaal, his presence was required at peace negotiations in Pretoria: his safe-conduct would be guaranteed by none other than Col Douglas Haig.

Leaving Maritz to carry on fighting, Smuts took Reitz with him to Port Nolloth, from where the pair travelled to Cape Town by ship, and on to Pretoria by train. Smuts was afforded every courtesy and military honour en route, but was in no mood to fraternise with the likes of General French, who met him in Matjiesfontein, or any other British officer.[21] At Kroonstad, he was met by Kitchener himself, who impressed upon him the hopelessness of further Boer resistance and urged him to help bring an end to the war.

Taken to meet Commandant-General Louis Botha at Standerton, Reitz described afterwards how appalled he and Smuts were at the condition of the 300 delegates from Boer commandos who had gathered to elect delegates to peace talks at Vereeniging. 'Nothing could have proved more clearly how nearly the Boer cause was spent than these starving, ragged men, clad in skins or sacking, their bodies covered in sores, from lack of salt and food. Their appearance was a great shock to us, who came from the better-conditioned forces in the Cape,' Reitz wrote.[22]

Smuts was not a delegate himself at Vereeniging, but at Botha's invitation, he and the Free State's legal adviser, General JBM Hertzog, participated freely in deliberations before the conference began. Earlier discussions between Free

State and Transvaal leaders had revealed deep differences of opinion among Boers over the question of unconditional surrender. An ailing President Steyn insisted that he would make peace only if the Republics were allowed to retain their independence.[23] The Transvaalers, on the other hand, realised the game was up; surrender had become unavoidable.

Milner insisted to Kitchener that victory over the Boers had to be total, and was not prepared to countenance any demands for independence. On 15 May 1902, the 60 Boer delegates gathered at Vereeniging (30 from each Republic) deputed Botha, De la Rey, De Wet, Smuts and Hertzog to parley one more time with Milner and Kitchener. On 19 May, in Pretoria, after the morning session of talks had ended in deadlock, Kitchener called Smuts aside and quietly told him that in his opinion a Liberal government was likely to come to power in Britain in two years' time and might be more sympathetic to the Republics' demands for self-government. In the afternoon, the still intransigent Milner insisted that if the Boers would affirm their surrender and acknowledge their allegiance to Britain, then he, Cape Attorney-General Sir Richard Solomon, Smuts and Hertzog would draft the remaining provisions of a treaty to be put forward for ratification by the delegates at Vereeniging.

A key element of the treaty was the question of the native franchise. Smuts re-drafted a key clause in the document that would have extended the franchise to a limited number of Africans to one that deferred a decision on the African franchise until after the introduction of self-government, thereby leaving the matter in the hands of the Republics rather than the British. The change, accepted by Milner, was to have fateful long-term consequences for a future South Africa.

Milner and Kitchener insisted on receiving a final acceptance of their terms by midnight on Saturday, 31 May. Smuts had made his own views known earlier in an impassioned address to his fellow Boer leaders, in which he spoke of their duty to the Boer people, rather than the Boer army. 'We commenced the struggle, and continued it to this moment, because we wished to maintain our independence and were prepared to sacrifice everything for it,' he cried. 'But we may not sacrifice the Afrikaner people for that independence ... No one shall ever convince me that this unparalleled sacrifice which the Afrikaner nation has laid upon the altar of freedom will be in vain. ... The war of freedom for South Africa has been fought, not only for the Boers, but for the entire people of South Africa. The result of that struggle we leave in God's hands. Perhaps it is His will to lead the people of South Africa through defeat and humiliation, yea even through the valley of the shadow of death to a better future and a brighter day.'[24]

After a tense and emotion-charged debate, the peace proposal was put to the vote, and carried by 54 votes to 6. At 11 pm, a peace agreement was signed in Kitchener's house in Pretoria. It was to become known as the Treaty of Vereeniging.

◆

Throughout the negotiations, however, Smuts had been preoccupied by alarming reports of the parlous state of Isie's health. On 26 May, two days after his thirty-second birthday, he had written lovingly to her from Pretoria, 'I know that you must be suffering horribly and that no calm of mind can make up for the ruin of the body. ... I have no doubt that, once this dark business is over and we are restored to each other again, you will soon recover your lost health and spirits. At any rate, I shall do everything in my power to make up for the long years of separation ...Without you I would not care to live, and with you life's noblest treasure is still left to me. I am prepared for all losses except for the loss of you ... To you I owe whatever is noblest and best in my life and work.'[25]

On 1 June, the day after the Peace Treaty was signed, Smuts left for the Cape Colony to fulfil his last duties as a Boer general, which included the orderly disbanding of his commando, still encamped at Soetwater, near Calvinia, and unaware of the outcome of the negotiations at Vereeniging. To him fell the unenviable task of telling his disbelieving comrades, who had fought so nearly to the death alongside him, that it was the Boers not the British who had surrendered and sued for peace. The more deeply affected among them refused to accept the news and accused him of betraying the Boer cause.

After visiting his father, who had remarried after the death of Smuts's mother, Cato, as well as members of the Krige family in the Western Cape, Smuts went briefly to Pietermaritzburg to see Isie. She had been operated on in June, but was not well enough to accompany him on the train journey home to Pretoria, only being fit enough to travel in mid-August. As Hancock records, another woman would have begged her husband to remain with her, but Isie took it for granted – as did Smuts, now a former minister and general – that duty came first for both of them.

CHAPTER 6

Aftermath

FRUSTRATING MILNER

The Anglo-Boer War left a legacy of bitterness among Boers that endured for decades. In the two former republics, now British colonies, there was devastation everywhere. Smuts had emerged from the conflict with a much enhanced reputation – his small force had tied up thousands of British troops charged with defending the Cape Colony and his skills as a soldier and leader of men had been forged in the heat of the guerrilla campaign. But the war's outcome had left him disillusioned and depressed, and deeply resentful of all things British. He particularly disliked the imperious Milner, who began, as soon as the war was over, to anglicise most spheres of life in the new Crown colonies. And although he might not have acknowledged it, now that Kruger had gone, he himself was sorely in need of a new leader to inspire him in the way the old president, and before that Rhodes, had done.[1]

He was fortunate to find such inspiration near at hand in his friend and fellow Boer general, the much-loved Louis Botha. When Botha moved to Pretoria after the war, he and Smuts drew even closer to each other and began discussing their own, Rhodes-like vision of a united South African nation of white Afrikaners and English-speakers, under the protection of the British umbrella. More aware now of where the power in international politics lay, the two men had come to the conclusion that South Africa could only grow economically with the support of foreign capital. Like it or not, the Empire could offer both trading opportunities and long-term physical security. In Smuts's mind, South Africa had to remain within the Empire not only for reasons of safety, but in order to carry out its mission also as the bearer of 'civilisation' to the African continent.[2]

Both men sensed that self-government for the Boer colonies would

41

eventually be forthcoming, probably sooner rather than later. As a deliberate tactic, therefore, they resolved to abide carefully by the provisions of the peace treaty, but to advance their case for self-government by withholding any help from Milner and his 'Kindergarten' – the handful of young, career-minded civil servants educated at Oxford and sent out by the Colonial Office to cut their teeth in far-off South Africa. They declined to help efforts at reconstruction and refused the offer of a seat on the Transvaal Legislative Council. While Botha attacked Milner in public, behind the scenes, it was Smuts who orchestrated most of his colleague's criticisms.

The campaign against Milner was given added impetus by a downturn in the Transvaal economy, brought about by severe drought and a shortage of labour on the mines. The war had been good for African tenant farmers, who had supplied both sides with food when Boer farms became inoperable. As a result, many Africans were unwilling to leave their communal land.[3] Yet mining was the bedrock of an economy whose recovery depended upon the expansion of mining operations to low-grade reefs. With the mine owners as reluctant as ever to raise black wages, Milner tried to boost economic growth by importing cheap labour from China, a remedy that outraged British Liberals and served to infuriate Smuts too, who feared it would deepen the racial problem in a future South Africa.

In Britain, the Liberals made the introduction of 'Chinese slavery' into South Africa an important plank of their election campaign against the ruling Conservatives. The furore over Chinese immigration helped to revive Afrikaner nationalism and add weight to demands for responsible government for the Transvaal. Milner was forced to respond to the protests by promising to draw a distinction between white labour, on the one hand, and black and Chinese labour on the other.

The depth of Smuts's anger may be gauged by a private letter he wrote in February 1904 to Emily Hobhouse – the well-connected Englishwoman who had become a heroine to the Boers as a result of her campaign to alleviate conditions in Kitchener's concentration camps. In the letter, he vented his spleen against both Milner and the 'exploitative' foreign mine-owners who supported the importation of indentured Chinese labour. Without obtaining the writer's permission, Hobhouse passed on the letter to The Times in London, where its publication caused a minor sensation in political circles and made Smuts worry for a time that Milner might deport him because of his anti-British hostility.

EMILY HOBHOUSE

Piet Beukes, journalist and author, describes Emily Hobhouse as the woman who made Smuts world famous.[4] The two met in 1903 when Emily came to Pretoria to seek help for Boer farmers in the Free State whose livelihood had been lost because of the war. Deeply appreciative of her pro-Boer concern, Smuts invited Emily to stay with him and Isie, and the pair began to correspond regularly. Impressed by Smuts, Emily decided to make him her ally in the political campaign she had mounted in Britain on behalf of the Boers. When he wrote her the intemperate letter referred to above, she decided quite deliberately to leak it. Although embarrassed by its unauthorised publication, Smuts never once scolded her for doing so – which endeared him to her even more.

Hobhouse was ten years older than Smuts, the daughter of a well-connected clergyman in St Ives, Cornwall. Chafing at the restrictions of her cloistered, small-town upbringing, and having nursed her father until his death, at the age of 35 she set out to find her mission in life. When the Anglo-Boer War broke out, she became aware of the existence of the two Boer republics for the first time, and was outraged when she learnt that concentration camps had been set up to house Boer women and children.

Helped by her aristocratic uncle, Lord Hobhouse, to travel to South Africa in late 1900 to see conditions in the camps at first hand, the impecunious Emily took herself from the Cape to Bloemfontein, where she was appalled at what she found. Wading in herself to alleviate the unhygienic conditions in the more than 30 camps where some 63 000 women and children were held – 23 000 of whom were to die there – she began a one-woman publicity campaign to demand an improvement in living conditions in the camps. If there had been no Emily Hobhouse, Beukes wrote, many more would have died.[5]

Back home in Britain, Emily's influential political friends had introduced her to the new Liberal leader, Sir Henry Campbell-Bannerman, whom she convinced of the barbarity of the methods being employed in South Africa. She was so effective that a Commission of Women was sent out from Britain to investigate and recommend improvements to the camps, which resulted in

Emily Hobhouse, a heroine to the Boers. Gallo Images/Alamy/The Art Archive

the death rate dropping substantially. By 1903 she had become a force to be reckoned with in British politics, and with the help of Smuts's letter, she set in motion a process that was to culminate in the replacement of the Conservative government by the Liberals, and lead to the granting of self-government to the former Boer republics.

Emily also introduced Smuts to the woman who, besides Isie, was to become his soul-mate and closest confidante. Margaret Clark was the daughter of a prominent Quaker shoe-making family, who were generous in their support for deserving causes. Her grandfather, John Bright, was a distinguished English Radical, whose Quaker beliefs were to have an important influence on Smuts in later life. In 1904, Margaret went out to South Africa as Emily's secretary to help in the rehabilitation of Boer families. While a student at Cambridge, she had heard tell of the intellect of Jan Smuts. She was to become, as we shall see, even more of an influence on Smuts than Emily.

HET VOLK

By the early 1900s, Botha and Smuts had become universally recognised as the leaders of Afrikanerdom.[6] Guided by a re-energised and resolute Smuts, the pair set about founding a political party – Het Volk – to put an end to restrictions on use of the Dutch language, advance the cause of self-government, halt the importation of Chinese labour, and improve relations between the white races – which was what 'race relations' meant in those days. In the Free State, a party with similar aims, the Orangia Unie, came into being, while in the Cape, the Afrikaner Bond broadened its appeal and changed its name to South African Party in order to attract non-Afrikaners.

In 1905, to Smuts's considerable relief, Milner's term of office as overlord of the Crown Colonies came to an end. The Queen's representative had hoped to thoroughly anglicise the Transvaal by introducing a new education policy and encouraging the immigration of large numbers of British settlers, before self-government for the gold-rich colony could be considered. However, he had succeeded mainly in further inflaming Afrikaner sentiment. He was replaced by the more emollient and tactful Lord Selborne, whose instructions were to conciliate rather than antagonise the Afrikaner population, which he did with some success.[7]

◆

Smuts's capacity to forgive if not to forget is apparent from the remarkable letter he wrote to Milner upon the proconsul's departure from South Africa in April 1905: 'Will you allow me to wish you "Bon Voyage" now that you are leaving South Africa for ever? I am afraid you have not liked us; but I cherish the hope that, as our memories grow mellower and the nobler features of our respective ideas become clearer, we shall more and more appreciate the contribution of each to the formation of the happier South Africa which is surely coming, and judge more kindly of each other. At any rate it is a consolation to think what is noble in our work will grow to larger issues than we foresaw, and that even our mistakes will be covered up ultimately, not only in a merciful oblivion, but also in that unconscious forgiveness which seems to be an inherent feature of all historical life. History writes the word "reconciliation" over all quarrels …'[8]

The letter must have come as a total surprise to Milner. He and Smuts, strong-minded and determined men who liked getting their own way, were to develop a much higher regard for one another when, years later, they served together as members of Britain's war cabinet.

◆

Tucked away at the back of Smuts's mind was Lord Kitchener's whispered hint to him that the Liberals might be more sympathetic to Boer aspirations than the Conservatives. No sooner had the Liberals won power, therefore, than he was on his way to London on behalf of Het Volk to sound out Campbell-Bannerman and his colleagues about responsible government for the Transvaal and Free State. A fellow passenger on the ship was Margaret Clark, whose family, along with Emily Hobhouse, were to help him secure an audience with the new prime minister.

Smuts's meeting with Henry Campbell-Bannerman at No 10 Downing St turned out to be one of the seminal experiences of his life. As Antony Lentin writes, 'It would be impossible to exaggerate its impact on him, even if his version of it in subsequent years may have been overdrawn.'[9] Although Smuts had carefully prepared a memorandum setting out the case for self-government for members of the new Liberal cabinet, whose luminaries included Asquith, Lloyd George, Edward Grey and Winston Churchill, it was his 'man to man' conversation with Campbell-Bannerman that proved to be decisive. He found Campbell-Bannerman to be 'the sort of sane personality – large hearted and honest – on whom people depend. He reminded me of Botha.'

As Smuts was later to write, 'I put a simple case before him … Do you want friends or enemies? You can have the Boers for friends, and they have proved what quality their friendship may mean. I pledge the friendship of my colleagues and myself if you wish it. You can choose to make them enemies, and possibly have another Ireland on your hands. If you do believe in liberty, it is also their faith and their religion.'[10]

The cautious Scot did not react immediately to Smuts's plea, but, having had his doubts about Boer loyalties assuaged, made a speech next morning in cabinet which Lloyd George hyperbolically called 'the most dramatic, the most important ten minute's speech ever delivered in our time'.[11] A hitherto unenthusiastic cabinet thereupon endorsed the Prime Minister's proposal to grant self-government to the two Boer colonies. As Smuts marvelled, 'They gave back our country in everything but name. After four years. Has such a miracle of trust and magnanimity ever happened before? Only people like the English could do it. They may make mistakes, but they are a big people.'[12] Campbell-Bannerman's 'magnanimity' was henceforth to infuse Smuts's own political philosophy and served to convince him (and Botha) that South Africa's future lay within the British Empire.

SELF-GOVERNMENT AT LAST

Self-government for the two Boer republics was not long in coming. The West Ridgeway Commission, appointed by the British government, was charged with making proposals for a constitutional settlement acceptable to all parties. The cautious commissioners busied themselves with the delimitation of constituencies rather than the much trickier question of the franchise in the Transvaal and Free State. It was taken more or less for granted that the vote would be restricted to white males only: the British still considered themselves bound by the Treaty of Vereeniging to defer any decision on an African franchise. They were under no such restraint, however, regarding Indian and 'coloured' citizens of the Cape Colony.

In December 1906, letters patent inaugurating a new constitution for the Transvaal were issued, and shortly afterwards for the Orange River Colony. Smuts immediately threw himself energetically into a two-and-a half month long election campaign, drafting a declaration of principles and programme of action for Het Volk as well as authoring a series of party manifestos.[13] Along with Botha, he toured the province and beyond tirelessly, calling for conciliation and goodwill between Afrikaners and English-speakers. Although the response was encouraging, the two men ran into occasional pockets of stiff resistance, and found themselves having to counter some suspicion-mongering by elements in the pro-British Transvaal press. Even Isie had not been able to overcome her own antipathy towards the British, staying behind at home so as not to embarrass her husband in public and at political meetings.

CHAPTER 7

Nation Builder

THE ARCHITECT

Jan Smuts was by common consent the architect and designer of the Union of South Africa. 'The Boer has fought for his independence, the Englishman for his Empire: all have fought for what they consider highest. Now the highest is Union … Let us have Union … not of top dog or underdog, but of brothers,'[1] he declared with a brio and optimism that now became characteristic. Other politicians, notably Louis Botha, John X Merriman, JBM Hertzog and WP Schreiner, played significant roles in the discussions about unification, but it was Smuts's views on the crucial choices between a unitary or federal constitution, political rights for other races, and the selection of capitals that finally prevailed. As Hancock says, more than any other national constitution within the Commonwealth, that of the Union of South Africa bears the imprint of one man's mind.

In the Transvaal election of February 1907, Het Volk had easily won power, gaining an absolute majority over the other parties. Wisely declining the premiership in favour of the more popular Botha, Smuts became colonial secretary and minister of education. In Britain, the Liberal government may not have realised that in conceding to Smuts's appeal for self-government, it would be putting a force of nature at the centre of events in South Africa, eager to apply his intellect and energy to the creation of a new country.

With the election behind him, Smuts drove himself with 'colossal industry and persuasive tact',[2] striving to undo the work of Milner and reluctant as ever to delegate any of his workload to less capable subordinates. He spent long hours in his office and took almost all the affairs of government upon his own head. A cartoon in a British newspaper depicting the Het Volk cabinet gave each minister the face of Smuts, while the accompanying caption read: 'The controlling interest of General Smuts in the cabinet is so apparent that the government may be said to be concentrated in him alone.'[3]

For Het Volk, reconciliation and the building of mutual trust between Afrikaners and English-speakers was not simply a matter of altruism or idealism.[4] Harmony between the two white groups was regarded as the prerequisite for a unified South Africa. In the almost unilingual Orange River Colony, Afrikaners were in the overwhelming majority, but not so in the Transvaal, where the white population was half English- and half Afrikaans-speaking: Het Volk needed the English vote to gain power.

Conciliation came at a high cost, however. Across the Orange River, Steyn and Hertzog differed fundamentally over the concept of nationality and became convinced that Botha and Smuts were intent upon selling out to the British Crown. Before long, this divergence in outlook was to split Afrikanerdom and have a decisive bearing on the next three decades of South African history.[5]

Having become prime minister, Botha deemed it necessary – as a gesture of goodwill – to appoint two English-speakers to his cabinet; Smuts, just as eager to conciliate, introduced a controversial education policy which decreed that, in government schools, a child's mother-tongue would be the medium of instruction until standard four, whereafter English would become the standard and Dutch taught only as a subject. There were cries of resentment from Afrikaners – and Smuts was charged with betraying his own people.

As his fellow Afrikaner, Piet Meiring, points out in his even-handed assessment of a man he admired, in view of Smuts's previous struggle for Afrikaans, as education minister he could easily have entrenched the Dutch language once and for all.[6] But he failed to do so, and had to live for years with the consequences. Whereas separateness and autonomy were fundamental to Hertzog, to Smuts conciliation and adaptation were much more desirable. Prior to the creation of Union, Meiring suggests, Smuts was so intent on wiping out differences between the two white groups that he failed to give proper consideration to what was so dear to Afrikaners.

BOTHA AND SMUTS

There was no man alive whom Smuts admired more than his fellow Boer leader, Louis Botha. Although their characters differed in almost every respect,

The guiding hand behind Union: Smuts with Transvaal premier Louis Botha (left) and Cape premier John X Merriman (seated), 1910.

the strengths of the one made up for the shortcomings of the other. Botha regarded the world through the eyes of a cattle-farmer, while Smuts had the outlook of a scientist. Their relationship was like that between David and Jonathan.[7]

Eight years older than Smuts, Botha was a large, heavily built, genial man of infinite tact and patience, readily available to the many who sought his advice. Smuts, a lean, smaller-framed dynamo of boundless energy, was a much more driven individual, often uncommunicative and inaccessible. His enemies, who claimed that he was too clever by half, called him *Slim Jannie*, a nickname that was to stick. Botha's personal magnetism made him better able to handle crowds than Smuts, whose cerebral approach could sometimes alienate an audience. A modern analogy might be the contrast between Nelson Mandela and Thabo Mbeki post-1994, where the older man was the more popular, public face of the ANC leadership, while the younger turned rhetoric into policy behind the scenes.

Smuts was much more dominant in Parliament than Botha. Although he used his mother tongue with family and friends, he had been taught to think in English and was fluently bilingual. Botha, on the other hand, thought in Afrikaans and spoke English only when he could not avoid it.[8] This put him at a disadvantage in a country in which the language of commerce and industry, and parliamentary politics, was predominantly English. So whenever Botha spoke in Parliament, he made sure that Smuts, the true voice of the government, was close at hand.

Smuts made up his mind quickly, and sometimes wrongly, on important matters of state; the more laid-back Botha, by contrast, preferred to take his time. 'Whereas Botha could charm, Smuts could overawe.'[9] Though Botha sometimes had to placate people put off or offended by Smuts's '*slim*-ness', he nonetheless had the highest regard for the younger man's intellectual ability and delegated most policy making to him, except on agricultural matters. Although Smuts had been the more obvious candidate to become premier of the Transvaal when the colony acquired self-government, he wisely stood back in favour of Botha. As he wrote to Merriman, 'I might have been Premier, but considered that it would be a mistake to take precedence over Botha, who is really one of the finest men South Africa has produced. If he had culture, as he has chivalry and common-sense, there would not be his equal in South Africa.'[10]

51

Where Smuts's and Botha's minds were at one was on the issue of 'concili-ation' – the building of mutual trust between Boer and Briton after years of bitterness and conflict. Both men believed it imperative that the two white races should unite and stand together, under an imperial canopy if necessary, if they were to survive in an overwhelmingly black environment. What made practical sense to the pragmatic Botha was for Smuts the guiding principle of his life: the need for various parts to be absorbed into the greater whole.

The much-reviled Milner had understood what Botha and Smuts were made to realise when Het Volk came to power: the Transvaal's problems were inextricably bound up with those of the other provinces. The northern colony was relatively wealthy, but its goods came and went via the ports and railways of the Cape and Natal. Divisive issues such as the railway system, education policy and qualifications for the native, coloured and Indian franchise could only be dealt with effectively by a central authority which derived its authority from political unity.

Milner had attempted to bring the four colonies closer together in a tem-porary Customs and Railways Union, for which the new Liberal government in the UK showed little enthusiasm. As friction between the colonies over tariff barriers and freight rates grew, Smuts gave notice in early 1908 that the Transvaal would withdraw from the customs agreement, but was ready to negotiate a new arrangement. The matter had to be decided at a forthcoming conference to be held in Pretoria. As he put it in a letter to the Cape's John X Merriman: 'Otherwise I am afraid we shall drift further apart and develop vested rights alien to the establishment of Union.'[11]

FEDERATION OR UNION

Smuts was the not the first to entertain the notion of political unification in southern Africa. At various times, Hofmeyr, Rhodes, Kruger, FS Malan and even Milner had urged closer co-operation among the four colonies. Yet it was Smuts who took it upon his own shoulders to transform an ideal into reality. Ironically – for he was later to be vilified for supporting the mining companies – it was his concern about the growing power of foreign capital that spurred him into action. In 1906, he wrote to Merriman warning that 'unless the power of the mining magnates in the Transvaal is broken by our entry into a Unified or Federal South Africa, the danger of their capturing supreme power here and so over the rest of South Africa (which they will rout piecemeal) will continue to exist …'

In another letter to Merriman, he cautioned, 'Believe me, as long as we stand divided and separated in SA, the money power will beat us. … let us proceed to lay the foundation of a united South African people.'[12]

Merriman, English-born but staunchly anti-imperialist, thought that the four South African colonies should be allowed to run their own affairs without interference from British politicians. This was the view of Smuts and former Free State president Steyn too, who both saw union as a way of lessening British influence. When Merriman's South African Party, backed by the Afrikaner Bond, won power in the Cape in 1908, it became the third of the four colonial governments to be in favour of unification. Yet, while Smuts and Merriman visualised South Africa as a self-governing dominion within the British Empire, Steyn on the other hand hoped that union would unite Afrikaners and hasten their independence.[13]

The British government was also in favour of a closer union that would include Southern Rhodesia. Its high commissioner, Lord Selborne, produced a memorandum which declared that true stability would remain impossible as long as there were five separate governments in South Africa, each developing its own systems, each potentially antagonistic to the other, and no national government able to harmonise the whole.

The time for unification had clearly come, although significant differences among its protagonists remained – chiefly over the question of colour. The Cape had always harboured reservations about the Transvaal's attitude to other races. After Smuts's meeting with Campbell-Bannerman, Merriman had upbraided him for omitting any mention of the 'native franchise' in his memorandum to the Liberal government. The Cape leader believed that not making provision for African voting rights would be 'building on a volcano'.[14]

◆

In Merriman's view, there were two options: the first was the Cape's more liberal policy of giving the vote to people of colour who achieved certain defined educational and economic standards; the second was the policy adopted by

53

the two Boer republics and Natal of giving the vote to whites only. Smuts declared himself at one with Merriman in sympathising profoundly with the 'natives' who had been dispossessed of their lands, but begged to differ with him on the franchise: 'It ought to be the policies of all parties to do justice to the natives and to take all wise and prudent measures for their improvement. But I don't believe in politics for them,' he wrote.[15]

The double standards were patent. As Bernard Friedman was later to ask pertinently, why should the 'natives' have been denied the use of the politics which Smuts himself was exploiting so successfully to gain freedom for the Boers?[16] Yet Smuts knew well that a non-racial franchise was unthinkable to most white citizens of a future South Africa. He held firmly to his belief that the franchise issue could only be addressed after Union had come about. 'The political status of the natives is no doubt a very important matter, but vastly more important to me is the Union of South Africa, which if not carried now will probably remain in abeyance until another deluge has swept over South Africa.'[17]

While liberal opinion in Britain, concerned about the absence of African voting rights, thought that a federal parliament with the powers to adopt (and alter) the franchise in each colony would be the most desirable option, Smuts argued otherwise. There was a danger, he insisted, that the (white) people who would have to ratify any constitution for a united South Africa would veto it on the grounds that it would give the vote to blacks.

While continuing to assert that benevolent paternalism was no substitute for political rights, Merriman chose not to allow the franchise issue or his other concerns to stand in the way of unification. He was at one with Smuts on the merits of a unitary over a federal system. Having studied the precedents of Australia and Canada, the two men preferred a constitution that would be unitary and flexible, rather than 'federalistic and rigid'.[18] Mindful, no doubt, that he would be primarily responsible for implementing the constitution, Smuts wanted one powerful national government, arguing in a letter to his British liberal friend JA Hobson, 'we must not be prevented in far-off years from going forward because we have an agreement which cannot be altered. What we want is a supreme national authority to give expression to the national will of South Africa, and the rest is really subordinate.'[19]

In the Orange River Colony, there were other concerns about Smuts's intentions. With non-Afrikaners making up some 10 per cent of the population, its new leader, JBM Hertzog, had no need to conciliate English-speakers as Botha and Smuts, out of necessity let alone conviction, simply had to do.[20] Hertzog, like Smuts a lawyer from the Cape, but educated post-Stellenbosch in Holland rather than England, was first and foremost an Afrikaner nationalist, determined that the Dutch language should be placed on an equal footing with English. The two men 'were to each other as fire and water. They were alike, and yet so different that they could never agree.'[21]

The Orange River Colony's leader was particularly opposed to the Transvaal's education policy, which made the study of English compulsory but left Dutch as merely optional. Botha's attendance at the Inter-Colonial Conference in London in 1908 had helped to reinforce his and Steyn's growing suspicion that Botha and Smuts had gone over to the British side. The gift of the Cullinan Diamond by Botha to King Edward VII added to their fear of what union on the Transvaal's terms might mean.

In the other British colony, Natal, where whites lived in far closer proximity to Africans than their Cape counterparts and were fearful of being 'swamped', official policy was close to that of the two ex-republics: only the few Zulus in possession of a certificate from the Governor were permitted to vote. White public opinion was in favour of political unification, though not necessarily in the form envisaged by Smuts. Hoping to keep close ties to Britain and retain its legislative powers, Natal politicians came out in favour of a federal rather than a unitary constitution.

At a meeting of the four governments in Pretoria on 3 May 1908, Smuts won unanimous approval for his resolution that the 'best interests and permanent prosperity' of South Africa could only be secured by an early union of the four colonies under the British Crown. He proposed further that the colonies should appoint delegates to a National Convention to meet as soon as possible after the next parliamentary session. In preparing for the event, he and Merriman engaged in a lengthy correspondence about the procedures and principles of constitution-making.

◆

Smuts knew he would not have matters all his own way at the Convention. For the reasons already mentioned, the Orange River Colony's representatives – Steyn, Hertzog and De Wet – were suspicious of him, and watchful. Natalians were reluctant to risk their future in the hands of Afrikaners, who in turn were equally hesitant about joining forces with the Natal English. He took the precaution, therefore, of circulating to the man chosen to preside over the Convention, Sir Henry de Villiers, Chief Justice of the Cape, as well as ex-president Steyn and other leading participants, the draft of a constitution which allowed delegates some room for manoeuvre.[22] To those colonies which feared union, he proposed a form of provincial government with limited powers, subject to the sovereignty of the national parliament – a concession to the form of the weak federalism that survives in South Africa to this day.

THE NATIONAL CONVENTION

The National Convention opened in Durban on 12 October 1908, with subsequent sessions in Cape Town and Bloemfontein over the next eight months. Only whites were represented. Smuts took upon himself the planning, preparation and direction of the proceedings, which the other 32 delegates were content to leave to him. As his biographer, FS Crafford, was to write, 'The work of the convention … ultimately amounted to little more than a gradual toning down of Smuts' original thesis, to satisfy preconceived notions, whims and sometimes fears of some of the delegates.'[23]

There were, however, some deep divisions to be bridged before consensus could be reached. Steyn and Hertzog, leading the Orange River contingent, remained exercised about equality between English and Dutch, so both languages were given official status. Natal's sound but poorly argued case for federation, by contrast, had little impact on the discussions, and was not taken seriously. As to the location of the nation's capital, Smuts would have chosen Pretoria, but after much haggling the delegates accepted his compromise that Pretoria should be the executive capital and Cape Town the parliamentary capital, while Bloemfontein would become the seat of the Appeal Court.

On the question of governance, delegates voted for the unitary system proposed by Smuts and Merriman, ignoring the fact that, as Hermann Giliomee observes, it would have required a different dispensation to accommodate a nation 'so diverse, so torn and so colour conscious as South Africa'.[24]

As for the 'native problem', it was agreed that the current franchise arrangements in each colony should remain, with future policy left for the Parliament of the future Union of South Africa. 'Give us,' Smuts said – in retrospect unwisely – 'a national Parliament, a national executive, and trust to them for a solution of those questions that have troubled us in the past'.[25] Trust, he emphasised time and again, had to be the foundation upon which the new Union would be built.

African and coloured opinion, not surprisingly, was hostile to the proposals for white unification and protest meetings were held throughout the country. In the Cape, the African Political Union resolved that federation was preferable to union and the Cape franchise should be the basis of a national franchise. The South African Native National Congress, comprising black leaders from the four provinces, met in Bloemfontein. While agreeing that union was 'essential, necessary and inevitable',[26] the SANNC rejected the colour bar and resolved to send a delegation to Britain to protest. Black newspapers were vehement in their criticism of the colour bar and warned presciently of a future 'filled with bitter hatred and even violence'.[27]

◆

During the course of National Convention, Smuts purchased the farm Doornkloof, in the Transvaal grasslands, 16 km from Pretoria. He moved there in 1909, and immediately felt at home. Whenever he returned to Doornkloof, he was later to write to Mary Gillett, 'all my wounds are healed, all my aches are gone and I feel almost reborn in this atmosphere of peace and loving kindness ... No peace this side of the grave [is] like the peace of Doornkloof.'[28] The farm was to remain his abode for the rest of his days.

TO LONDON

Once the National Convention had approved the draft constitution for the new Union, it was referred to the four parliaments for formal ratification. The Cape, Transvaal and Orange River Colony passed it, while Natal held a referendum in which a large majority voted in favour. A delegation from the Convention, led by Botha and Smuts, took the draft to London, where it was warmly received. No heed was paid to the pleas of WP Schreiner and his colleagues that the Act of Union would in time become an Act of Separation between the minority and majority of South Africans. Their argument that it was Britain's duty, as the colonial power, to protect the rights of all in the new country fell on deaf ears.

The Colonial Secretary, Lord Crewe, took the view that Britain was still honour bound by the agreement reached at Vereeniging in 1902 that any decision on the franchise would be postponed until 'after the introduction of self-government'.[29] Sir Henry de Villiers was of the opinion that 'no worse blow could have been struck at the cause of sound relations between the races [Boers and British] than this notion of attempting to induce the British to override the almost unanimous wish of South Africa on the question of native policy'.[30] Botha himself insisted that the franchise question had to be settled in South Africa by South Africans, who had always 'shown a spirit of justice and fair play toward the native races'[31] in the past and could be relied upon to do so the future.

The South Africa Bill was debated in the House of Lords on 27 July 1909. As Privy Councillors, Botha, Merriman, De Villiers and Moor (from Natal) sat in the chamber, while Schreiner, MK Gandhi – whose campaign for Indian rights was already a thorn in Smuts's side – and others looked on from the public gallery. In the House of Commons, Prime Minister Asquith, while recognising the reservations expressed at the lack of protection for Africans and coloureds, claimed that whites would deal with these issues more wisely if they were united rather than divided. Any intervention from outside would be 'in the very worst interest of the natives themselves,'[32] he declared. The South Africa Act was passed unamended by both Houses and received the Royal Assent on 9 September.

On 31 May 1910, shortly after Smuts's fortieth birthday, his painstaking handiwork came together in the formation of the Union of South Africa. He played down the extent of his extraordinary achievement. Typically, he described Union as 'not a man's work; it bears the impress of a Higher Hand.'[33]

CHAPTER 8

Rebellion

TENSIONS SURFACE

The atmosphere of peace and goodwill which accompanied the birth of Union in 1910 was short-lived. As Crafford wrote, for the defeated Boers 'the healing hand of time had not as yet been able to expunge soreness from the heart and bitterness from the soul'.[1] And South Africa's first national election lay ahead.

As the political leader enjoying the most popular support, Louis Botha rather than a hopeful John X Merriman was asked by the Governor-General, Herbert Gladstone, to form an interim cabinet of members of the ruling party in each province. In September 1910, this coalition of governing parties, led by Botha and Smuts, easily won the general election. Proof of how necessary it was for the Afrikaner-led parties to conciliate English-speakers was provided in Pretoria, where Botha himself lost his seat to Sir Percy Fitzpatrick, largely as a result of Hertzog's aggressive language policy in the Free State. A year later, the South African Party (SAP) was formed to replace the coalition: Botha remained prime minister, Smuts was given no fewer than three portfolios (interior, mines and defence), and Hertzog was reluctantly given the ministry of justice.

This being South Africa, it did not take long for underlying tensions to rise to the surface. Smuts, as usual, was at the centre of any controversy. There was a furious row about an *ex gratia* payment made by the new government to outgoing members of the Transvaal parliament to thank them for voting in favour of Union. Merriman and his colleagues in the Cape were especially mortified by the gesture. To deflect criticism, Smuts put the Transvaal's money at Sir Herbert Baker's disposal to construct the Union Buildings.[2]

In trying to reconcile Boer and British interests, Botha and Smuts were at great pains not to antagonise the mining industry and the business community.

English-language newspapers, however, were up in arms over Hertzog's language policy; so promoting conciliation meant overruling Hertzog and curtailing Afrikaner language rights. This infuriated the uncompromising Free Stater, who argued in a speech at Nylstroom that there were 'two streams' in South Africa, each different in language and culture, which could flow alongside without the one imposing on the other. To the press, 'Hertzogism' was synonymous with 'racialism'.[3]

It was not so much Hertzog's argument that non-Afrikaners found offensive, but the angry, aggressive manner of its delivery. At De Wildt on 7 December 1912, he declared 'I am not one of those who always talk of conciliation and loyalty; they are idle words which deceive no one. I have always said I do not know what this conciliation means.'[4] He seemed to be doing his best to exacerbate and deepen divisions between the two races.

By now Botha, who could not stand Hertzog and vice versa, had had enough. After a Natal cabinet member, Sir George Leuchars, resigned in protest over Hertzog's speech in which he described two English-speaking MPs as 'foreign adventurers', the Prime Minister himself resigned, and on being invited to form a new cabinet by the Governor-General, appointed neither Hertzog nor Leuchars as ministers. Matters came to a head at the SAP conference in Cape Town in November 1913, when Hertzog and his supporters, with Christiaan de Wet at the forefront, walked out and formed their own National Party. In the 1915 election, the Nationalists won 30 per cent of all votes cast: five years later it was the strongest single party in the country.

◆

At this point, almost half-way through Smuts's life, it is opportune to consider where he stood in relation to Afrikanerdom. As Hancock observes, he was no longer as close as he had been to the old centres of Afrikaner nationalism. And although he remained a churchgoer, he had become uncomfortable with the conservatism of the Dutch Reformed Church.[5] While he believed that Afrikaners should hold dear the language in which they honoured their forefathers, their families and God – as he always did himself at home – he felt that English was more suitable as a literary and intellectual medium. Accordingly, he underestimated the link between language and nationality, and failed to support the growing campaign for Afrikaans to replace Dutch as one of the two official languages. This turned out to be a political mistake. It allowed Hertzog to put himself forward as the true champion of his people and don the mantle of Afrikaner leadership that Botha and Smuts were equally entitled to. But, as the Free Stater's popularity demonstrated, the one-track mind can often be an advantage in politics.

◆

The new SAP government's post-election priorities were to centralise administration and consolidate the civil service. With three portfolios to look after,[6] far more than anyone else, Smuts had his hands full on several fronts. Relations with Britain were left in the hands of Botha, who represented South Africa at the first Imperial Conference in 1911, while Smuts busied himself trying to resolve Indian grievances, establishing a Defence Force and putting down a violent strike on the mines.

AN AWKWARD OPPONENT

Of the many issues confronting Smuts at this time, the Indian question vexed him more than any other. It brought him up against the passive resistance or *satyagraha* of the immigrant lawyer, Mohandas K Gandhi – an instance of one believer in soul force confronting another.[7] The political struggle between these two men, closely watched throughout the Empire, foreshadowed the looming ideological and constitutional battle between Imperial Britain and India.[8]

Indian labourers, mostly of Hindu origin, had been brought to Natal in the 1860s to work on the sugar plantations. Thirty years later, after another influx, this time of Muslim merchants, Indian numbers had increased six-fold and, by the end of the 1900s, were greater than the white population. The immigrants' interests were represented by the Natal Indian Congress (NIC), founded by Gandhi in 1894. Theoretically, the NIC was open to all but in reality it was supported by a small and relatively privileged group only. Many Indians, mostly small traders, had left Natal and relocated in the Transvaal, where Kruger's determination to limit their movements had brought him into

61

Mohandas K Gandhi and the staff of his attorney's firm in Durban. INPRA

conflict with the Imperial government. Milner was as strict about immigration as Kruger, but Smuts, who was colonial secretary under Kruger, was even
tougher, introducing legislation which made provision for the registration of
'Asiatics' and the carrying of passes. The measure drew protests from the NIC
and liberal opinion in Britain and, more volubly, from the government of
India.

Gandhi had come to South Africa from London in the early 1900s, not
to stay but to fight a court case on behalf of some friends of his brother's.

A cultured, British-trained barrister, the Indian-born lawyer ran up against institutionalised racism wherever he turned. As he travelled north from Natal to the Transvaal, it occurred to him that his true vocation in life should be to confront racial prejudice wherever he found it. It was here in South Africa that the tactic of *satyagraha* was conceived. Those whites who humiliated him, had they but known it, were driving him into political activism – with incalculable consequences for South Africa, India, Britain and the world.[9]

Gandhi first came face to face with Smuts in January 1908, after he and 150 other *satyagrahis* were imprisoned for refusing to register or leave the Transvaal. The first meeting between the two men was cordial, even though they were at cross-purposes over what they had actually agreed. Smuts recognised in the Indian lawyer and activist a spiritual dimension similar to his own. Gandhi, for his part, understood Smuts's concerns about immigrants and went so far as to acknowledge that whites had legitimate concerns about Indian backwardness 'in hygiene, in civic seemliness and similar matters'. He asserted vigorously, however, that his fellow countrymen should not be obstructed in their attempts to improve their standard of living.[10]

As minister of the interior and the upholder of law and order throughout South Africa, Smuts found Gandhi's pacific tactics difficult to fathom or counter. He tried persuasion, concessions, threats, and eventually imprisonment with hard labour, without success. In desperation, he even sent Gandhi two religious books as a gift. The Indian sage returned the compliment by bringing Smuts a pair of sandals he had made for him in prison. Smuts wore the sandals every summer.

After Union, the battle of wills between the two men intensified. Smuts could not agree to Gandhi's plea for equal rights for Indians and introduced a new bill into Parliament to limit Asiatic immigration. As he told Gandhi, 'You are a simple-living and frugal race, in many respects more intelligent than we are. You belong to a civilisation that is thousands of years old. Ours, as you say, is but an experiment. Who knows but that the whole damned thing will perish before long. But you see why we don't want Asia here.'[11]

In 1913, Gandhi led 2 700 of his supporters into the Transvaal, for which he was again thrown into jail. By now, Smuts had become eager to settle the Indian question, so he set up a commission, which a defiant Gandhi refused to recognise. After an exchange of letters, however, the two men came to an arrangement – known as the Smuts-Gandhi agreement – which was taken up into the Indian Relief Bill. Both sides had been forced to compromise: the government abolished the special tax on Indians and gave official recognition to Indian marriages and other 'vested rights'; in response, Gandhi called off his defiance campaign. Left in abeyance was the vexed issue of the Indian franchise. Declaring nonetheless that his demands had been met, Gandhi set sail for India, via Britain. 'The saint has left our shores,' wrote Smuts, 'I sincerely hope for ever.'[12]

DEALING WITH STRIKERS

As minister of defence, it fell to Smuts to create a new military structure out of the forces of the two former British colonies and two Boer republics. 'We want an organisation that shall not be Boer or English, but a South African Army,' he told the staff college in Bloemfontein. His Defence Act of 1912, which took effect two years after the creation of Union, provided for a Permanent Force of career soldiers, an Active Citizen Force of voluntary soldiers, and various coastal protection units. It also made provision for a National Reserve of white males between 17 and 60, to be called upon only in a grave emergency. The new Union Defence Force (UDF) was headquartered in Pretoria; and Brigadier Generals Henry Lukin and Christiaan Beyers were appointed as heads of the PF and ACF respectively, reporting directly to Smuts.

It was not long before the need for such a force became evident when violence broke out once again on the mines. Back in 1907, Smuts had crossed swords with striking miners and used forceful measures to put down the strike. He was quite prepared, if necessary, to do so again. In mid-1913, another rash of strikes broke out among white miners and railway workers on the Witwatersrand. By this time industrial trade unionism had spread to South Africa, urged on by 'apostles of syndicalism'[13] from abroad. Their slogan was 'Workers of the world unite and fight for a White South Africa' and their purpose the protection of white workers' interests in the face of competition from large numbers of lower-paid blacks.

A strike on a Benoni mine led to the downing of tools elsewhere and the declaration of a general strike of miners on the Rand. As unrest spread to other industries, mobs of poor whites and the unemployed joined the strikers, looting shops and burning the houses of strike-breakers. The small police force was unable to cope, and as the UDF was not yet operational, Smuts was forced to ask for the help of Imperial troops. Refusing at first to heed the mine-owners' requests for intervention, he tried to prevent a mass meeting of workers in Johannesburg's Market Square on 4 July, but the strikers took no notice. At the meeting, fighting broke out between troops and demonstrators, who set fire to the railway station and *The Star* newspaper's offices later that evening. Next day, the Rand Club came under attack. In the fighting that ensued between policemen, troops and protesters, 21 people were killed and 47 wounded, not all of them strikers.

Smuts decided to deal with the crisis personally, taking Botha with him. He and the Prime Minister bore no weapons as they braved the hostile mob and drove slowly through the streets of Johannesburg to negotiate with the heavily armed strike-committee members at the Carlton Hotel. With the cards stacked against him, Smuts had no choice but to sign a document in which he undertook to reinstate strikers, set up a judicial committee into the miners' grievances and recognise trade unions. As he drove away from the meeting, he resolved never to be caught unprepared again.[14]

Smuts's struggles with strikers were only beginning. A few months later, in January 1914, retrenchments on the railways resulted in a general strike of workers being declared. This time, the minister of defence was ready. Calling up the ACF and commandos, he proclaimed martial law and ordered that strikers should be handled with the 'greatest severity'.[15] To the Trades Hall where the leaders of the strike had gathered, he sent his old comrade Koos de la Rey with orders to blow up the building if necessary. The strikers quickly capitulated.

A determined and resolute Smuts did not stop there. Without consulting Parliament or seeking cabinet approval, he ordered the deportation of nine British immigrant unionists who had instigated the strike. Before the courts could intervene, the men had been sent to Durban by special train and put on a boat to England.[16] Labour MPs, led by Colonel Fred Creswell, and their supporters were outraged, but Smuts defended his action in a five-hour speech in Parliament in which he argued that he had resorted to 'illegal' deportations because revolutionary syndicalists had declared war on the government and Parliament would never have given him the authority to take the action necessary to maintain law and order.

His argument failed to find favour in the House of Commons or with his Liberal friends in Britain, who thought he might be setting a dangerous precedent. Though some parliamentary opponents of the government, Hertzog among them, endorsed the deportations, many SAP members were perturbed that Smuts could deliberately flout the law when it suited him. Merriman described him as a 'ruthless philosopher'.[17] Creswell and his Labourites attached themselves more closely to Hertzog's National Party.

SCHISM DEEPENS

It took the outbreak of war in Europe to widen the growing divide within Afrikaner ranks. Many former Boer combatants believed the Union should stay well out of any European conflict; but Botha and Smuts did not. To both men, lending support to Britain in a time of crisis was a matter of national honour. The Empire was protecting South Africa internationally and it was now the country's moral obligation – as a faithful ally – to contribute to Imperial security.[18] As soon as Britain declared war on Germany, Botha wrote to the Imperial government accepting responsibility for South Africa's defence in order to allow British troops still in the country to be released for service elsewhere. Smuts, in turn, announced plans to recruit a volunteer force of four regiments in response to Britain's request for an invasion of German South West Africa.

Before the final commitment was made, Parliament was called into special session to give its approval for the invasion. The debate demonstrated what Crafford called 'an almost unbelievable recrudescence of race hatred … and a complete fading out of the convention spirit'.[19] Hertzog seized the opportunity to berate Botha and Smuts for their pro-British sympathies and plead that South Africa should remain neutral, a stance that found no support from either the SAP or Creswell's Labour Party. On 14 September, a motion in favour of the government taking the necessary measures to protect the Union and maintain the integrity and security of the Empire was carried by a comfortable margin of 92 votes to 12. Later that night, the first troopships left for German South West Africa.[20] In the meantime, the South African Native National Congress, in conference at Bloemfontein, had passed a resolution of support of the Empire and promised to suspend criticism of the government as long as the hostilities lasted.[21]

Botha and Smuts, however, had sorely underestimated the extent of internal resistance to their plans. Many Afrikaners felt that a German invasion of the Union was unlikely and were strongly opposed to creating unnecessary trouble across the border in South West Africa, where many hundreds of their kinsmen had settled.[22] On the day after the parliamentary vote, General Beyers resigned as commandant-general in the UDF in protest at the government's intentions. That evening, he and General Koos de la Rey, on their way to further plans for rebellion at a meeting in the Western Transvaal, failed to stop at a police roadblock outside Johannesburg. Shots were fired at their car tyres and De la Rey was killed by a ricocheting bullet. Boer sentiment was inflamed and Botha and Smuts were held responsible for De la Rey's death. For Smuts, the loss of his old friend and comrade was particularly heart-breaking. 'We were almost brothers,' he said in tribute, 'before the war, during the war and after the war'.[23] At De la Rey's funeral in Lichtenburg, which he and Botha attended without an escort, the two ministers had to brave the mourners' bitter hostility.

As soon as the funeral was over, Beyers, Christiaan de Wet and other Boer leaders began mobilising opposition to the government's plans to invade German South West Africa. On 9 October, General 'Manie' Maritz, commanding South African troops on the border, defected to the German side, taking most of his men with him. Elsewhere, large numbers of former commandos were refusing to serve in the UDF and flocking to join Beyers and De Wet in rebellion.

The government declared martial law in an attempt to impose its authority and avoid bloodshed, but by interfering with recruiting and holding up trains, the rebels made armed conflict inevitable. In this crisis, wrote Hancock, 'Botha rose to his full stature as a political and military leader, and as a man'. He announced that he would use volunteers only in the invasion of South West Africa and that he would take command of the UDF and go into the field himself. At pains to ensure that English-speakers were kept out of the intra-Afrikaner conflict, he and Smuts assembled a force of some 40 000 loyalists to put down the insurrection of 11 500 rebels. Fighting began in earnest in November 1915.

The internal conflict was more than just about support for Britain in war. Three years of drought had devastated areas of the Free State, Transvaal and

Northern Cape, and many 'poor white' Afrikaners were lured into rebel ranks by the promise of a Boer republic and a better life for all.[24] In clashes between UDF troops and rebels, Christiaan de Wet's youngest son was killed, while Beyers himself was drowned while trying to cross the Vaal River under fire.

By December, the UDF's superior numbers had prevailed and De Wet and other insurgent leaders forced to surrender. As many as 190 rebels and 132 government troops had lost their lives. When hostilities were over, the government had the problem of what to do with the insurgents. Special courts were set up, but Botha wisely called for a spirit of 'forgive and forget'. Prison sentences were imposed, but by the end of 1916, all rebels had been released.

All, that is, but one. Captain Jopie Fourie had defected to the rebels in UDF uniform without resigning his commission. He had led his commando into a skirmish with a UDF force in which twelve soldiers had died. Charged with high treason, he was tried by military court-martial and sentenced to be shot. A delegation of DRC churchmen, which included DF Malan, took a last-minute petition signed by hundreds of Afrikaners to Smuts's home at Doornkloof, but were not able to see him. Early next morning, the sentence was carried out by a firing squad and Fourie instantly became an Afrikaner-Nationalist martyr, a symbol of the bravery and defiance of his people. As Meiring notes, the echoes of that salvo were to follow Smuts to the end of his days.[25] He was left in no doubt that he had been deserted by a significant number of his fellow countrymen.

One man who appreciated Smuts's role in putting down the rebellion was Prime Minister Botha, who paid his lieutenant this tribute: 'Nobody can sufficiently appreciate the great work General Smuts has done. It has been greater than any man's throughout this unhappy period. He was at his post day and night. His brilliant intellect, calm judgment, his undaunted courage have been assets of inestimable value to the Union in the hour of trial.'[26] Smuts, in turn, declared that South Africa owed much more to Botha. Few knew, he said, what Botha had gone through in the rebellion: 'He lost friendships of a lifetime, friendships he valued perhaps more than anything in life. ... No one else in South Africa could have stuck it out.'[27]

CHAPTER 9

On Britain's Side

GERMAN SOUTH WEST AFRICA

One of the Kaiser's subsidiary war aims in 1914 was to extend Germany's reach across Africa south of the Sahara and challenge other European interests there. 'Mittel-Afrika' (Central Africa) was the term for a geo-strategic region that stretched from German South West Africa, through the Cameroons and Togoland in West Africa, all the way to German East Africa (Tanganyika, Ruanda-Urundi and other small pieces of territory). If Belgium were to be defeated in the war, the Belgian Congo could be added to a band of resource-rich colonies that would contribute to German economic self-sufficiency.

The huge, arid, underpopulated territory of South West Africa, with its long coastline, had been in German hands since 1884, when it was annexed by Bismarck. Its strategic value lay in its ports of Lüderitzbucht and Swakopmund, from which U-boats could wreak havoc along Atlantic sea routes, and a wireless facility which linked the capital, Windhoek, to Berlin. The Germans had built a 2 000 km rail network in the territory and stationed 8 000 German troops there to defend what was little more than a military outpost in a remote part of Africa.

For Smuts, going to war with Germany aroused mixed feelings. From his student days, he had always admired German thought and culture. He understood, however, that Germany's drive for colonial possessions could eventually threaten South Africa's interests and, unlike some of his fellow Boer leaders, knew exactly why the Kaiser had to be stopped. Also at the back of his mind was a hope that the German colony might become part of a greater South Africa. While his Quaker friends in England such as Emily Hobhouse implored him to keep his country out of the conflict, he chose to disregard their well-meant advice. As he wrote to Arthur Gillett, 'Botha and I are not the men to desert England in this dark hour. Many Boers cannot forget the past and bitterly disapprove of our action. But I think we are doing our duty.'[1]

South Africa's incursion into South West Africa, the first mounted by the new UDF, began in September 1914, but was put on hold for three months while troops returned to crush the Boer rebellion. The force assembled under Botha's command was a remarkable one. As Gerald L'Ange observes in *Urgent Imperial Service,* it was not only that every man was a volunteer that made it remarkable, nor that it was led by the Prime Minister himself – sometimes riding on a large white horse at the battlefront. What was remarkable was the nature of the men in it, nearly half of whom, only 12 years earlier with little more than their horses and rifles, had defied the might of Victorian Britain and kept the most powerful army in the world at bay.[2]

Some of these men, says L'Ange, were there out of loyalty to Botha and some because they felt honour-bound to Britain. But many were there because of their love of war. When General Coen Brits was asked by Botha to join his forces, he responded: 'My men are ready. Who do we fight, the English or the Germans?'[3]

Although Botha commanded a much greater force than the enemy's, the Germans' well-placed railway system enabled them to transfer troops rapidly across the country. Until the railway lines were secured, the South Africans had to march for long distances through searing heat across desert sands. But the UDF army combined the mobility, social cohesion and initiative of Boer commandos with the more orthodox and disciplined approach of largely English-speaking infantry regiments. For a fighting force, it proved to be a potent mix.

The C-i-C himself arrived in Swakopmund in February 1915 to take personal command of operations in the north. Three months later, he called on Smuts to take charge in the south. Splitting his troops into four units and outflanking the enemy with a series of daring thrusts, Botha and his men quickly cut the German colony in half.[4] By May, Windhoek had been captured and 4 000 German troops forced to capitulate in conditions that severely tested the mettle of the new UDF. 'If it were not for the thousands of sheep wandering around the countryside,' wrote a soldier in the Natal Carbineers, 'we would die of starvation … Some days we get half a biscuit and other days

Smuts and Botha on the South West Africa campaign

nothing not even salt ... Nobody shaves, we have no soap; our clothes are with (*sic*) dried animal blood.'[5]

In the south, Smuts mounted a three-pronged attack on the remaining German forces at large, driving them up against Botha's lines in the north. As in his days on commando, Smuts did his own scouting and drove his men relentlessly through the heat and sand. Water was in desperately short supply as the retreating Germans poisoned wells and laid land-mines and booby traps around installations in an effort to deter their pursuers. One of Smuts's columns rode for almost 1 200 kilometres through the desert on horseback in order to surprise the enemy at Keetmanshoop.

Within six months, the South West Africa campaign was over; on 9 July 1915, the Germans formally surrendered. Botha's and Smuts's tactics had proved remarkably effective. Although 530 South Africans had been killed and wounded, that was less than half the number of casualties in the rebellion. On 12 July, Smuts proudly declared the conquest of German South West Africa to be the 'first achievement of a united South African nation, in which both races have combined all their best and most virile characteristics'.[6]

He was entitled to boast: no other Dominion army had achieved as much on its own so quickly.[7] As the historian Bill Nasson observes with tongue in cheek, while little New Zealand had indeed seized nearby German Samoa, that was not of much significance 'other than to enlarge the pool of potential All Black rugby players once hostilities had ended'. A German observer noted sourly that the 'first British victory in the war was won by a Boer general'.[8]

News of the German surrender in South West Africa brought cheering crowds onto the streets of South African cities and raised spirits in the Allied trenches in Europe. Kitchener cabled Botha to express his 'sincere admiration for the masterly conduct of the campaign'.[9] There was wildly extravagant enthusiasm in sections of the South African and British press. *The Argus* in Cape Town, for instance, described the capture of Windhoek as 'the greatest blow which has ever been dealt to the German ambition of world dominance'. Even the usually circumspect London *Times* claimed that victory – in what had really been a colonial sideshow – 'will leave its mark on the history of the world'.[10]

1915 ELECTION

On returning home, Generals Botha and Smuts were treated as conquering heroes by one section of the white population and as 'sell-outs' to the British Empire by the other. Soon afterwards, the first five-year term of the Union Parliament came to an end, and the two soldier-politicians had to take to the campaign trail again. In the urban areas, they were given huge ovations, but in the countryside they were met with hostility. Tensions heightened after the sinking of the *Lusitania* by a German U-boat, with the loss of 1 198 lives, and anti-German rioting broke out in some of South Africa's cities.[11] Smuts's public meetings gave his opponents the opportunity of venting their loathing of him, which they did by screaming insults, attacking him physically and breaking up his meetings. At Newlands in Johannesburg, where he had brushed aside warnings of threats to his person, he was knocked to the ground by an angry mob and his car fired upon as he was driven away.

The election itself was a bitter affair. Nationalist newspapers, *Die Burger* in particular, railed at Smuts day after day, while Hertzog's supporters routinely accused the government of having deliberately murdered De la Rey, Beyers and Jopie Fourie. To whip up hatred of Smuts, even the widow of Jopie Fourie was brought into the fray.[12] Within the Dutch Reformed Church, congregations were split and families quarrelled; while at Stellenbosch, the university turned its back on its most eminent graduate.[13]

The results of the election were a severe disappointment to the SAP, which lost every contest in the Free State and half of the country's rural seats. Although the governing party won 54 seats, the Nationalists polled more than 30 per cent of the vote and increased their parliamentary representation from five to 26. The Labour Party, deserted by many immigrant workers after the *Lusitania* tragedy, lost heavily to the pro-British Unionists, who won 40 seats. The tide of anti-government propaganda had clearly found its mark: Botha and Smuts had lost the support of many of their fellow Afrikaners and needed Unionist help to remain in power.

The stresses of the campaign left their mark on Smuts, who confessed to an audience: 'I would like nothing better than to be out of this hell into which I have wandered, and in which I have lived for the last two years … But the Government cannot leave you … We have to exterminate this spirit of rebellion and unrest. Briton and Boer must combine to make a great nation. You can take my assurance that I shall work with my last breath for the good of South Africa.'[14]

Philosophically, he had already come to terms with the hatred he aroused, accepting it as the price to be paid for doing his patriotic duty. And, as always, he was convinced of his own well-intentioned rectitude. His spirits were raised by the news that he had been elected a Fellow of Christ's, his old college at Cambridge.

Shortly after the election, he turned down an invitation from Britain to take command of the army fighting the Germans in East Africa, to which the Union was about to commit 20 000 volunteers. But when the British came calling a second time in early 1916, he was prevailed upon to become commander-in-chief of the Imperial Forces in East Africa, with the rank of lieutenant-general. He accepted the appointment despite 'many a pang and many a grave misgiving' because, as he told Merriman, victory over the Germans might enable South Africa to expand its territory. However, it meant another of his long separations from Isie and the family.

EAST AFRICAN CAMPAIGN

As Kenneth Ingham observes, Britain's decision to invite Smuts to take command in East Africa was a strange one.[15] Despite being a general in the UDF, he had never commanded a large number of troops and his lack of experience of military planning put him at a disadvantage. But the British campaign in East Africa had not been going well, mainly because of the brilliance of Von Lettow-Vorbeck, the wily German commander and expert in guerrilla warfare. From his mountain bases on the northern border between British and German East Africa, Vorbeck had been successfully raiding British territory and threatening its lifeline, the railway between Mombasa and Nairobi. The British decided that a dose of Boer unorthodoxy was required.

In January 1915, with its forces on the Western Front bogged down, the Imperial government had taken a decision in principle to transfer more troops to the German-held territories in Africa, as the latter might eventually become vital assets 'when peace terms are discussed'.[16] Its already large force in East Africa was a polyglot collection of men from all parts of the world, including Britain, the Gold Coast, Uganda, Nigeria, India, the West Indies, Rhodesia

Accused of being a sell-out to the interests of mining capital and the British Empire – a typical attack on Smuts by *Die Burger*'s DC Boonzaaier. Museum Africa, Johannesburg

and South Africa, and varied in size between 55 000 and 114 000 – far more than the enemy had mustered.

The vast German East African terrain, twice the size of Germany itself, was not at all conducive to military operations. It ranged, according to historian

75

Ross Anderson, from tropical jungle and swamps to forested mountain ranges and undulating, parched scrubland.[17] The combatants had to advance, often in single file, over long distances on narrow, unsurfaced tracks. Communications were primitive: there were few roads and only two unconnected railways; the rivers were wide and unbridged.

The climate was equally inhospitable. In the dry season, conditions were unbearably hot and dusty on the plains, while during the six-month-long rainy season much of the countryside was impassable. Snakes and other wild animals were a constant hazard, as were swarms of mosquitoes, jigger fleas and tsetse flies, the latter accounting for thousands of transport animals. For Smuts's forces, it was as much a battle against the unforgiving environment as against the German army.[18]

Von Lettow-Vorbeck knew that he could not win the war in East Africa, but pinning down large numbers of Imperial troops might keep them away from the battlefields of Europe, where he believed the Great War would be decided. His own army consisted of some 14 000 men, most of them 'askaris', locally born and better able to withstand most tropical diseases, who were placed under the command of German officers.[19]

Smuts landed at Mombasa on 19 February 1916, and set up base at Nairobi in British East Africa. Refusing invitations to socialise, he set forth immediately into the thick bush to reconnoitre. Across the border in Tanganyika, the German front-line extended all the way from Mount Kilimanjaro, along the Pare mountain range, down to the sea. The way into German East Africa was via a single gap in the mountains, near the town of Taveta, which was heavily defended by Von Lettow's men.[20]

As usual, Smuts was in a hurry. Rallying his dispirited troops, some of them grumbling about being commanded by an amateur colonial, he launched a frontal attack on the enemy's forward positions, supported by flanking movements across the Kilimanjaro foothills led by Brigadier-General Jaap van Deventer, and to the south by General Stewart. Within twelve days, the Imperial forces had driven through the strategic Taveta gap and captured the Moschi-Arusha region, the most fertile area in German East Africa. But because General Stewart had taken his time and failed to cut off the retreating Vorbeck, he was promptly replaced.[21] Further follow-up operations were thwarted by the ferocity of the spring rains.

Within a month of his arrival, Smuts had managed to transform the military situation in East Africa.[22] Two-thirds of the territory, including the key rail link from Lake Tanganyika to Dar es Salaam, was now safely in British hands, and the Germans were pinned south of the railway line. Yet conditions for the troops were dire. The tropical heat was exhausting and the supply of provisions and medicine was frequently held up by the torrential rains, which washed away bridges and roads and turned large areas into swamps. Most of the South African troops, including Smuts himself, fell ill with malaria, while horses and mules died in the thousands. With the enemy on the defensive, Smuts began repatriating British and South African troops and replacing them with askaris from the King's African Rifles.

Ironically, as Ingham observes, Smuts now found himself in a similar position to that of Lord Roberts in the Boer War. He had far superior numbers to Vorbeck, but was unable to use his troops decisively against an elusive adversary. It was far easier to occupy enemy-held territory and win sporadic skirmishes than force his opponent to surrender.[23]

◆

At home, the growing UDF casualty list gave rise to allegations in some newspapers that Smuts was driving his forces too hard. Yet he never asked his men to do what he would not do himself; he ate the same food, endured hunger and thirst, went without sleep, and took pills and quinine to fight off malaria.[24] His troops respected and admired him because he was willing to face danger and possible death, just as they did. The novelist and poet Francis Brett Young, a medical officer at the time, wrote that 'the personality of that one man dominated the course of the whole war in East Africa'.[25]

Some of his officers were not so appreciative of their leader's 'austere message and spartan endurance', however.[26] According to Bill Nasson, when they heard the rumbling of his approaching Buick, they would flee their tents for the Cape Corps mess, 'where there were bottles to be hit'.[27] As on commando, Smuts kept mostly to himself in the evenings, reading the books that his old friend HJ Wolstenholme had sent him from Cambridge and developing his thoughts on holism. He had little success, though, in persuading his sceptical correspondent of the validity of holistic theory; 'Please think about this,' he once wrote, 'and don't merely pooh pooh what I say. There is something in it.'[28]

Boosted by the arrival of Nigerian reinforcements, towards the year's end Smuts's men made another concerted attempt to drive the German forces out of the jungle south of the great Rufiji River. Yet once again the elusive Vorbeck, aided by the drenching rains, was able to evade his pursuers and escape to fight another day.[29]

By this time, January 1917, Smuts had accomplished what the British government had asked of him. He had also become fascinated by the landscape and flora of East Africa, which he regarded as the loveliest he had ever seen[30] though the most difficult in which to wage war. Hoping to stay on in his post, he wrote to Isie to say that he would be home in a few months, but out of the blue a telegram arrived from Louis Botha asking him to represent South Africa at the forthcoming Imperial Conference in London, because he (Botha) felt unable to leave the country at such an unsettled time.

Declaring, once again like Roberts, that the battle against Vorbeck was effectively at an end – which it was not[31] – Smuts turned over command to his highly capable deputy Van Deventer and returned home for a 'honeymoon' week with Isie and the family. He spent most of the time on his bed, stricken by an attack of malaria.

◆

Like Winston Churchill, Smuts believed that the way to make history was to write it oneself. He wrote a long and detailed foreword to a book by a British artillery officer which became an authoritative account of the East Africa campaign and enhanced his own reputation as a commander. It also contained glowing references to the gallantry and fortitude of his men, as well as a tribute to the military skills of Von Lettow-Vorbeck, with whom he eventually came face to face after the war was over.

Military historians have always argued about Smuts's performance in East Africa. General French thought his campaign plan revealed 'unmistakeably the mind of a great strategist and tactician', but Colonel R Meinertzhagen, a British intelligence officer who liked Smuts and regarded him highly as a man, did not think much of his strategy and risk-taking tactics.[32] As the acerbic Briton recorded in his diary, '[Smuts] is a bad tactician and strategist, an indifferent general but in many ways a remarkable soldier.'[33] The historian Ross Anderson wrote: 'If the standard of military success is victory on the battlefield then it is difficult to judge Smuts a success. While he captured a great deal of territory, he never seriously threatened the existence of the enemy who left the theatre with their morale and fighting power unharmed. On the debit side, he had to evacuate the bulk of his army and those who were left were in no condition to carry on the advance.'[34]

Back in South Africa, Smuts's Nationalist detractors, who had opposed the recruitment of troops and the supply of materiel to the campaign, lamented its 'ruinous' human and financial costs. Hertzog-supporting newspapers called Smuts an 'Afrikaner traitor' who had a nerve to compare himself with the Voortrekkers, an empire builder who was the 'reincarnation of Rhodes'. In the eyes of the Hertzogites, South Africa might be officially at war with Germany, but the real enemy was 'English domination'.[35] Botha and Smuts, they insisted again and again, had gone over to the other side.

Smuts retaliated before his departure by talking up South Africa's successes in East Africa. 'Through our own efforts and our sacrifice, we have secured a voice in the ultimate disposal of this sub-continent. ... I trust ... that South Africa, instead of being a small, cramped, puny country, gnawing at its own entrails, will have a larger freedom and a better life and will become the great country which is its destiny,' he declared.[36]

CHAPTER 10

'On Service for Humanity'

A RAPTUROUS RECEPTION

Smuts arrived in London quite unprepared for the reception that greeted him. Food was in short supply in Britain as a result of German U-boat activity and public morale was low following the slaughter in French trenches – especially on the Somme. In Russia, the Bolshevik Revolution was under way. Britain was desperately in need of a hero and it found one in the Boer leader and former enemy, 'the destroyer of German power in Africa', who was now fighting on the side of Empire. In the press and on public platforms Smuts was referred to in overblown terms as 'the most conspicuous figure in Great Britain ... a remarkable combination of talents not usually found in one person, unless, indeed, that person belongs to the small and select class of which the Caesars, the Cromwells and the Napoleons are the outstanding types'.[1] Winston Churchill greeted Smuts as 'a new and altogether extraordinary man from the outer marches of the Empire'.[2] Yet amid the hyperbole, there was genuine admiration for the visitor and gratitude for his achievements. Invitations to speak poured in, and honours of all kinds were lavished upon him.

The warmth of Smuts's reception in Britain – in such stark contrast to the chilly atmosphere at home – as well as the many accolades, honours and invitations heaped upon him served to persuade him that the international arena might be where he truly belonged. He now enjoyed greater fame and prestige than any Afrikaner before him and would have been less than human had he not felt a deep pride in what he, and his new country, had achieved. Never short of idealistic self-belief, he even imagined that he could shorten the suffering brought about by the Great War, writing to Isie that he was now 'on active service for humanity'.[3] To requests that poured in from all sides for advice and opinion on a wide range of subjects, he responded with alacrity and 'astonishing speed'.[4]

Still a simple Boer at heart, he was determined not to allow celebrity or adulation to go to his head. Although he could have had London society at his feet, he much preferred to slip away into the countryside at weekends, to the Liberal and Quaker households of the Gilletts, Hobhouses, Hobsons and Clarks, where he could relax among friends. Although he could never bring himself to be as pacifist as they were, he understood and sympathised with their aversion to war of any kind.

Writing again to Isie in September 1917 from Windsor Castle, where he was a guest of King George V, Smuts told her that he felt lonely and alone in England, and would much rather be at home in 'my beloved South Africa'.[5] When the King made him a Privy Councillor and a Companion of Honour a year later, he confessed his embarrassment to Margaret Gillett, saying 'these things go against my Boer grain'.[6] His homesickness in London was compounded by letters telling him of Louis Botha's poor state of health. He longed also to be back with Isie and the children, writing to her, 'Once this war is over, I hope that we shall be together for ever and that there will be amends for all the separation that has been our portion in the bitter years behind us ...'[7]

◆

As a newcomer to Great Power politics, however, Smuts's self-assurance was truly remarkable. The Imperial Conference to which he had been called was actually two gatherings in one: the Imperial War Conference, which was to discuss matters of common interest to Britain and the Dominions (Canada, Australia, New Zealand and South Africa); and the Imperial war cabinet, chaired by the British prime minister and attended by the Dominion leaders, which co-ordinated the conduct of the war.[8]

To the unease of some Dominion representatives, the British seemed concerned not only with matters of war, but also with expanding their influence over the Empire. Smuts's former *bête noire*, Milner, now a cabinet minister, and his resurrected Kindergarten were dead set upon creating a federal imperium, run by a central parliament and an executive, in order to keep the Empire together.

Britain's Imperial war cabinet, 1917, seated in the garden of No 10 Downing Street. Smuts is at far right in a front row that includes Lords Milner and Curzon, Bonar Law and Lloyd George. INPRA

Knowing what his enemies back home would make of this proposal, Smuts countered that federation would be disastrous. He put forward an alternative resolution, in terms of which the Dominions would be recognised as autonomous nations of an Imperial Commonwealth, retain their existing powers of self-government, and keep control over their own affairs. Any constitutional amendments that might be necessary should be dealt with at a special conference to be called after the war. His argument won the day. From here, as Professor Ockie Geyser notes, the constitutional road ran straight on to the Statute of Westminster of 1931 – a milestone in the emancipation of the Dominions from Britain.[9]

The visionary Smuts, his eyes fixed on the post-war world, wished not to obstruct but rather to transform British imperialism and adapt it to the coming international order. While accepting that the Empire's roots would always be British, it should be founded, he asserted, on 'principles which appealed to the highest aspirations of mankind, the principles of freedom and equality'.[10] Invited to address both Houses of Parliament jointly on 15 May, Smuts argued that the Empire 'was not a State but a community of States and nations. ... not a stationary but a dynamic and evolving system, always going forward to new destinies'.[11]

'If we are not an Empire,' he continued, 'why call ourselves one? Let us rather take the name of "Commonwealth". ... the fundamental fact ... is

that the British Commonwealth of Nations does not stand for standardisa-
tion or denationalisation, but for the fuller, richer and more varied life of all
the nations that are comprised in it.' With characteristic enthusiasm, he predicted that a diverse but unified Commonwealth would be 'far greater than
any empire that has ever existed'.[12]

While the Imperial War Conference was in session, the first meeting of the
Imperial war cabinet took place. In March 1917, Smuts was invited to join the
cabinet by Lloyd George who described him as 'one of the most brilliant generals in this war'. It was here that Smuts's intelligence and far-sightedness really
stood out. He spoke rarely, but when he did he was listened to with attention
and respect. He soon found himself being consulted by colleagues, political
leaders, generals and admirals on a variety of matters. In June, at the suggestion of Milner – of all people – and in a move greeted with incredulity as well
as some hostility in Britain, Lloyd George invited Smuts to become a seventh
member of Britain's hitherto six-man war cabinet. (See Chapter 25, 'Counsellor
to Kings', for more on this subject.) Here in London, at the centre of events, he
had found his métier, bringing his intelligence to bear on practical matters of
war as well as more high-minded issues such as the future of mankind.

After the Conference was over and Dominion heads began leaving for home,
Lloyd George would not let Smuts go. As he wrote later, 'so deep was the
impression that General Smuts made at this time upon his colleagues, nay upon
the nation, that we would not let him leave us when the Conference ended. We
insisted on keeping him here to help us at the centre of our war efforts.'[14]

AT THE FRONT

One of Britain's most intractable problems was the situation in Ireland, where
nationalist anger had been exacerbated by the Easter Rebellion in 1916. Lloyd
George regarded Smuts, an impartial outsider, as the ideal person to preside over an Irish Convention. Smuts was urged by HJ Wolstenholme and
other friends to accept the challenge, but after taking further advice, he wisely
heeded warnings that he would be accepting a poisoned chalice. The opportunity to become deeply involved in the affairs of Ireland was to recur.[15]

Smuts's first assignment on behalf of Lloyd George was to visit France and
the Western Front to discuss the war's progress with the Belgian king, the

French president and Allied generals. On his return, he submitted a lengthy memorandum of his findings to the war cabinet in which he suggested that British strategy in France should be more flexible but supported his old foe General Douglas Haig's proposed offensive in Flanders. He came to regret that decision when, to his consternation, Haig's tactics led to the bloodbaths of Ypres and Passchendaele.

Smuts also suggested to the war cabinet that the campaign to drive the Turks – one of Germany's props in Europe – out of the war should be switched from Salonika to Palestine, so that British forces could be supplied from Africa and Australia and not have to brave the dangerous Mediterranean. He was promptly invited by Lloyd George to take over the Palestine command, spanning a territory which ranged from Egypt to the Caucasus. The idea of rescuing the Holy Land from the infidel appealed greatly to Smuts, and he consulted Louis Botha about the appointment. The Prime Minister, who regarded his fellow Boer soldier as a fine guerrilla leader but not a great general, felt that Smuts had to accept the implied honour, but should remain a member of the South African cabinet as a minister without portfolio rather than go onto Britain's payroll. In the end, Smuts thought better of the idea. The War Office was opposed to it and he sensed, correctly, that without proper support, he might become mired in one of the war's backwaters. A disappointed Lloyd George sent General Allenby to command Palestine instead.

At the end of May 1917, Smuts made another attempt to go home, but the British government would not countenance his departure. As a Dominion politician without a seat in the British parliament or any domestic constituency, however, his position remained 'constitutionally and politically anomalous'.[16] Was he a British or a South African public representative – or neither? At a time of national emergency, no one in London seemed too concerned about political or constitutional niceties, however.

Conscious of the anomaly, Lloyd George tried his utmost to persuade Smuts to become a member of the House of Commons, but after consulting Botha, Smuts declined, no doubt with an eye to the potential political fallout at home.[17] So South Africa's minister of defence stayed on as a member of the British war cabinet on indefinite loan from his country and its government. Smuts had concluded that it was in South Africa's best interest for him to remain in Britain, for he and Botha had already decided that when peace came, they would lay claim to German South West Africa. He looked forward to the day, too, when even Hertzog and co would have to acknowledge that he (and Botha), far from being Britain's lackeys, had led South Africa along the right road to national sovereignty.[18]

HANDYMAN OF EMPIRE

The British government, as had become clear, had plans to deploy Smuts in a variety of capacities. In July 1917, London had come under sudden attack by a squadron of German airplanes. In Crafford's words, 'public indignation was surpassed only by public anxiety'.[19] The war cabinet responded by deputing the Prime Minister and Smuts to examine the state of Britain's defences against air raids and remedy the debilitating lack of co-ordination between the fledgling air services of the Army and Navy. Lloyd George was too busy to do much committee work himself, so the task was left to Smuts, who sprang immediately into action. Within a mere three months, he had devised effective air-defence plans for London and other strategically important cities. Overriding the protests of turf-conscious admirals and generals, he proposed the merger of their air arms into one fighting service under a new ministry. As Lloyd George was to acknowledge in his memoirs, Smuts more than any other man had the right to be called the Father of the Royal Air Force.[20]

With German air raids on the increase and the British army bogged down in the mud of Flanders, Smuts turned his mind to the possibility of an air offensive as a means of turning defence into attack. That entailed coercing British industry into the production of aircraft, so the Aerial Operations Committee, with Smuts in the chair, was enlarged to become the War Priorities Committee, charged with bringing all of the country's industrial resources to bear on the war effort. By this time, Smuts's administrative burden had become immense, but he was in his element. Not for nothing had he become known in the UK press as the 'Handyman of the Empire' – a soubriquet that his detractors in South Africa latched on to with glee. 'Honest broker of the Empire' might have been a more accurate term.

◆

At around this time, Smuts came to know Professor Chaim Weizmann, a chemist at the University of Manchester, who had invented a new and simple way of manufacturing acetone, used in the production of explosives. Weizmann sought no personal reward from the British for doing so, but hoped that Palestine might be designated as a homeland for his fellow Jews. Since the Anglo-Boer War, Smuts had always harboured an affection for the Jewish people, whom he regarded as similar to Afrikaners in being God-fearing, hard-working and without a homeland to call their own. He envisaged a free Palestinian state as part of the British Empire. Pragmatic as always, and with Allied fortunes in 1917 declining, he understood the need to win wealthy and influential Jews in America, in particular, over to the Allies' side. He encouraged Lloyd George and his foreign secretary Arthur Balfour, therefore, to issue what became known as the Balfour Declaration – a formal but ambiguously worded promise that in the event of an Allied victory, Britain would establish a national homeland for the Jews in Palestine. He recorded that the undertaking was given 'to rally Jewish sympathy for the Allied cause at the darkest hour of the war.'[21]

◆

By late 1917, the Russian revolution was coming to a head, socialism was on the march and Marxist slogans resounded across Europe. In Britain, the war effort was being hampered by a series of industrial strikes. The situation was particularly serious in the South Wales coalfields, where a walkout by miners threatened supplies of coal to the Royal Navy. The war cabinet decided it had to face down the challenge to its authority. Having helped to settle a police strike in London and a munitions strike in Coventry, Smuts was asked to make a last effort at conciliation. At home, he had always cracked down forcefully on any worker insurrection but in Wales more peaceful tactics were required.

Arriving at Tonypandy, the town at the centre of the strike, he was confronted by a huge assembly of hostile miners, intrigued by the presence of this white man from Africa with a high-pitched voice and funny accent. Remembering a remark by Lloyd George that his countrymen were great singers, Smuts began by saying, 'Gentlemen, I come from far away, as you know. I do not belong to this country. I have come a long way to do my bit in this war … I have heard in my country that the Welsh are among the greatest singers in the world and before I start, I want you first to sing me some of the songs of your people.'[22] Suddenly, a man in the crowd began singing 'Land of My Fathers' in Welsh and then with deep fervour the rest of the throng joined in. When the anthem ended, Smuts spoke again: 'Well, gentlemen, it is not necessary to say much more tonight. You know what has happened on the Western Front. You know your colleagues in their tens of thousands are risking their lives. You know that the front is as much here as anywhere else … I am sure you are going to defend the Land of Your Fathers, of which you have sung here tonight.' After he had successfully addressed other meetings on the coalfields in a similar vein, the strike was over. Back in London, an admiring cabinet colleague, Lord Curzon, called him 'a crafty fellow'.[23] In South Africa, people would have nodded their heads and called him *slim*.

Of more immediate concern to Smuts and the war cabinet was the dire situation on the Italian front, where German and Austrian forces had inflicted a heavy defeat on the Italian army at Caporetto. Smuts's advice to Lloyd George was to send several British infantry divisions and heavy artillery to Italy to shore up Allied defences. The two men hurried to a conference at Rapallo, where Smuts's suggestion was endorsed and plans made for a Supreme War Council drawn from all the Allied armies.

Shortly before the year's end – at a most inopportune moment, given the scale of the disaster at Caporetto – Lloyd George decided to respond positively to a secret peace overture from Austria. He sent Smuts under an assumed name to Geneva to meet an Austrian envoy, Count Mensdorff. Smuts's hopes of inducing the Austrians to conclude a separate peace were dashed when Mensdorff declared that idea to be out of the question. Smuts for his part told Mensdorff that Britain would not settle for peace until Germany had been defeated.

Although their two days of talks ended inconclusively, Smuts was able to brief the Austrian on Allied plans for the establishment of a League of Free Nations, along the lines of the British Empire, into which the Habsburg empire might be brought once it had severed its links with Germany. Mensdorff, on his part, asked for a statement of British war aims that would make it clear that destroying her enemies was not the objective of British policy. The war cabinet agreed to this request and delegated the drafting of the document to Smuts and two others.

THE WAR ENDS

Nineteen eighteen began with Lloyd George setting out Britain's (and the Dominions') war aims in a speech at Caxton Hall in London. Not surprisingly, Smuts warmly approved of the speech, having drafted most of it himself. The Prime Minister made it clear that Britain's war aims were limited and based on a desire for justice for those who had suffered rather than any wish to see Europe in ruins. (He was to harden his stance later.) His speech was followed days later by President Woodrow Wilson's famous declaration of 'Fourteen Points', which prepared the way for his (and Smuts's) ideal of a post-war League of Nations to settle international disputes and advance the cause of peace.

In mid-January, Smuts was asked to go to France to report once more on conditions on the Western Front. By this stage, Lloyd George had become deeply suspicious of the information he was being fed by his generals. He asked Smuts to recommend a replacement for Haig, but Smuts came to the conclusion that there was no one better than his former foe. The PM then turned his attention to Palestine, where he suspected the War Office of trying to undermine his (and General Allenby's) plan to defeat the Turks and knock out one of Germany's supporting pillars. Smuts was sent post-haste to Palestine, and then to Egypt, from where he and Allenby hatched plans for an Allied advance into Syria.

No sooner was Smuts back in England than an all-out assault by the Germans on the Fifth Army's lines in France began. The stakes could hardly have been higher. If the Germans broke through, the way to the Channel ports lay open. If the attack failed, it would mean an end to the Kaiser's hopes of victory. Staring defeat in the face, the Allies agreed to appoint France's General Foch as supreme commander. Because of the gravity of the situation, Smuts turned down an invitation to leave Britain for America to try to prod President Wilson into more vigorous action on the Western front. Despite having declared war on Germany a year ago, America had yet to begin fighting.

Smuts's impatience with American inactivity and his lack of regard for the leadership of America's General Pershing led him to make the remarkable proposal to Lloyd George that he (Smuts) be put in overall charge of US forces in France. He suggested that, with his military experience, he could lead the long-overdue American offensive in support of the Allied forces, with Pershing left in charge of arrangements in the rear. Lloyd George wisely declined the offer – which would have been a severe slap in the face for the Americans – and tactfully kept it to himself. (It only became public knowledge in 1954.) Instead, he suggested that Smuts should go secretly to Russia – which the fiercely anti-Bolshevik Smuts turned down because he did not see how revolutionary Russia could contribute to the Allied cause.

With an Allied victory now a distinct prospect, Smuts set out his ideas about a post-war settlement in a speech in Glasgow on 17 May, when the freedom of the city was bestowed upon him. It was here that his views and Lloyd George's began to diverge. Fearful that what had essentially been a European conflict, with some digressions, might develop into a full-scale world war across all seas and involving all continents, Smuts warned the Allies against prolonging the fighting until they had delivered 'the knock-out blow' to the Germans.[24] Pointing out that the Allied armies had been waging a *defensive* war with limited objectives against Germany's *offensive* war with unlimited objectives, he argued that once Germany's war aims had been thwarted, it was unnecessary to march to Berlin and beat the Germans into submission. But, as became apparent in Paris, the war cabinet and Lloyd George were intent on teaching the Germans a lesson and – under pressure from a vocal 'Hang the Kaiser' lobby at home – viewed matters rather differently.

By July 1918, American forces had entered the war in numbers, enabling Allied forces under Marshal Foch to beat back Ludendorff's last desperate onslaught on the Allied front. It became apparent even to the Kaiser that the war could no longer be won, and on 8 August a demoralised Germany sued for peace. The Central Powers abruptly imploded: Austria, Turkey and Bulgaria surrendered; revolutions broke out in Hungary and Germany; the Kaiser fled into exile in Holland. On 11 November 1918, an Armistice based on the principles of President Wilson's 'Fourteen Points' was signed in Foch's railway carriage in a French forest.

◆

If Smuts thought that Armistice might lessen the burden upon him, he was mistaken. The war cabinet gave him the task of guiding the demobilisation and 'return to normalcy' of Whitehall departments and Lloyd George charged him with drafting Britain's brief for the Peace Conference in Paris. He was also hard at work writing a memorandum on the League of Nations, preparing the case for Dominion representation at Versailles, and setting out South Africa's territorial claim to German South West Africa. The demands on his time remained relentless.

Many in Britain (including Winston Churchill), as well as nations such as France, objected to Smuts's proposal that the Dominions should each be represented in their own right and given a vote at the Paris Peace Conference, but Smuts eventually had his way. As for South Africa itself, he regarded membership of a British 'Commonwealth' as an enhancement of the country's international status and a guarantee against the isolationist path of Hertzog and his allies at home. Looking further into the future, as he had done throughout the war, he viewed the establishment of a League of Nations, based on the principle of Commonwealth, as the primary goal of the forthcoming Peace Conference.

On 16 December 1918, Smuts brought his thoughts on the future of the world together in an intellectually brilliant paper presented to the Imperial war cabinet. In the paper, he synthesised three concepts – Imperialism, Commonwealth and a League of Nations – into one, by so doing lending support to President Wilson's efforts to counter the isolationist tendencies so deeply rooted in American politics. In a series of 21 propositions, he laid out a constitutional blueprint for the proposed League. As the Peace Conference drew closer, he issued his paper in the form of a pamphlet: *The League of Nations – A Practical Suggestion.*

President Wilson was one among many who were captivated by it. The President latched on to the words 'Europe is being liquidated, and the League of Nations must be heir to this great estate' and repeated them time and time again. He also rewrote his own proposals to take account of Smuts's suggestions. The pamphlet, described by Lloyd George as 'the ablest state paper he had seen during the War'[25] attracted much public support and was privately circulated among delegates at the Paris Conference. A leading historian of the League of Nations wrote, 'here in language worthy of Milton or Burke, were high idealism, acute political insight, a profound understanding of the hopes and sentiments of the rank and file of soldiers and civilians, [and] clear and practical administrative planning'.[26]

In his recent study of the formation of the United Nations, Mark Mazower notes that, by now, Smuts had become one of the leading theorists of international order and played an important role not only in shaping the League of Nations, but in brokering accords between Whitehall and Washington.[27] Smuts's proposal for a peacetime international organisation was the most radical proposal to emerge from British policy makers and took internationalism much further than the Lloyd George government really wanted to go. Its 'genius' lay in its link to the questions of Atlanticism and imperial cohesion that the British so strongly valued.

With the war at an end, Smuts laid down his responsibilities in Britain in December 1918 and resigned from the war cabinet. Louis Botha was about to join him in London and accompany him to Paris to represent South Africa at the Peace Conference. Botha was in poor health and battle weary, having had to put up with a relentless campaign of denigration waged by Hertzog and his followers, intent on capitalising on the hardship produced by war to press their claims for a republic. Both men felt acutely the insults their fellow countrymen were heaping upon them, but duty had to come before any other consideration.

CHAPTER 11

Losing the Peace

THE JUDGEMENT OF PARIS

Smuts went to the Paris Peace Conference in a pessimistic frame of mind. The Allies had won the war, but he was doubtful they could win the kind of peace that he, Woodrow Wilson and others wished for Europe and the world. Now no longer a member of the British government, and with his own prime minister in attendance, he was South Africa's junior representative at the Conference. Although his prestige remained high, he felt frustrated at no longer being at the centre of affairs.

The Peace Conference was presided over by a Committee of Ten, but effectively run by the Big Four (Britain, France, Italy and the USA). Smuts was not on either of the main committees, but was elected to the Commission of the League of Nations, chaired by President Wilson, which was given the task of drafting a constitution for the proposed organisation. The idealistic American president proved to be no match for France's Clemenceau, Lloyd George and others who were determined, first and foremost, to extract reparations from the Germans and were in no mood to adopt any of Wilson's 'Utopian' schemes. The Conference resolved, nonetheless, that a League of Nations should be created as 'an integral part of the Treaty of Peace',[1] and approved the initial draft of its Covenant – in essence the work of Smuts. But an assassination attempt on Clemenceau and the temporary departure from Paris at a critical juncture of Wilson, Lloyd George and Smuts himself who fell seriously ill in London while on a brief visit there, resulted in further discussions about the League being overtaken by events. Pleas from Smuts and Botha for the magnanimity shown to them after the Anglo-Boer War to be extended to the defeated Germans found little resonance with elected politicians from Britain and France, bent – quite understandably after years of loss and sacrifice – on punishment and revenge. Smuts wrote repeatedly to Lloyd George warning of the dangers to Europe of destroying the German economy, but the British prime minister was no longer in receptive mood.

The question of what to do with Germany's former colonies, including South West Africa, was dealt with in Article 22 of the League's Covenant. Although Wilson adopted the essence of Smuts's proposal for a system of 'mandates', he went much further than the South Africans had expected or wished. In devising the concept of mandates, Smuts had in mind not only the new states formed out of the ashes of the former Austro-Hungarian Empire, but Germany's overseas possessions as well. The latter, he believed, should be annexed to the Dominions, but the anti-imperialist Wilson disagreed. If the responsibility for colonial mandates was not vested in the League of Nations, the American president asserted, the mandate system would merely be a way for the Allies to share out the spoils of war.[2]

Smuts's formula separated the territories to be assigned by the League into 'A', 'B' or 'C' mandates, according to their readiness for independence. South West Africa fell into the 'C' category and was entrusted to South Africa on terms amounting to virtual annexation.[3] Wilson's anti-imperialist stance and insistence on the principle of 'national self-determination' as the *sine qua non* of any new world order was a setback for Botha and Smuts, however. Their grand vision of a Greater South Africa under white rule, stretching beyond the Zambezi to the Congo and including the British colony of Basutoland, the protectorates of Bechuanaland and Swaziland as well as Portuguese East Africa, began to recede into the Parisian mist.

DEVASTATION IN EUROPE

An out-of-sorts Smuts was persuaded to undertake one further mission on behalf of Lloyd George and the Peace Conference. Hungary had fallen victim to a Bolshevist dictatorship, led by Bela Kun, and neighbouring Rumania was attempting to advance across the border in contravention of the Armistice. Smuts was sent to Budapest ostensibly to settle the territorial dispute, but really to see whether Kun could persuade the Russians, especially Lenin, to come to Paris. Travelling by train through central Europe, he was appalled by the poverty and degradation he witnessed. Stopping over in Vienna, he resisted attempts by the

In agreement on the subject of German reparations: Smuts and John Maynard Keynes in conversation. Museum Africa, Johannesburg

British military attaché to entertain him lavishly and was equally unimpressed by Bela Kun's offer of a welcoming banquet in the midst of his country's poverty. No admirer of Bolshevism, Smuts refused to budge from his train in Budapest station and made Kun come and see him four times. When the Hungarian dictator continued to haggle over the definition of the military frontier, Smuts gave him an ultimatum and ordered his train to depart at the precise time he had stipulated, leaving Kun and his colleagues on the station platform 'looking up in blank amazement'.[4] The impatient Smuts had already concluded that Kun had little influence with his masters in Moscow.

From Budapest, he travelled to Prague at Lloyd George's request for talks with Tomas Masaryk, president of Czechoslovakia, and to Vienna to discuss trade issues with the Austrian finance minister, Josef Schumpeter. He returned to the Paris Conference profoundly affected by the harrowing sights he had seen, convinced that Austria-Hungary should remain a single economic unit and be put back on its feet via a substantial international loan. Few in Paris were listening, however.

◆

The Peace Conference attracted delegations from ethnic groups and tribes from many countries, each intent on bringing its demands to the attention of the world's leading statesmen. From South Africa came a deputation of Afrikaner nationalists, headed by General Hertzog, to make their case for a republic. Their passage had not been smooth. When they were about to embark from Cape Town, the crew of the Union-Castle liner had refused to man the vessel taking them to Europe. Although the Royal Navy put a warship at Hertzog's disposal, he rejected the offer and boarded a Dutch ship en route to Europe via New York instead.

Hertzog knew full well that his mission had little chance of success, but was certain to win him votes at home. Lloyd George gave the delegation a courteous reception, but explained that Botha and Smuts were South Africa's official representatives in Paris and that Hertzog and company had no *locus standi*. Though the Nationalist leader went home empty-handed, he had succeeded in his mission to make propaganda against Smuts and Botha and portray them as being more concerned with the affairs of Empire than the welfare of ordinary South Africans.

◆

By the end of May 1919, Smuts had come to realise that his hopes that the Allies would treat the Germans with 'pity and restraint' were unlikely to be realised, especially after President Wilson had given way and accepted Clemenceau's proposals for the military invasion of Germany. He soon found himself caught up in the most vexed issue at the Conference – the amount of German reparations.

As Margaret Macmillan explains, the question of German reparations was 'at once both very simple and very complicated'.[5] Simple because, in Lloyd George's words, someone had to pay for the damage caused by the war, and if it were not to be Germany, it would be the British taxpayer. Complicated because no one in Paris could agree on the amount, or how much Germany could actually afford by way of compensation.

Britain's cleverest economist and chief Treasury adviser, John Maynard Keynes, believed, as did Smuts, that imposing a crippling burden on Germany would merely deepen the economic hardship caused by war. Smuts, for his part, could not understand how the British government could believe that the destruction of one of its most important export markets would help British industry back onto its feet. Another of his memoranda to Lloyd George, followed by impassioned letters to both him and Wilson, drew no response. His letter to Lloyd George ended with these prescient words, 'This treaty breathes a poisonous spirit of revenge, which may yet scorch the fair face – not of a corner of Europe, but of Europe.'[6]

The wily British prime minister was not above exploiting the high regard in which Smuts was held by President Wilson to Britain's advantage, nonetheless. When an argument arose over whether German reparations should include state pensions to British serviceman and their dependants, George asked Smuts – about to leave for Budapest – for a quick legal opinion. When Smuts opined that Germany should indeed pay for all British war pensions and separation allowances, the Prime Minister used his argument to persuade Wilson to support British demands 'to make Germany pay'.[7] Keynes was appalled, and Smuts himself was widely criticised for apparently contradicting himself, not least in South Africa where Hertzog and his supporters leapt upon any opportunity to vilify him.

◆

During these discussions, it was Smuts who put the word 'appeasement' into international circulation,[8] long before it acquired its pejorative connotation in World War II. Writing to Lloyd George from Paris in March 1919, he argued that Germany's appeasement might turn her into a bulwark against the Bolshevist threat in Eastern Europe. By appeasement, he meant an attitude of generosity, the magnanimity of the strong towards the weak, such as the British had displayed to the Boers. After World War II, however, appeasement came to mean the abandonment of principle and abject capitulation by the weak to the strong.

◆

Smuts had many reservations about the draft peace treaty when, after much Allied haggling, it saw the light of day. He regarded it as a war rather than a peace treaty and agonised over whether or not he could sign a document with which he so profoundly disagreed. He was worried, however, about the implications in South Africa if he did not sign and decided instead to renew his efforts to have the treaty amended. In a letter to President Wilson, he warned presciently that the peace might well become 'an even greater disaster to the world than war was'.[9] To his disappointment, the American president did not bother to reply.

None of the Allied leaders shared Smuts's concerns or seemed to care what might happen if Germany refused to sign a treaty it regarded as grossly unfair. Smuts feared that the British naval blockade, imposed during the latter stages of the war and lifted by Lloyd George over the objections of the French, might have to be re-imposed, which would bring further hardship and starvation to millions in Europe. His hopes were raised, briefly, when Lloyd George called together the war cabinet, the Dominion prime ministers and other leaders at the Peace Conference to discuss Germany's counter-proposals to the treaty. After Smuts had made a strong plea for the terms to be revised, the meeting resolved to give Lloyd George a free hand to make any changes he thought fit.

Smuts was extremely angry when the British prime minister declined to alter any of the treaty's provisions. The tenseness of relations between the two is reflected in their exchange of letters in June 1919, in which Lloyd George wrote, 'The Germans repeatedly request the return of their colonies. Are you prepared to allow German South West Africa or German East Africa to be returned to Germany as a concession which might induce them to sign the peace?'[10] Smuts replied, 'Please do not have the impression that I would be generous at the expense of others, as long as the Union gets South West Africa. In this great business, South Africa is as dust in the balance compared to the burdens now hanging over the civilized world.'[11]

Smuts now found himself in a minority of one, however.[12] His fellow Dominion prime ministers were supportive of some of his objections, but were not prepared to cross Lloyd George. Even Botha, a simpler, less moralistic and more pragmatic politician who shared Smuts's doubts about the treaty, counselled caution. The two of them were in Paris, he said, to look after the interests of South Africa; Europe should be left to settle its own affairs.[13]

If Smuts had hopes that Germany might refuse to accept the peace terms, they were dashed when Marshal Foch issued an ultimatum, threatening to re-open the war if the treaty was not signed forthwith. On 23 June, the Germans agreed to accept the terms of the treaty unconditionally. Smuts announced, at first, that he would refuse to sign what he regarded as 'a death sentence on Europe',[14] but was persuaded to change his mind by Botha, who thought that if he signed and his deputy did not, his position as prime minister would be untenable. Consulted by Botha and Smuts over their dilemma, Lloyd George advised Smuts to sign the treaty under protest and express his criticisms afterwards.

On 28 June 1919 in the Hall of Mirrors at Versailles, representatives of all nations gathered at the Paris Conference affixed their signatures to the Peace Treaty, Smuts (but not Wilson) among them. The next day, British newspapers carried a statement from Smuts expressing his belief that the treaty merely marked the end of the war; real peace would not come 'unless the victors can effectively extend a helping hand to the defeated and broken peoples [of Europe]'.[15]

A BITTER-SWEET HOMECOMING

As soon as the treaty was signed, a very ill Botha left for South Africa. Smuts went back to London for two more weeks before he too left by sea for home. Arriving in Cape Town, where Botha awaited him, he and the Prime Minister embarked on a 1 000-mile train journey to the north. Hertzog and his sup-porters might not have been pleased to see them, but the two were welcomed as conquering heroes along the route home.[16] Smuts had been away from his wife and family for two and a half years and his youngest children hardly knew him, but his long-awaited rest at home was to last barely four days before his presence was required at a party conference.

After the conference, he and Botha were due to visit Natal together, but the Prime Minister felt too ill to accompany Smuts, who went ahead on his own. On receiving the news that Botha's life was ebbing away, he hurried back to Pretoria on 27 August, but early next morning en route word reached him that Botha had died at midnight. Writing to a friend in England after hearing the news, an emotional Smuts described his old colleague as 'South Africa's greatest son and among men my best friend'.[17] In a poignant graveside tribute to Botha on 30 August 1919, Smuts said that 'in the deepest sense', his friend was not dead. 'The grain does not grow unless it first falls into the earth. From this grave, Louis Botha speaks more eloquently than ever to his people.'[18]

By then, the Governor-General had already called upon Smuts to become South Africa's new prime minister.

CHAPTER 12

A Reluctant Prime Minister

IN AT THE DEEP END

It was a reluctant Smuts who became prime minister of the Union at the age of 49. Now a figure of world renown, he had reflected wistfully on having to turn his back on a Britain in which he was admired and appreciated to return to 'a land where too often my countrymen hated my ideas and despised my larger hopes'.[1] But, as his son observed, there was never any question of his not returning to complete the task he had begun.[2] He well knew that he lacked Botha's popularity and temperament, but his experience on the international stage had bred a confidence in his own ability which, in Kenneth Ingham's words, 'was gradually to envelop him in a protective cloak of intellectual rectitude'.[3]

Botha's death so soon after his return from Paris gave Smuts no time to acclimatise after three years away from South Africa. He was out of touch with political trends and public opinion. He was also worried about the effect of his long absences on Isie and his young children, who had grown up hardly knowing their father. As he wrote plaintively to Margaret Gillett, 'Public life has to me been one long sacrifice of family life. Isie must surely feel this all very much and looks very thin and worn out ... Now I am prime minister and things will be worse than ever.'[4]

At his first SAP caucus meeting Smuts warned his colleagues that, unlike his predecessor, he had 'neither tact nor patience and they must take him for what he was worth'.[5] As Crafford notes dryly, they had little option. Henceforward, both party and cabinet were to be ruled with a rod of iron.[6] Besides being prime minister and minister of defence, he also took upon his shoulders the ministry of native affairs – despite not having spoken a single sentence in Parliament about 'native' policy in nine years.[7]

Soon the autocratic Smuts was perceived as more than just the head of the government: he *was* the government – held responsible for the country's dire economic situation after the Great War and the target of hostility from those who clamoured for secession.[8] The suddenness of his elevation to the premiership heralded 'an almost fanatical revival of bellicosity' on the part of his political opponents.[9] He was blamed for virtually everything. In his first speech as premier, he appealed to his fellow-Afrikaners to focus on the present and future, instead of dwelling incessantly on the past. His plea fell on deaf ears.

In early March 1920, South Africa held another general election, the most prominent issues on the hustings being the country's ties with Britain, the high cost of living, the Indian question, and the administration of the country during the war. Voters clearly wished to send a message to the government and the election results came as a nasty shock to the SAP. The Nationalists had won 44 seats, the SAP 41, the Unionist Party 25 and a revived Labour Party 21. To survive in office, Smuts needed the support of Sir Thomas Smartt's Unionists – the party of the hated Rhodes, Jameson, Fitzpatrick and the mining magnates – to give him a majority of four votes and enable him to govern.

Despite the SAP government's slender majority, it managed nonetheless to enact legislation dealing with a wide range of economic, industrial, agricultural and social issues, most notably the Native Affairs Act of 1920, which gave effect to the findings of various commissions and made provision for the appointment of a three-member, all-white Native Affairs Commission to represent the interests of black Africans. It also extended Rhodes's Glen Grey Act throughout the Union, making it possible for Africans to be elected to local government councils in their own areas. Giving 'natives' their own institutions, Smuts fondly imagined, would foster their own indigenous culture and 'avoid forcing them into a European mould'.[10] Not for the first time, instead of being consulted, Africans were advised to accept what was good for them.

Having to modify his policies to satisfy the pro-British Unionists made Smuts more unpopular than ever with the Hertzogites, and undermined attempts that had begun to heal the breach in former Boer ranks and bring about Afrikaner re-unification (*hereniging*). The stumbling block, as always, was the question of secession, and Smuts's cause was not helped by a statement

Prime Minister of South Africa, 1919. South African Library

from the British foreign secretary, of all people, that if Dominions wished to secede from the Empire, Britain would not try to stop them.

Three *hereniging* congresses of Afrikaners were held, at Paarl, Robertson and Bloemfontein, but Smuts declined to attend any of them, suspecting that their real objective was to bring about South Africa's withdrawal from Empire. Instead, he called a party conference in Bloemfontein in October 1920, where he proposed the amalgamation of the SAP and the Unionists into one party. 'Now that the Nationalist Party is firmly resolved to continue … fanning the fires of secession and of driving the European races apart from each other, the moderate elements of our population have no other alternative than to draw closer to one another in order to fight that policy,' he declared.[11] The Unionists, alarmed at the resurgence in republicanism among Afrikaner Nationalists and their own dwindling fortunes at the polls, were ready to accept Smuts's offer of two (later increased to three) cabinet seats and willing to be absorbed into an enlarged SAP.

Buoyed by his success in uniting the two parties, Smuts immediately called another general election in early 1921. His decision was well-timed, for the climate within the country had changed significantly. The Labour Party, which harboured many communists within its ranks, had suffered a significant fall-off in support because of the atrocities committed by the Bolsheviks in Russia. Smuts also raised the spectre of secession from Empire, which would mean international isolation. The SAP's new-found assertiveness won it 79 seats to the Nationalists' 45 and Labour's nine, giving the government a parliamentary majority of 24.

The election in South Africa was observed with keen interest throughout the Empire, where Smuts's resounding victory was seen as a triumph for imperialism over narrow nationalism and hailed with delight. In the UK, Lord Curzon described it as 'a triumph for the whole Empire'.[12] In truth, however, it was a pyrrhic victory. The SAP had been kept in office by its erstwhile Unionist opponents, and in the rural areas the Nationalists had gained more ground. Smuts had not helped matters by admitting candidly, in a speech at Kimberley, that in his conception of South Africa's place in the world, the spirit of Rhodes was still alive. His critics promptly threw back in his face some of his bitter utterances in his tract *A Century of Wrong*.

REMARKABLY SHORT-SIGHTED

The Smuts government may have been far-sighted with regard to Dominion autonomy, but it was myopic about the impact of its racial policies upon international opinion.[13] Its action, in 1922, in sending in troops and aircraft to crush a revolt by the 500-strong Bondelswart tribe, of mixed origin, in newly mandated South West Africa caused consternation at the League of Nations. Before that, the Bulhoek Rebellion – an uprising in the Eastern Cape in which 163 members of an African religious sect were killed and 100 wounded by a police unit – had occurred. As minister of native affairs, Smuts was accused of being far more concerned with the affairs of Europe than South Africa, in some cases by white politicians less troubled about the loss of life at Bulhoek than with making political capital out of the tragedy. Nonetheless, as Kenneth Ingham observes, his decision to absent himself for the Imperial Conference and leave the Bulhoek matter in the hands of officials was 'a pointer both to his attitude towards Africans and to his personality'.[14]

He had been looking forward to the Conference as a chance to define post-war constitutional relations between the member countries of the Empire. The Hertzogites, still insisting on their right to self-determination, raised a clamour about what they called the Smuts–Milner conspiracy against South African independence.[15] Yet Smuts was never less insistent than his National-ist opponents that South Africa should have the right to determine its own destiny, even if he differed with them over what that destiny should be. He believed that his economically small and geographically remote country could best exert what influence it had as a fully fledged member of the League of Nations by co-ordinating its own interests 'with those of the British Empire and the world as a whole'.[16]

Mark Mazower observes perceptively that in his efforts to create a new national consciousness at home, Smuts promoted internationalism *because* he was a nationalist at heart himself. Nationalism was a real force in the world, Mazower writes, and in Smuts's view a good one in the African context because it brought whites together and promoted their civilising mission on the 'Dark Continent'.[17]

Oddly enough, the South African prime minister's outspoken views on Empire alarmed not only his critics at home, but – for different reasons – some Whitehall mandarins also, who believed that London should speak with one voice on foreign policy and regarded Smuts's independent streak as a threat to Imperial unity. If self-government were to extend to foreign policy, they claimed, and the King were to receive conflicting advice from the Dominions, the Empire might implode under the weight of its own contradictions.[18] But British ministers, who knew Smuts better, did not take the argument seriously and the South African leader's reputation remained extraordinarily high. No sooner had he arrived in England than he was on his way to Windsor Castle to be consulted by the King about the crisis in Ireland. Looking to conciliate, as always, he advised George V to use the opening of the new Ulster parliament to send a conciliatory message to the rebellious South.

Following their meeting, at the King's special request Smuts drafted a speech in which the monarch expressed his desire that the ideals of freedom and co-operation upon which the Empire was based should be extended to the whole of Ireland.[19] Smuts sent a copy of his draft to Lloyd George with the suggestion that dominion status for Ireland should be adopted as official British government policy. Lloyd George responded by softening his aggressive attitude towards the Irish to one of conciliation and negotiation, and invoked Smuts's help in reaching out to the pro-republican leadership. Wishing to call a conference in London to which the Sinn Fein leader, Eamonn de Valera, and the Northern Ireland premier, Sir James Craig, would be invited, he sent Smuts – as 'an outsider and a Boer' – secretly to Dublin to discuss Sinn Fein's grievances with de Valera and his colleagues and persuade them to attend the conference. Smuts made it clear that he would only go once he had been formally invited by de Valera.

◆

Arriving in Dublin as a private citizen under the pseudonym 'Mr Smith', Smuts was taken to meet the Sinn Fein leadership, assuring them that he had not come as an emissary of the British government.[20] It was a truly extraordinary occasion: a strongly anti-republican South African prime minister seeking to persuade pro-republican Irishmen of the need to attend a conference called by their arch-enemy Britain. Smuts tried valiantly to persuade de Valera of the advantages of accepting dominion status and – conveniently ignoring the vehement opposition to him among pro-republicans at home – spoke in glowing terms of the advantages of being a member of 'a sisterhood of equal nations rather than a small, nervous republic which had to rely on the good-will and assistance of foreigners'.[21]

It was characteristic of Smuts to brush aside the concerns of de Valera and his colleagues in the same way that he dismissed the opinions of the Hert-zogites as being misguided and unworthy of serious consideration.[22] Before departing from Dublin, he asked de Valera for an immediate ceasefire with the British army and urged him to attend the London conference, to both of which requests the Sinn Fein leader surprisingly agreed.

Three days later, the still sceptical de Valera and his colleagues accepted the invitation to travel to London. Smuts played no part in the conference which began on 10 July and ended in deadlock two weeks later. The British offered dominion status to Ireland, but only on condition that the six counties in the north were not coerced into joining a united Ireland. The Sinn Feiners, for their part, would only agree to become a dominion if the six counties were included. 'I have brought both mules to the water,' Smuts wrote later, 'but the drinking is their own affair.'[23] Shortly after the conference, it became known that the ceasefire he had negotiated with de Valera had averted a bloody massacre: a posse of gunmen had been assembled to shoot, at an appointed time, all uniformed British citizens in Dublin.

◆

Smuts's most pressing purpose in attending the 1921 Imperial Conference was to settle the status of the Dominions. Unless that was done, he wrote, we must look for separatist movements not only in South Africa but in the other Dominions as well.[24] As was his custom, he put his thoughts into a long and carefully worded memorandum in which he called on the Imperial government to draft a series of resolutions which would clarify relations between countries of the Empire and be ratified at a constitutional conference a year hence. He also proposed that the term 'Empire' be changed to 'Commonwealth of Nations' and pleaded for the adoption of a declaration of rights for member countries.

To his surprise and chagrin, however, he found himself in a minority among Dominion leaders – and hoist by his own petard. Having insisted upon the principle of unanimity in Dominion affairs, he was thwarted by the prime minister of Australia, WM Hughes, in particular, who was vehemently opposed to further constitution making and wished to leave matters where they stood. The outspoken Hughes persuaded his colleagues to repudiate Smuts's call for a constitutional conference and a declaration of rights. On his return to Australia, he proudly informed his countrymen 'that he had soldered up the constitutional tinkerers in their own tin can'.[25]

Smuts departed for home on 5 August 1921, chastened by the rejection of his views yet hopeful that at least an Anglo-Irish settlement might be achieved. In a long letter to de Valera, he urged the Sinn Fein leader to do as he and Botha had done. 'My belief is that Ireland is travelling the same road as South Africa and is destined to achieve the same success,' he wrote.[26] The fiery de Valera was not convinced by the parallel, but his colleague Michael Collins was more impressed. On 6 December, a historic agreement was signed between Ireland and Britain which provided for the establishment of an Irish Free State as a self-governing dominion within the 'British Commonwealth of Nations', the first time the term that Smuts had coined was used officially. Far from producing the outcome that Smuts ardently desired, however, the Anglo-Irish agreement contained the seeds of bitter strife.

CRACKING DOWN ON MINERS

If Smuts's forceful handling of the uprising at Bulhoek had raised eyebrows among liberals at home and abroad, it was his treatment of the miners that cost him even more support. In the aftermath of World War I, South Africa was in a parlous condition: the economy was in decline, inflation had pushed up prices by as much as 50 per cent, and jobs were being shed in industry and on the railways. The flashpoint, however, was on the mines, where Afrikaners had stepped into the most dangerous underground jobs after immigrant miners had returned home. The forcible end to the mining strike of 1920, in which eleven African miners were killed and 120 injured, was a prelude to even greater conflict.

In late 1921, in the midst of the growing economic crisis, the Chamber of Mines announced plans to do away with the colour bar in semi-skilled jobs in order to lower costs and make mines more profitable. The possible loss of white jobs and reduction in pay brought the Mineworkers' Union, many of whose members were Hertzogites, out on strike. The Labour and Nationalist parties were quick to make common cause with the miners, and the dispute degenerated into a battle between the Industrial Federation and the Chamber of Mines, or between labour and capital.

Smuts understood only too well that the country's economic fortunes depended on the mines producing gold at a profit. As in 1913, he refused at first to intervene. Yet although not minister of mines, he soon found himself – as the framer of mining policy in the past – personally involved in negotiations. The miners believed, rightly or wrongly, that the Chamber had white workers in its sights and suspected that the government had been given advance notice of the mine-owners' plans. When Smuts's attempts to persuade the miners to call off their protest failed, he warned that a strike would be ruinous for the country and profitless for themselves. Yet neither the Chamber nor the workers was prepared to compromise, and an industrial struggle turned into political conflict. To the strikers, it appeared that the government had taken the side of the mine-owners and should therefore be overthrown and a republic declared. As tempers rose, Smuts made a statement in Parliament he would come to regret. When asked by a Labour MP on what terms the strikers should return to work, 'on the terms of the Chamber' was his reply.[27]

Disturbances broke out around the Reef as strikers, now organised into commandos, picketed mines and threatened 'scabs' with retribution. On 28 February, three miners in Boksburg were killed in clashes with the police. By this time a radical group, the five-member Council of Action, had taken control of the strikers. Although the Council claimed to represent all workers, a communist faction chose to march under the banner, 'Workers of the world fight and unite for a white South Africa'. After a general strike was declared, thousands swarmed through the streets of Rand towns sowing murder and mayhem in their wake. Blacks found themselves a particular target of the commandos.

By now, Smuts had had enough. On 10 March, he mobilised the Active Citizen Force and declared martial law. Secretly leaving Cape Town by special train for Johannesburg, he was halted 80 miles from his destination when the railway line he was travelling along was blown up. Hurrying into a car, whose tyres were flattened by strikers' bullets, and ill with gastric flu, he arrived at the Johannesburg Drill Hall at midnight to assess the situation for himself.

The next day, he and the 20 000 strong security forces retaliated. Strikers were driven 'systematically and relentlessly'[28] from their strongholds in the Reef towns and suburbs of Benoni, Boksburg, Brixton and Langlaagte. Within three days, the white flag had been raised and the insurrection was over. However, the loss of life had been high: 43 members of the army, 21 policemen and 81 civilians had been killed, and 650 civilians injured. Smuts had saved the country from anarchy, but, as he wrote ruefully to Alice Clark, 'I have earned an additional claim to the titles of butcher and hangman'.[29]

◆

The Prime Minister returned to Groote Schuur in chastened mood; the revolt had been costly in damage to life and property and he had paid a high political price for victory over the workers, driving the Labour Party into the arms of the Nationalists. His first act on returning to Parliament was to ask for the government to be indemnified for declaring martial law, which gave Hertzog the opportunity to denounce him as a partisan politician whose career was drenched in blood. The Leader of the Opposition complained that Smuts had declared martial law no fewer than three times in ten years and on each occasion had asked to be indemnified afterwards.

Low in body and spirit and sensing that the electorate were tiring of the SAP government, Smuts made an attempt in October 1922 to draw Rhodesia into the Union as a fifth province. Having never lost his expansionist aims, Smuts hoped not only to acquire an area rich in minerals, but also to recruit English-speaking Rhodesians into the ranks of the SAP. But put off by the Nationalists' republican sentiments and South Africa's official policy of bilingualism, white Rhodesians decided by a narrow majority of 2 785 votes against incorporation into South Africa. Smuts refused to accept the vote as final and predicted that Rhodesia would eventually bow to the inevitable and come into the Union.

◆

A year later, Smuts again disengaged from mounting problems at home to attend what turned out to be his last Imperial Conference. He had not lost his concern for the future of Europe and was determined to make his views known about France's 'illegal' occupation of the Ruhr after Germany had failed to meet its reparations payments. Drawing once more on his Boer past, he used the occasion of a speech to the South African Luncheon Club on 23 October to plead for sympathy for the Germans: 'Defeated, broken, utterly exhausted, my little people also had to bow to the will of the conqueror ... But it was not an impossible peace. The Boers were not treated as moral pariahs and outcasts.'[30] The speech caused a sensation in Britain and around the world, but the French, who resented anyone telling them how to be good Europeans, were not amused. The government must have paid heed, however, because by the time Smuts's ship had reached Cape Town on his return voyage, France had agreed to consider alternatives to the provisions for reparations.

Smuts's attendance at yet another Imperial gathering merely increased the determination of the Nationalist and Labour parties to form a pact to force him from office. Hoping to attract voters who had lost faith in the SAP, Hertzog took an expedient leaf out of Smuts's book by promising that his government would not seek to 'upset the existing constitutional relationship of South Africa to the British Crown'.[31] Smuts could sense what was coming. Mentally exhausted by mid-1924 and suffering badly from rheumatism, he wrote to Margaret Gillett, 'The pace is terrific ... How I shall get through it I don't know ... The grind of politics is really more than one can bear. Times are hard, everybody is cursing the government, and I know nobody will do better than we do.'[32]

When the SAP, against expectations, lost a by-election in the hitherto safe seat of Wakkerstroom, Smuts decided, on impulse, to bring matters to a head. Without consulting his cabinet or his party, he resigned and called a general election. Within the party, there was fury at his high-handedness. Politicking through cities and the *platteland,* he was forced to realise the depth of resentment against him. His countrymen had had enough of his high-minded speeches on world affairs and defence of Empire; Hertzog, who spoke 'the language of food, clothing and shelter'[33] and his Pact ally Labour now had the electorate behind them. It was time for change.

In an election noteworthy for the bitterness of the personal attacks on Smuts, the SAP was badly beaten: the party lost 17 seats to the Nationalists and seven to Labour, giving the Pact a majority of 27 in Parliament. One of the seats lost to Labour was the Prime Minister's own constituency in Pretoria-West. In calling the election, Smuts had made a tactical error: if only he had waited, he would have benefited from the economic upturn that began in the following year.[34] But impatient as always, he had been defeated by what he regarded as his opponents' 'defect of political narrowness'.[35] At the age of 54, he found himself a prophet without honour in his own country – and even in his own Transvaal bailiwick.

Stunned by the extent of his rejection, he briefly considered retiring from politics but quickly dismissed the idea because he regarded the inexperienced Pact government as being incapable of running the country. He also felt that 'under these distressing circumstances, the South African Party might go to pieces in the rout and that irreparable mischief might be done to South Africa'.[36] Offered the safe seat of Standerton, he returned to Parliament as leader of the opposition, determined to be ready for another general election that he regarded as inevitable. He had been prime minister for little over five years and would have been astonished had he known that his successor, Hertzog, would remain in power for the next 14 years.

CHAPTER 13

Model of Restraint

TAKING A BACK SEAT

Frustrating though they were politically, the years from 1924 to 1933 were some of the most fulfilling and productive of Smuts's life. Freed from the burdens of high office, he found time to read, think and write. Working in his study at Doornkloof, it took him eight months to complete the manuscript of *Holism and Evolution*, begun many years previously. The book was published simultaneously in London and New York in 1926, where it received a mixed reception. The philosopher Gilbert Murray thought it was the most interesting philosophical work he had read for many years. Winston Churchill wrote to Smuts to say that he had 'peered into the book in awe' – which suggested he had no desire to read it.[1] The distinguished scientist JBS Haldane discussed the concept of holism admiringly in his Gifford lectures of 1927–28 on 'The Sciences and Philosophy'. Albert Einstein read the book shortly after it was published and wrote that there two mental constructs which would direct human thinking in the next millennium: his own theory of relativity, and Smuts's theory of holism[2]. Others were less impressed: Lancelot Hogben, chair of zoology at the University of Cape Town, for instance, was scathingly dismissive of a theory under which, he claimed, 'all the superstitions huddled'.[3] The poet Roy Campbell mocked Smuts in verse:

> Statesmen-philosophers with earnest souls
> Whose lofty theories embrace the Poles
> Yet only prove their minds are full of Holes.[4]

Smuts hesitated to describe the book as either a philosophical or a scientific work; rather it set out an overarching theory which sought to link the physical to the metaphysical and make sense of the vast complexity of the world around us. As he modestly asserted, 'I have simply tried to hammer out some rule of thought to carry my action along.'[5] The fundamental character of the universe, he suggested, is based on a pattern in which the whole is always greater than the sum of its parts, with human personality being the highest 'whole'.[6] Upon this fundamentally optimistic and hopeful assessment of the human condition he had based his own personal philosophy and political career. Because he deliberately did not bring the Deity into the discussion, choosing to keep his deepest religious beliefs to himself, he was accused in some theological and political circles of being an atheist. His relationship in his twilight years with Dutch Reform pastor Johan Reyneke gave the lie to these claims; he was a believer in a Divine Spirit to the end.

Politically, it took some time for Smuts to become accustomed to being leader of the opposition in Parliament; he was determined, however, to keep his upper lip stiff and not let any traces of hurt or discomfort show. Scrupulous in his attendance in the House, he sat impassively on his front bench as the new government continued to make him the scapegoat for most of the country's troubles. On one celebrated occasion, he allowed Hertzog to harangue him for more than an hour, using 20 different epithets, most of them libellous.[7] After the diatribe was over, with both Mrs Hertzog and Mrs Smuts in the public gallery watching, he wandered over to the Prime Minister's seat and sat with him, 'chatting amicably'. Friend and foe alike found his self-discipline and composure remarkable.

As SAP leader, he also had to rebuild the organisational structure and morale of his defeated party, and hone its responses to the Pact government's policies. The SAP reacted positively to Interior Minister DF Malan's proposal, in 1925, that South Africa should adopt its own national flag, but protested volubly when Malan insisted on excluding the Union Jack entirely from the new design. A bitter argument dragged on until a joint sitting of Parliament in 1927 failed to resolve the matter, and the Governor-General had to be called in to mediate. A compromise was reached whereby the flags of the old Transvaal, Orange Free State and the Union Jack were superimposed upon Van Riebeeck's tricolour of orange, white and blue.[8] This flag was to endure until it was redesigned in 1994.

Smuts was more irked by the failure of his prediction that Hertzog and his

The Leader of the Opposition. Freed from the burdens of high office, he found
time to read, think and write – and for long walks.

bunch of amateurs would be unable to run the country successfully. Soon
after the new government took office, the drought broke and South Africa
experienced its best rains for many years. And, as the global economic climate
improved, so mineral sales increased, commerce and industry recovered and
the country began to produce its own iron, steel and electricity.

◆

Having extended an invitation to the Prince of Wales to visit South Africa,
Smuts found it ironic that it fell to the Hertzogites to lay out the welcoming mat for the prince on his official tour in 1925. He observed that it was

as well that the royal visit came after the change in government: 'Instead of the Nationalists now standing aloof and pointing to us as jingoes and snobs, they now have to do the job themselves, with our approval, and the national unanimity of South Africa is therefore far greater than it otherwise would have been.'[9] On taking office, Hertzog had displayed his anti-imperial sentiments, however, by abolishing British titles for South Africans, disposing of the preferential tariff for British goods and promoting 'economic nationalism'.[10] All these actions drew an angry response from sections of the SAP, but the party nonetheless supported the government's motion to recognise Afrikaans instead of Dutch as one of the country's two official languages.

In order to placate his Pact partner, Creswell, Prime Minister Hertzog decided that it was not necessary for the National Party to press for a republic: South Africa's free association with other Dominions within the Commonwealth was sufficient to satisfy the aspirations of Afrikaner nationalists – a view with which DF Malan and his supporters strongly disagreed. Inheriting the constitutional issue from Smuts, Hertzog dusted off his predecessor's memorandum of June 1921, which proposed a declaration of rights for member countries of the Empire, and headed to London for the Imperial Conference of 1926. The memo, according to Hancock, had anticipated almost every demand that Hertzog intended to make.[11] With new leaders in Australia and Canada more sympathetic than their predecessors to Smuts's views, the outcome of the conference was the seminal Balfour Declaration of 1926, which established the legislative independence of the Dominions from Britain and enabled both Hertzog and Smuts to claim that their approach had been vindicated.

In time, both the Balfour Declaration and the subsequent Statute of Westminster of 1931 were to become the source of unending disagreement between Smuts and Hertzog. The latter continued to allege that Smuts wanted Britain to exercise a kind of 'super-authority' over the Dominions. Smuts, for his part, believed that the Statute confirmed South Africa's independence as a self-governing nation, but one that owed a loyalty to the British Crown. The differences were to surface many years later when Hertzog claimed that South Africa was entitled to remain neutral in the event of Britain declaring war. Smuts, on the other hand, maintained that neutrality would violate the terms and spirit of the Balfour Declaration, as well as the Statute of Westminster.

115

'SWART GEVAAR' ELECTION

Of much more significance than the argument over the flag issue were the differences between the two men over 'native' policy. Although shaken by the 1922 Rand Revolt, the Smuts government had not enshrined the colour bar on the mines in law because it would have been an admission that whites needed to be 'artificially protected against the native and coloured man'.[12] Pressed by Creswell, however, who was intent on protecting the interests of white labour, Hertzog introduced a Mines and Works Amendment Bill in 1925 which imposed an industrial colour bar for the first time. 'Self-preservation is the first law of Nature', the responsible minister declared, and the purpose of the legislation was 'the preservation and perpetuation of the white race'. Smuts vehemently opposed the statutory protection of white labour, perhaps with an eye to the provocation it might cause elsewhere in Africa and in India. Speaking in Parliament, he warned that the government was bringing in a law under which 'we are going to declare to the Natives: You shall in future be debarred from rising above the level of hewers of wood and drawers of water. I am all for the white man, but there is something in my breast that cannot stand this.'[13]

Hertzog, now minister of native affairs as well as prime minister, took his time before outlining his new 'native policy'. In a speech at Smithfield in November 1925, he spoke of his intention to provide the extra land promised to Africans under the Land Act of 1913, but also to reduce the size of the 'scheduled reserves' and make more land available for purchase by Africans and others on the fringes of the reserves. Politically, Africans would lose their franchise rights in the Cape and be placed on a separate voters' roll to elect white representatives to Parliament. They would also be given their own separate administrative bodies, local councils and a Native Representative Council.

Hertzog needed the support of the SAP if he was to obtain the two-thirds majority needed to alter the Union Constitution. Although he had no alternative to offer, Smuts was determined that existing political rights should not to be tampered with, and refused to support Hertzog's impending legislation. He proposed, instead, the holding of a National Convention to discuss Hertzog's proposals, but the Prime Minister rejected his suggestion and tabled four Bills in Parliament – the Native Land Act Amendment Bill, the Union

Native Council Bill, the Representation of Natives in Parliament Bill and the Coloured Persons Rights Bill – in July 1926.

Within a month, Smuts responded on behalf of the SAP with a lengthy memorandum in which he criticised the proposals to set aside more land for 'mixed' ownership. He also opposed the measures to curb labour tenancy on farms (as it would drive workers into towns); remove black voters in the Cape from the common roll; and for seven whites to represent Africans in Parliament. After a select committee of Parliament had failed to iron out the differences between the two sides, Hertzog drew Smuts into a series of consultations, but the latter flatly refused to compromise, suggesting that the Cape's form of qualified franchise should serve as a model for the whole country. To Hertzog, this was anathema.

With a general election looming, Hertzog re-introduced two of the four bills in Parliament, knowing that a two-thirds majority was beyond reach but intent on giving his party an emotive issue with which to arouse the electorate. The election of 1929 became known as the '*swart gevaar*' election, as the Nationalists went out of their way to persuade voters that the future of white civilisation was endangered by a growing black tide. When Smuts played into their hands in a speech in Ermelo by calling for 'a British confederation of African states … a great African Dominion stretching unbroken throughout Africa', Hertzog and his followers gleefully denounced him as 'the man who puts himself forward as the apostle of a black Kaffir state … extending from the Cape to Cairo'.[14] The SAP, they claimed not unjustifiably, stood for a policy of *niksdoen* (do nothing) in the face of the racial threat, and was out to impose *gelykstelling* (equality) between white and black. Claiming disingenuously that a vote for Smuts was a vote for black domination, the Nationalists romped to a 17-seat victory over the SAP and no longer needed to rely on Creswell's much-diminished Labourites to remain in office.

◆

From time to time, Smuts continued to involve himself in world affairs. After being contacted by his old friend Chaim Weizmann, he criticised a White Paper setting out British policy in Palestine for failing to meet the undertakings given in the Balfour Declaration, for which he said he felt partly responsible.

He was also critical of British policy in India and on a visit to London in 1931 was asked to intervene in discussions between the British government and Gandhi. He and Gandhi had several cordial meetings, and he also held discussions with Prime Minister Ramsay MacDonald. Smuts regarded Gandhi as an asset in the negotiations, 'an honest man despite his vagaries',[15] but independence for India was not to come about until more than a decade later. These interactions with foreign leaders kept Smuts abreast of international developments and alleviated some of the frustration he felt at no longer being in charge of South Africa's fortunes.

◆

Hertzog's popularity with the white electorate was enhanced even further when he returned from the Imperial Conference of 1930 having finally secured South Africa's constitutional status as an equal partner in the Commonwealth. Now that the Afrikaners' language and culture had been established, he declared, there was no longer any reason why the two (white) cultures should not come together 'in the spirit of a consolidated South African nation'.[16] The republican cause had been shelved, he proclaimed; his immediate priority now was to achieve 'national unity'. This change of heart caused predictable unease amongst DF Malan and his diehard republicans, who feared that – like Botha and Smuts before him – Hertzog had been seduced by the pageantry of London, and was beginning to betray the Afrikaner nationalist cause.[17]

ON THE LECTURE CIRCUIT

Disillusioned at the thought of having to spend another five years on the opposition benches, Smuts took refuge in solitary walking, plant collecting, reading and – as always – thinking. In mid-1929 he undertook a nine-day safari to the Zimbabwe Ruins and the Copper Belt, a prelude to a more strenuous five-week plant-gathering trip with friends and family a year later. In October, he went to Oxford to deliver a series of Rhodes Memorial Lectures on the topics 'African Settlement', 'World Peace' and 'Native Policy in Africa'. He hoped, he said, to influence Britain's colonial policy in East and Central Africa by encouraging more white settlement: world peace, he claimed, could be achieved by expanding the colonial policy of the British Empire under the aegis of the League of Nations.

Yet the tone of his addresses might best be described as 'paternalistic and patronising'.[18] What was needed in Africa, he asserted, was policies to promote the cause of civilisation 'without injustice to the African'... a 'child type, with a happy go-lucky disposition, but with no incentive to improvement'.[19] In South Africa, he suggested, there should be a set of 'parallel institutions', based on the Glen Grey Act of 1894, which made provision for 'white settlement to supply the steel framework and the stimulus for enduring civilisation', to which should be added, 'indigenous native institutions to express the specifically African character of the natives in their future development and civilization'.[20]

A liberal critic in Britain labelled his prescriptions as 'well-meaning but slightly outdated and largely unworkable'.[21] Back home, the usually supportive *Cape Times* was far more critical, describing the 'native question' as presented by Smuts to the guileless and unworldly eyes of Oxford as having scandalously little resemblance to local realities.[22]

While in London, Smuts attended a dinner for veterans of the East Africa campaign at which he came face to face with Von Lettow-Vorbeck for the first time. The two men became friends and Smuts was to send the ailing German food parcels after the end of World War II.

After staying with the King at Sandringham, Smuts paid visits to Edinburgh and Glasgow where he lectured to large audiences on the famous African explorer, David Livingstone. Journeying on to the tenth annual meeting of the League of Nations in the US, he was given the honour of a ticker tape parade in New York and an audience with President Hoover at the White House. He was feted everywhere he went, even by American Negroes who took to him warmly until he remarked artlessly in a speech that they were 'the most patient creatures next to the ass,' which caused unintentional offence.[23]

Showered with civic and academic honours, he embarked on an exhausting lecture tour of America and Canada, giving 26 addresses in 18 days in support of the Jewish cause in Palestine and the embattled League of Nations – the latter a contentious issue in American politics. He left for home early in 1930, exhausted but happy.

On board ship, he learned to his consternation that the government had

introduced a Quota Bill to restrict Jewish immigration to South Africa; worse
still, his entire SAP caucus, with the exception of five Jewish members and
two others, had supported the Second Reading. Arriving at Parliament during
the Third Reading, an infuriated Smuts took his party to task so effectively
that during the final division on the Bill, every SAP MP voted against it. Government members taunted him for being the 'King of the Jews'.[24]

◆

While the Quota Bill was being fought in Parliament, Smuts received what
he regarded as the greatest honour of his life – an invitation from the British
Association for the Advancement of Science to preside over its Centenary
Meeting in London in September 1931. In the words of his son, Jannie, his
biographer, 'Science held no higher honour, for this was the greatest meeting
of scientists of the world.'[25]

His opening lecture on 'The Scientific World Picture of Today' to 5 000 of
the world's most distinguished scientists was, in Kenneth Ingham's description, 'a formidable survey of recent developments in mathematics, physics,
biology, physiology and astronomy, followed by a leap to philosophy and
theology'. It was the first of many other addresses to smaller groups at the
gathering on subjects ranging from philosophy to farming.[26] On one particular day, he made no fewer than 13 speeches. To those who regarded the
origins of humankind as accidental, he had this to say, 'The human spirit is
not a pathetic, wandering phantom of the universe, but is at home and meets
with spiritual hospitality and response everywhere. Our deepest thoughts and
emotions are but responses to stimuli which come to us not from an alien, but
from an essentially friendly and kindred universe.'[27]

It was during this visit that the University of London conferred on Smuts
– for only the third time in its 100-year history – a DSc, its highest honorary
degree. On his way home, inspired by Louis Leakey's book on East African
prehistory, he began marshalling his thoughts about South African prehistory,
which later became a scientific paper, 'Climate and Man in Africa'[28] – still
regarded in this country as a landmark in the history of geology and climatology and their relation to human history.[29]

CHAPTER 14

Achieving the Unthinkable

DEPRESSION GRIPS

Soon after the 1929 election, South Africa began to feel the fall-out from the collapse of Wall Street and the ensuing economic depression that swept the world. Mineral and maize prices dropped sharply and, to make matters worse, the most severe drought in living memory ravaged the countryside, causing agricultural production to slump. As always, it was the government of the day that took the blame. When the salaries of civil servants were reduced and taxation increased, confidence in the ruling party began to wane. Smuts observed that 'the psychology of the desert is creeping over South Africa'.[1]

Throughout the 1920s, the crisis of white unemployment had been growing. In 1922, the number of whites out of work was estimated at 120 000 out of an economically active white population of 540 000. As a leading liberal politician, Margaret Ballinger, observed, 'It is difficult now to remember or to appreciate the dark shadow which poor whiteism cast over this country in the 1920s and 30s … yet it was the formative force in standardizing the relationship of black and white in this country.'[2] It is generally agreed by historians that 'poor-whiteism' was a primary driver of the segregationist policies of both the Pact government and Smuts's SAP.

In Britain, an emergency coalition under Ramsay MacDonald was formed in late 1931 to deal with the economic crisis. The new government immediately took the country off the gold standard, causing a loss of confidence in sterling. In London at the time, Smuts pleaded repeatedly by cable for South Africa to follow suit, but his urgings met with firm opposition from Hertzog, who threatened to resign rather than go off gold. It was typical of Smuts, he asserted, to follow where England led. Even members of Smuts's own party – not to mention the mining industry – thought it would be folly to abandon gold. It took another 15 months of acute of economic misery, and the intervention of the maverick Nationalist politician Tielman Roos with his slogan 'Off Gold', before the government came to its senses.

Sensing that the mood of the country had turned against Hertzog but not necessarily towards him, no sooner had the gold standard been abandoned than Smuts began putting out feelers to his rival about political co-operation 'in the national interest'. In Parliament, Hertzog laughed openly when conciliation was suggested, but behind the scenes his lieutenants were already sounding out SAP MPs. A few weeks later, on 28 February 1933, Hertzog announced in Parliament, to general bemusement, that he and his former opponent had agreed to form a coalition government, based upon a seven-point programme of principles. After 20 years of bitter rivalry, the unthinkable had happened: the breach between Smuts and Hertzog appeared to have been healed.

In truth, the two old foes had much more in common than they were prepared to concede or recognise. Their long struggle, as Hancock observes, had always been more about means than ends.[3] Both were Afrikaner idealists acting in what they perceived were the best interests of their people: Hertzog wished to ensure Afrikaner survival by looking inwards and fighting for his language and culture; Smuts, with his holistic vision, saw security for Afrikanerdom within the wider British Commonwealth. Both had fought in their own way for South Africa's sovereign equality in the community of nations.[4] And despite their political differences, and the angry tone of Hertzog's public rhetoric, the two men got on well privately. In his book, Jannie Smuts wrote that his father had never taken Hertzog's 'wild outbursts' to heart, and not once complained privately about his opponent's often unfair attacks on him.[5]

Coalition, however, was not welcomed on either fringe of the white political spectrum. Cape NP leader DF Malan resigned from the Hertzog cabinet to form what was called the 'Purified' National Party, while in pro-British Natal, Smuts was roundly accused of selling out to the Nationalists. But the electorate gave its approval, even if the number of seats won by the Coalition in the general election of May 1933 (144 out of 150) gave a misleading impression because the overall majority of votes was a mere 43 637.

A MARRIAGE OF CONVENIENCE

Smuts took office under Hertzog as deputy prime minister and minister of justice, sublimating his desire to run the country again to what he believed was the greater national interest. Yet he still continued to wield considerable influence, Hertzog once telling an American writer that although he was prime minister, 'it is General Smuts who runs the Government'.[6] On international matters, Smuts's advice continued to be eagerly sought.

While the Deputy Prime Minister was away at the World Economic Conference in London in 1933, preliminary talks began among *platteland* Afrikaners intent on fusing the two Coalition parties in order to build a 'white South Africa'.[7] Detecting an opportunity to drive a wedge more deeply into his opponents' ranks, Smuts threw down the gauntlet to Hertzog upon his return. The Prime Minister, he declared, had to choose between Fusion – which meant the exclusion of the Malanites, with their insistence on the rights of neutrality, secession and republicanism – or the failure of Fusion and the perpetuation of white disunity.

Hertzog wavered before putting his own wishes to the test at the Cape National Party congress in Port Elizabeth. After receiving a stinging rejection from Malan and his followers, the Prime Minister and his supporters walked out of their old party. As Ingham observes, this was a significant step for both sides of the divide in Afrikanerdom: it was now apparent that Malan did not represent all Afrikaans-speakers, but only those who, like Herzog and Kruger before them, saw their future in a limited Afrikaner republic rather than a broader and united (white) South Africa.[8]

The new Hertzog-led United Party turned out to be more of a marriage of convenience than a union of hearts and minds, however. Deep differences remained over 'native policy' and what South Africa's obligations would be in the event of another war in Europe. Hertzog believed that, as a sovereign country, South Africa had the right to remain neutral; Smuts maintained that as a fully fledged member of the Commonwealth, the country had a moral duty to support Britain. As Malan was quick to point out, the Fusion government was at odds over 'fundamental issues of peace and war'.[9] Many Afrikaners who supported Fusion remained in two minds about where they really stood: some were repelled by the 'jingoes' in United Party ranks; others were isolationists who would have been more comfortable under Malan.

Prime Minister Hertzog and Deputy Prime Minister Smuts, 1938.

Nonetheless, Fusion held, largely as a result of South Africa's growing prosperity. The impact of going off gold and maintaining the link to sterling was
immediate: as the gold price rose sharply, low-grade mines became profitable,
the stock market boomed and money flowed back into the country. Yet while

124

protectionism restored health to the farming sector, many Afrikaners were still in straitened circumstances. A lengthy study by the Carnegie Commission estimated the number of poor whites in South Africa to be 17 per cent of all whites. While recognising that the problem of black poverty was as acute as that of white indigence, the Commission suggested that uplifting whites would ultimately be to the benefit of other races as well.[10] Yet the implementation of its recommendations served only to increase the dependence of poor Afrikaners upon the government, and widen further the divisions between white and black South Africans.

DEFENDING FREEDOM

Smuts regarded the Status Act of 1934, which clarified South Africa's constitutional position after the passing of the Statute of Westminster, as quite unnecessary, but it smoothed the way for the transition from Coalition to Fusion. A key issue which remained unresolved between the parties, however, was the 'native question'. Before matters came to a head, Smuts took himself off to Britain to deliver two important addresses on the deteriorating international situation. Accepting the rectorship of Scotland's oldest university, St Andrew's, he immediately won over his audience by telling them of the old Hottentot at the battle of Majuba, in the First Anglo-Boer War, who was asked who would win the war and replied, 'The English.' Does that make the English the greatest nation in the world, he was asked. 'No,' was the answer, 'because the English are very much afraid of the Scots.'[11]

With one eye on the growing tensions in Europe and speaking on the subject of 'Freedom', he warned his young audience that civilisation was under threat from a new tyranny, disguised in attractive patriotic colours, which was enticing 'youth everywhere into its horrid service.' The issue of freedom, he cautioned, cannot be evaded. 'Individual freedom, individual independence of mind, individual participation in the difficult work of government seem to be the essential of all progress … Freedom must make a great counter-stroke to save itself and our fair Western civilisation.'[12]

This cry from the heart was followed by a wide-ranging speech to the Royal Institute of International Affairs, in which he pleaded for Germany to be treated more generously and, sixteen years after Versailles, given complete equality of status with her European neighbours; for notice to be taken of Japanese intentions in Manchuria, and for the strengthening of the League of Nations – 'the only forum for discussion among the nations.'[13] The driving force in the world, he asserted, should not be 'morbid fears and sickly obsession, but the inner urge towards wholesome integration and co-operation'.[14] The press went into raptures. Typical of many newspapers, the *Manchester Guardian* wrote that 'General Smuts, erect, neat, pink and white, speaking in a high voice with a touch of accent more Latin than Dutch, gave a speech worthy of his powers. No politician in England for many a day has combined his sweep, his detachment and his subtlety.' *The Times* published his address in the form of a pamphlet, which ran to no fewer than three editions.[15] At the Lord Mayor of London's reception, he was given a standing ovation.[16]

Leaving London trailing clouds of glory, Smuts returned to South Africa to decide his party's response to Hertzog's long-deferred 'Native Bills'. Since 1926, he had opposed these bills, hoping that delaying tactics might forestall their implementation or force their abandonment through a lack of support.[17] Without any clear policy of his own, his approach was essentially Fabian and gradualist: he could not imagine how he or Hertzog or anyone else could devise a policy that sought to solve South Africa's social, racial and economic problems once and for all.[18] He feared that disagreement within the government might only serve to foment racial discontent, however. Still a believer in the limited franchise provisions laid down in the Act of Union, he argued that improving African education, health and access to land was more meaningful by far than the matter of the franchise.

BLACK REPRESENTATION

Hertzog was determined, however, that whites and blacks should not vote together in an election. He had followed up his victory in 1929 by appointing a 27-member Joint Select Committee to consider and report upon the issue of black political representation, and invoked the support of right-wing reactionaries in the SAP such as Heaton Nicholls in Natal and Colonel CF Stallard to further his aims. This placed Smuts in a difficult position; he disagreed with the Hertzogites, but was the deputy leader of the party. He resolved the conflict

Smuts's right-hand man in the SAP, JH Hofmeyr (left), and Professor DDT Jabavu of Fort Hare University (right). South African Library

in his own mind by eventually accepting the recommendations of the Select Committee that Africans should be given more land, as well as increased representation in the Senate, in return for relinquishing their franchise rights in the Cape. This would be of greater value to Africans in the long run than the existing franchise arrangements, he reasoned. Within his wing of the United Party, he left it to his liberal lieutenant JH Hofmeyr to vote against Hertzog's legislation, while allowing Stallard to oppose it for being 'too liberal'.

An intellectual phenomenon, who had been an enthusiastic supporter of *hereniging*, Hofmeyr had graduated and been awarded a Rhodes Scholarship at the age of 15, become a professor at 22, principal of what was to become Witwatersrand University at 24, and Administrator of the Transvaal (appointed by Smuts) at 29. He had wavered in declaring his support for either Hertzog or Smuts, before throwing in his lot with the SAP, for whom he won a parliamentary by-election in 1929. As a party politician, Hofmeyr found himself moving steadily towards a more liberal position on colour policy, while most

127

of his colleagues were moving the other way.[19] His public statements were to put a great strain on the cohesion of his party during the years of Fusion.

African reaction to Hertzog's bills was divided, and cautious: shortly before the vote in Parliament, Prof DDT Jabavu, a foundation member of the academic staff at Fort Hare University with whom Smuts had had a long-standing and friendly relationship, summoned an All-African Conference in Bloemfontein to rally opposition to the plan to remove black voters from the Cape roll. However, a motion calling for nationwide strikes and demonstrations failed to find favour with delegates; the majority voted in favour of a qualified franchise for Africans throughout the Union instead.[20]

Speaking in Parliament, Smuts declared himself thankful that after years of bitter wrangling, he could assent to legislation that 'was not an ideal measure but contained the elements of justice and fair play, and the promise of fruitfulness in the future'. Defending his own actions in supporting the bills, he declared, 'Of course I could have died in the last ditch, so to say, I could have said "I fight to the bitter end for the Cape Native franchise", but what would have been the result? It would have been not I who died, but the Natives, metaphorically speaking.'[21]

The measure aroused disappointment and anger, not only in educated black circles, but among whites in the Cape especially, led by the ex-Chief Justice, Sir James Rose Innes. Hofmeyr immediately resigned his cabinet position in the Fusion government in protest, a step that annoyed Smuts, who said to his son: 'It's all very well Hofmeyr talking about principles and conscience and resigning. How does he think I feel about the whole business myself? Where would we be if we all lost our heads and resigned? It's the very thing the Nationalists want.'[22]

THE END OF FUSION

The Hertzog-Smuts coalition held together for six years, largely because of Smuts's determination to keep Afrikaners and English South Africans together in the common interest. Two major infrastructural developments during the years of Fusion were the completion of the huge Vaal-Harts irrigation scheme, originally proposed by Rhodes, to bring water to a drought-plagued land, and the expansion of the Kruger National Park as a wildlife sanctuary, under the supervision of Deneys Reitz. But the debate over disenfranchising Africans had laid bare the gulf in opinion between conservatives and liberals within Smuts's own ranks, let alone that between the Hertzogites and Malanites within Afrikanerdom. Many of Hertzog's supporters were Malanite hard-liners at heart and it was only Smuts's genius for compromise that had held the disunited party together. In the general election of 1938, the UP won 111 seats against the Purified Nationalists' 27; but the result showed that Malan and his followers were beginning to build momentum. The centenary celebration of the Great Trek in 1938 gave further impetus to their isolationist cause.

It took the gathering storm in Europe to bring the uneasy détente between the supporters of Smuts and Hertzog to an end. Smuts had been watching the growth of Nazism in Europe with mounting alarm. The Munich Agreement offered a temporary respite, but all hopes of peace disappeared when Hitler invaded Czechoslovakia on 15 March 1939. As minister of justice, Smuts took the precaution of sending armed police reinforcements to Windhoek in case Germany made good on its threat to reclaim its colonies. The move enjoyed Hertzog's support, but brought protests from the opposition that Smuts was once again trying to draw South Africa into a European conflict. The wisdom of his decision became evident later when pro-Nazi organisations reared their heads in South West Africa and South Africa.

By now, South Africa's neutrality had become a red-hot political issue. At the time of Munich, Hertzog and the cabinet had taken a resolution that the country would remain neutral in the event of war in Europe, and the Prime Minister saw no reason to alter that decision. But after Hitler's invasion of Poland on 1 September, followed by Britain's and France's declaration of war on Germany, Smuts came to a different conclusion. On 2 September, Hertzog called a special meeting of the cabinet at which he proposed a 'qualified' neutrality. Smuts dissented, arguing that as a member of the British Commonwealth, South Africa should also declare war on Germany. Seven members of the cabinet supported him and six were behind Hertzog, who called another cabinet meeting on the next day, Sunday 3 September. At that meeting, Hertzog proposed that the matter be put to the vote in the House of Assembly.[23]

Addressing a hushed and overflowing House of Assembly on 4 September 1938, Hertzog claimed that in going to war, Germany was only trying to recover from the humiliation of Versailles; South Africa should remain neutral unless the Union's interests were directly threatened. To take the side of Britain, he contended, would revive the bitter relations between Afrikaans- and English-speakers. Rising to his feet immediately, Smuts told the House that Hitler was intent on world domination, and had to be stopped. Anxious though he was not to destroy the co-operation which had existed between Hertzog and himself, and between the two language groups, South Africa had no choice but to sever relations with Germany. Union troops should not be sent overseas, but used to protect South Africa's interests, he declared. It would be suicidal for the Union, 'poor as it is in defence, rich in its resources to dissociate itself directly or indirectly from its associates in the Commonwealth'.[24]

When put to the vote, Hertzog's motion was defeated by 80 votes to 67. He immediately requested the Governor-General to dissolve Parliament and call an election (which he might well have won). The King's representative in South Africa declined on the grounds that the question of neutrality had already been raised in the May 1938 election, whereupon Hertzog resigned. Smuts was called upon to form a new government, which he did without great enthusiasm. At the age of nearly 70, he was prime minister of South Africa once again.

CHAPTER 15

War Leader

REBUILDING A DEFENCE FORCE

Smuts's keen understanding of world affairs had brought home to him that neutrality in war was never going to be an option for South Africa: the country's strategic situation in the south Atlantic would draw it inevitably into a conflict that would come quickly to Africa.[1] While he had promised not to send South African troops to fight *overseas*, the continent of Africa was different and had to be protected. With vigour renewed, he set about reviving the almost moribund UDF and preparing the country for the demands – and privations – of war. He met with resistance at every turn.

For the next six years, he had no choice but to prosecute South Africa's war against the Axis powers on two fronts: domestic and military. At the outbreak of hostilities in Europe, the Union – in Hancock's words – was 'militarily naked'.[2] For the preceding 15 years, Hertzog had been content to rely on the British Navy to defend South Africa's coasts and preserve its trade routes. The UDF had no navy of its own to speak of, a handful of mostly obsolete aircraft, a tiny Permanent Force of only 260 officers and fewer than 5 000 men, and an Active Citizen Force of about 950 officers and 14 000 men.[3] Knowing how controversial conscription would be, the SAP government dared only recruit volunteers to fight outside the country's borders.[4]

Hertzog's minister of defence, the pro-Nazi Oswald Pirow, had neglected to maintain a fighting force of any consequence, so until material support could be received from the UK and US, South Africa remained vulnerable. Smuts had to act quickly. For seaward defence, he converted fishing trawlers and other vessels into mine-sweepers and patrol craft. For air reconnaissance, he took over airplanes from SA Airways, trained pilots and recruited air crews; while army numbers were built up by the recruitment of volunteers for service 'anywhere in Africa'. These 'Smuts men' wore distinctive orange-red shoulder flashes known as *rooi lussies*, and were to become a common – and in some places provocative – presence on urban and rural streets. Some 190 000 whites out of a population of 570 000 men of fighting age volunteered for service in the UDF navy, army or air force – of whom two-thirds were Afrikaners.

A NATION DIVIDED

As had been feared, the war was a bitterly divisive issue in the white community. While English-speakers supported Smuts in large numbers, Afrikaners in general were opposed to being drawn into 'England's war'. Most Afrikaners who joined up were motivated by a wish to defend freedom and democracy, but some of the unemployed were attracted simply by the wages on offer – the highest in the Commonwealth.[5]

Many die-hards opposed to the war joined Oswald Pirow's Nuwe Orde vir Suid-Afrika, or the more militant Ossewa Brandwag (OB), led by former Administrator of the Free State, Dr Hans van Rensburg. Both were quasi-military, pro-Hitler organisations, in favour of an Afrikaner republic based on Nationalist-Socialist principles. The OB had its own division of storm troopers, which resorted to bombings and sabotage and provoked fierce clashes between soldiers and civilians. Malan's National Party, in stark contrast, set its face against violence and continued to express its opposition to the war via Parliament.[6]

When the House of Assembly reconvened in January 1940 for the first time after the decisive war vote, Hertzog proposed that South Africa should enter into peace talks with Germany. The motion was put to the House on 27 January and once again defeated by 80 votes to 67. Smuts then moved the War Measures Bill to indemnify the government for its actions in furtherance of the war effort. The opposition fought the bill at every stage and for the remaining four months of the session put up a spirited resistance to wartime legislation, making Smuts unable to absent himself from the House for any length of time.[7]

At Smithfield, Hertzog complained to a large crowd that Smuts's destruction of the great United Party had revived nationalist Afrikanerdom.[8] Across the country, impassioned anti-war demonstrations were held: in Bloemfontein,

70 000 pro-republican Afrikaners gathered at the Women's Monument to commemorate the deaths of Afrikaner women and children in the Anglo-Boer War and demand secession from the British Commonwealth.

Faced with a mounting threat to internal security, Smuts resorted to tough measures to put down insurrection. Many militants – including a young law-yer, BJ Vorster, who would one day become prime minister – were detained without trial in internment camps. A measure which caused special outrage was the order that all civilians, including famers, had to turn in their weapons and ammunition. Had General Christiaan de Wet not famously said: 'A Boer and his gun and his wife are three things always together?'[9] The opposition complained, not without reason, that the government was politicising the formerly non-partisan civil service, as well as the security forces and armed services.[10]

The war also brought Malan and Hertzog together again in an uneasy alli-ance. In early 1940, the two men formed a new Herenigde Nasionale Party/ Volksparty (Reunited National Party/People's Party, or HNP), under Hertzog's leadership, to demand South Africa's withdrawal from the war. While Malan was pleased to reconcile with Hertzog, his pro-republican supporters in the north had become suspicious of their former leader and were determined that Hertzog should go. On the other side of Afrikanerdom, the Nationalists' incessant anti-war propaganda served only to alienate the families of those who had signed up for the fight against Hitler.

1940 – A DISASTROUS YEAR

As Smuts had predicted, South Africa was drawn into the war almost imme-diately: the country's main harbours were soon filled with ocean liners and warships avoiding the dangers in European waters by sailing around the Cape. As they did so, German submarines began sinking shipping off the South African coast – until naval and air defences were strengthened. Allied vessels seeking repairs and convoys carrying war supplies imposed new demands upon local agriculture and industry. Dr HJ van der Bijl, managing director of Iscor, was given authoritarian powers to develop the country's manufacturing sector, which he did to such effect that South Africa became known as the 'great repair shop of the Middle East'.[11]

With Winston Churchill in Cairo, 1942.

As for recruitment, no attempt was made, in the war's early stages, to enlist soldiers of colour into the UDF, but in time an auxiliary force of non-combatants was formed to assist the men in arms. The Cape Coloured Corps, which had seen service in World War I, was revived initially as a non-combatant unit, but was soon in action in North Africa, notably at the battle of El Alamein. An Indian and Malay Corps and several thousand white women also enlisted in the armed services.

Nineteen forty proved to be a disastrous year for the Allied forces in Europe. Poland, Belgium, Holland and Denmark fell quickly to the Nazis and when Norway was unable to resist invasion despite Britain's help, Winston Churchill replaced Chamberlain as Britain's prime minister and war leader. One of Churchill's early actions was to send Smuts his greetings: 'It is a comfort to me to feel that we shall be together in the long and hard *trek*; for I know you and the Government and peoples of the Union will not weary under the heat of the day and that we shall make a strong *laager* … at the end,' he wrote.[12]

On 24 May, two days before the evacuation from Dunkirk, Smuts celebrated his seventieth birthday. After a brief celebration with Isie and the family, he turned his attention to developments in Africa, where he expected Mussolini to enter the war and strike from his country's bases in Abyssinia, Eritrea and Italian Somaliland. In July, with an attack by Italian forces on British-held Kenya imminent, Smuts sent the first contingent of South African troops to East Africa, under the command of Brigadier Dan Pienaar. In bidding the men farewell, he was at his rhetorical best: 'In taking part in this war we are not merely defending ourselves, our country, our future. We are standing by our friends in the Commonwealth of Nations in all loyalty and good faith, as we know they will stand by us. … The world cause of freedom is also our cause, and we shall wage this war for human freedom until God's victory crowns the end.'[13] Smuts's fundamental optimism, according to Ingham, sprang from his religious conviction that the evil of Nazism could not triumph in a universe shaped by Divine Providence.[14]

EAST AFRICA AGAIN

Late in 1940, Smuts accepted an invitation from the British Foreign Secretary, Anthony Eden, to fly to Khartoum to discuss plans to counter Italy's activities in Africa. On the way, he was able to visit 'his' troops – including his son, now Second-Lieutenant Jannie Smuts – on the Abyssinian border, and view from the air the spectacle of Mounts Kilimanjaro and Kenya and the 'great crater-land of East Africa'.[15]

His visit was not without dramatic incident.[16] Without informing anyone properly, he, General van Ryneveld and other top brass took off in two converted Junkers 86s and flew over the well-camouflaged air-base at Archer's Post in northern Kenya. To those on the ground, the German planes appeared hostile. Two Hawker Fury fighters were sent up to intercept the Junkers aircraft and shots were fired before it was realised that visitors were friendly. When Smuts's plane landed, it had eight holes in its fuselage, and one bullet had actually passed between his legs. Afterwards, he made light of the episode.

From bases in Kenya, the tiny South African Air Force had begun launching a series of bombing attacks on Italian military targets in Abyssinia. Though the damage inflicted was relatively slight, the SAAF's aggression gave ground forces in East Africa the breathing space they required to build up a substantial presence in the region. Pienaar's South African Brigade scored one of the Allies' first successes in the war when it captured the Italian fort at El Wak, 400 miles east of Nairobi, on the Kenya-Somali border. Together, East African and South African troops braved mountainous countryside and deserts, often in appalling weather conditions, in marching over 4 000 miles in 53 days to Addis Ababa, which they captured in April 1941. After the Italians' surrender, the Emperor of Abyssinia, Haile Selassie, was restored to the throne and the Union Jack hoisted alongside his nation's flag. The successful East African campaign neutralised the Italian threat to Allied shipping lanes and helped General Wavell, in command of British forces in the Middle East, to drive the enemy out of Egypt and Cyrenaica (now Libya).[17]

Shortly before the fall of Addis, Smuts flew to Cairo to confer once more with Eden and General Dill – this time over whether Commonwealth troops, mainly Australians and New Zealanders – should be switched from northern Africa to help in the defence of Greece. Smuts's support for the plan was born of his admiration and affection for the Greeks. On his return home, he was asked to send South African troops urgently to Egypt, where the diversion of British forces to Greece had created an opening for Rommel's Afrika Korps to come to the aid of the beleaguered Italians.

YEAR OF DESTINY

In a New Year's Day broadcast to the people of Great Britain, Smuts predicted that 1941 would be a year of destiny for the democratic world, and so it proved. Although Vichy France was collaborating with Germany, Hitler's invasion of Russia and Japan's attack on the US at Pearl Harbour had brought Russia and America into the war on the Allied side. He also foresaw that Vichy-German co-operation and Hitler's successes in the Balkans would result in Syria becoming Britain's weak point in the Middle East – a launch pad for Axis attacks on Egypt and the strategically important Suez Canal. Aware that he was putting all 'our South African eggs into one basket', he nonetheless moved the First South African Division from Abyssinia to the Western Desert as a precaution.

On Smuts's seventy-first birthday, King George VI conferred on him the rank of Field Marshal in the British Army, an honour bestowed on the monarch's behalf by the Governor-General, Sir Patrick Duncan, who described Smuts as 'a great rock in a weary world'.[18] Though proud of the singular honour, the new Field Marshal expressed the hope that those who had known him as 'General' Smuts for the last 40 years would continue to use his old, familiar title.

In August 1941, Smuts was accompanied on a three-day visit to Cairo by Isie – flying for the first time in her life – who received a 'tumultuous' welcome from South African troops.[19] As she had done in World War I, 'Ouma' Smuts had organised a nationwide Gifts and Comforts Fund which collected small luxuries, clothing and books to ease the harshness of daily life in the armed services.[20] Work parties of housewives were invited to join her at Libertas, Groote Schuur and Doornkloof to knit and sew for those 'up North'. In her son Jannie's opinion, his unpretentious and warm-hearted mother was no less active in wartime than his father. Her tireless efforts to improve conditions for 'her boys' made her hugely popular among all those in uniform.

Germany's early successes in Europe brought much encouragement to Smuts's Nationalist opponents, but it was not long before the alliance between Malan and Hertzog fell apart – over the republican issue. Their respective supporters were unable to agree over whether non-republicans could be members of the new HNP, and neither side was willing to compromise. At a conference of the HNP's federal council in December 1940, an ailing and short-tempered Hertzog led his followers out of the party because – irony upon irony – its new constitution did not make adequate provision for the equal treatment of English-speakers.[21] The walk-out brought an end to Hertzog's long political career. Dispirited and saddened by his fellow Afrikaners, he died on his farm near Pretoria less than two years later. Smuts, who was in Europe at the time, expressed deep regret at not being able to attend the funeral. 'General Hertzog,' he said in tribute to his old comrade and foe, 'maintained a standard of manliness, patriotism and honesty which I hope will always be maintained in South Africa.'[22]

SETBACKS

Towards the end of 1941, Britain's Eighth Army, comprising troops from all corners of the Commonwealth including two divisions from South Africa, assembled under the command of Generals Auchinleck and Cunningham to defend the Middle Eastern oilfields and Egypt against an Axis advance under Rommel. The fighting in the North African desert had become a tug of war as the British pushed Italian and German forces westwards only to be batted back by Rommel and his troops moving eastwards. In the brave fight to drive the enemy out of Cyrenaica and retrieve the coastal base of Tobruk, South African forces sustained heavy losses, most notably at Sidi Rezegh, where the 5th Infantry Brigade ran into a large Panzer force and was 'wiped out'.[23] In May 1942, while on another visit to Cairo, Smuts was able to inspect 'Springbok' troops stationed in the Tobruk area. Addressing the men from the back of a truck, he predicted that a great trial of strength lay ahead, for North Africa was destined to become 'one of the great battlefields of this war'.[24]

After a brief lull in hostilities, during which both sides built up their tank forces and regrouped, Rommel renewed his drive towards the Suez Canal. In his way were two South African divisions, at Gazala and Tobruk. After heavy fighting, the First South African Division under Maj-Gen Dan Pienaar was ordered to evacuate Gazala and retreat. The Second South Africa Division, under Maj-Gen HB Klopper, was ordered to hold Tobruk, which it failed to do against Rommel's superior Panzer Division. On 21 June 1942, Klopper surrendered: 33 000 men, 10 722 of them South African, were taken prisoner – a grievous blow to Smuts's and the nation's morale. Opponents of the war were quick to make political capital out of the setback.

The loss of Tobruk was felt deeply not only by Smuts but also by Winston Churchill, who requested an urgent meeting in Cairo, in August 1942. Smuts helped the British prime minister to reshuffle his top commanders in the Middle East: General Alexander was put in charge of Middle East Command and General Montgomery of the Eighth Army. Churchill told the media that he had been fortified in his decision making by the 'massive judgment of Field Marshal Smuts who flew from Cape Town to Cairo to meet me'.[25]

TIME TO TAKE THE OFFENSIVE

Smuts's ability to view the war objectively, and holistically, had made a deep impression on the indomitable Churchill, who invited him to London for further strategic discussions. This time, Smuts allowed himself five weeks in

England, the longest period he had been away from South Africa in five years. Landing in London on 13 October, he went immediately into a meeting of the war cabinet. British newspapers heralded his appearance as an indication that an important new phase of the war was about to begin. The editor of the *Guardian* wrote that the arrival of 'the father' of African strategy (whatever that meant) was a conspicuous sign 'that the Allies mean business in a new sense'.[26]

On 21 October, Smuts addressed members of both Houses of Parliament and their guests (a gathering of over 1 000). Introduced by Lloyd George, who described him as one of the foremost statesmen of his generation, of whom 'no one in calmness or discernment exceeds him in this age',[27] Smuts gave a masterly analysis of the course of the conflict from the fall of France to the attack on Pearl Harbor. The defensive phase of the war, he declared, was now over; the time had come for the Allies to take the offensive. Of the war's successful outcome, he was in no doubt. Mindful of the future, as usual, he invited the audience to consider what kind of social and international order would be needed to win both the war and the peace. His words of hope and encouragement were received with enthusiasm in Britain and around the world. A writer in the New York *Post* described the speech as 'one of the great political documents of the war … In unequivocal words the South African leader announced the offensive.'[28] (*For a fascinating video clip of Smuts's stirring speech, go to YouTube on the Internet and type in 'General Smuts addresses the Mother of Parliaments in London (1942)'.*)

THE TIDE TURNS

Two days later, in Egypt, General Montgomery's Eighth Army launched his 'great thunderbolt of an assault'[29] on Rommel's lines at El Alamein, driving the Germans out of Egypt and across the North African desert to Tunisia. In the forefront of the advance was the First South Africa Division, under the inspiring leadership of Dan Pienaar. As they retreated, the Axis forces lost over 70 000 prisoners of war, 8 000 of them German, as well as substantial quantities of war materiel. South African forces re-entered Tobruk on 13 November, but torrential rains enabled Rommel to elude the pursuing Allies and live to fight another day. Only five months after Smuts and Churchill had met in Cairo, the tide of the war had begun to turn in the Allies' favour. In London,

Churchill famously declared the 'Battle of Egypt' as 'not the beginning of the end, but the end of the beginning'.

Returning to South Africa after one of the busiest few weeks of his life – during which he was called into twice-daily discussions of the war cabinet as well as meetings of the Defence Committee, Privy Council, Pacific War Committee and the War Office, often until late into the night – Smuts set about preparing for the forthcoming session of Parliament. On 6 December, he broadcast another message to the British people, eulogising the effectiveness of the Empire's war machine and paying special tribute to the leadership of Churchill, in whom he had found 'open-mindedness and single-mindedness as Prime Minister, and fanatical inflexibility only in his objective of winning the war'.[30]

WINNING RE-ELECTION

The demise of Hertzog had served to make Malan's Nationalists more vehement than ever in their denunciations of Smuts. When troops were sent to Egypt, they asked scornfully what Britain's war in Egypt had to do with the defence of South Africa. When Smuts was forced by Stalin's declaration of war on Hitler to accept the Russians as allies, he was accused, absurdly, of being 'a champion of Bolshevism'.[31] And when Japan entered the war, he committed the ultimate sin – in the Malanites' eyes – of declaring in Parliament that, if necessary, blacks and coloureds would be given arms to defend their country. 'Fancy arming the Natives who are likely to use their weapons against the Whites,' he wrote with sarcasm to Margaret Gillett: 'Think of arming the Natives after I had *disarmed* the Europeans only a year or more ago. Manifestoes are raining, the Church has been mobilised to pass angry resolutions ... It is of course all purely party politics.'[32]

With the war turning in the Allies' favour, and South Africa's international prestige at a high, Smuts pressed home his advantage. Public opinion had turned in his favour: thousands of voters who opposed him at the outbreak of the war were now having second thoughts. The 1943 general election became a battle between him and Malan for the allegiance of the uncommitted Afrikaner voter.[33]

◆

In the run-up to the election, both party leaders had to paper over divisions within their own ranks. Attempting to appeal to middle-of-the-road voters put off by Pirow's and Van Rensburg's extremism, Malan downplayed the demand for a Christian National Republic and sought instead to exploit bread-and-butter issues as well as highlight the danger that Smuts was supposedly visiting upon the country by spreading the poison of communism among blacks, coloureds and Indians.[34] Smuts, for his part, had to bring his United Party into line with the smaller Dominion and Labour parties, the former deeply concerned about the growing Indian presence in Natal. He could also count on the support of 12 000 coloured voters on the Cape's common roll.[35]

By returning 110 pro-war members to Parliament against 43 for the anti-war parties, the electorate gave Smuts his most emphatic mandate ever. In every province except the Free State, the United Party won spectacularly. Yet Malan's Nationalists had not done too badly either: the party had obliterated the far right, pro-Hitler wing of Afrikanerdom while remaining 'uncompromisingly republican, secessionist and anti-war'.[36] More ominously for Smuts, by preying upon the fears of whites, the Malanites were turning the colour issue to their advantage.

Reflecting on his decisive win in a letter to Margaret Gillett, Smuts wrote, 'And when I think of my years in the wilderness ... and at sunset, I find such recognition of what I have stood for and suffered for, I feel that at last I have been repaid with more than compound interest ... it is indeed a famous victory.'[37] It was also to be his last.

One who observed Smuts at close quarters at this time was the British High Commissioner in South Africa, Lord Harlech. In a personal letter home, he gave an affecting description of South Africa's leader. 'He is 72 years of age, still erect, spare of body, dapper in his clothing, and intensely full of vitality. He keeps himself physically fit by eating little, and taking long walks ... He is a non-smoker and almost a teetotaller. At Irene he leads a patriarchal Afrikaner life, surrounded by his wife, daughters and many grandchildren. The ramshackle house was bought by him over thirty years ago and is completely "unmodernised" and always gloriously untidy.'[38]

CHAPTER 16

'We, the United Nations'

INFLUENCE DIMINISHES

At Churchill's urging, the newly re-elected Smuts paid a second wartime visit to London in September 1943. His son Jannie accompanied him as aide de camp, a role the younger man described as 'exacting'. On the Italian mainland, where British and American forces had landed after driving the Axis powers out of North Africa, Mussolini had resigned shortly before his dispirited troops capitulated. Within the Allied ranks, the balance of power had begun to tilt, with Washington replacing London as the locus of decision-making. The re-opening of the Mediterranean to shipping meant that, to Smuts's vexation, the strategic importance of the Cape sea route – and of South Africa – had been diminished.

En route to London, Smuts touched down at Tunis to confer with Generals Eisenhower and Alexander and RAF commander Tedder. From there he flew on to Sicily, Malta and Algiers, where he boarded an aircraft sent by Churchill to collect him. He was annoyed to learn that his advice that the Allies should attack Nazi Germany via defeated Italy and the Balkans was being disregarded in favour of Operation Overlord, the US-led, cross-Channel invasion of Europe along France's Atlantic seaboard. By dithering for so long, he believed, the Allies were fumbling a great opportunity.[1] Preparations to cross the Channel, he argued, should be slowed down or put on hold while the bombing of Germany was intensified.

Churchill, who took Smuts's views seriously, secretly agreed, but by this stage of the war had to yield to the Americans. He wrote to Smuts saying 'there can be no question whatever of breaking arrangements we have made for Overlord ... I hope you will realise that British loyalty to Overlord is a keystone of [the] arch of Anglo-American co-operation ... I think enough forces exist for both hands to be played, and I believe this to be the right strategy.'[2]

Although Smuts was in London officially for a meeting of Commonwealth prime ministers, he had many other engagements to fulfil. He was drawn immediately into meetings of the war cabinet, whose members were much concerned about the threat of German long-range rockets aimed at London. He also paid a visit to the RAF's Bomber Command, where Air Vice-Marshal 'Bomber' Harris, a Rhodesian who had served under him as an infantryman in South West Africa in World War I, was in charge. At Chequers, the British prime minister's country retreat, he spent a convivial weekend with Churchill, who – according to Jannie – tried to persuade Smuts to deputise for him during his and Eden's forthcoming absence from the UK on business. Another weekend was spent with the royal family at Windsor Castle, where the King invited him to preach the Sunday sermon in St George's Chapel – one of the most difficult requests, Smuts said afterwards, he'd ever had to comply with.[3]

On 19 October, he told an audience of over 2 000 in London's historic Old Guildhall that the turning points of the war had been Stalingrad and El Alamein, and urged a tremendous effort to end the fighting.[4] On 25 October, a week before returning to South Africa, he made what became known as his 'Explosive Speech' to the Empire Parliamentary Association, on the theme 'Thoughts on a New World'. In a *tour d'horizon* of the globe, he predicted the emergence after the war of three Great Powers, America, Russia (the new Colossus) and Britain, who would form a trinity at the head of a United Nations Organisation that would lead the fight for humanity.

It was because the League of Nations had lacked leadership, he declared, that matters had gone wrong.[5] If Britain, the smallest of the trinity, were to play a leading role after the war, the British Empire and Commonwealth would have to be strengthened, perhaps by the addition of Europe's smaller democracies. Germany, he predicted, would disappear in its old form and in France, the upward climb would be a bitter and a long one. The suggestion that their country was no longer a Great Power and might as well join the British Commonwealth did not go down well with de Gaulle and the French, who ever since Versailles had regarded Smuts as a thorn in their flesh.[6]

On his way home, Smuts stopped over in Cairo for a dinner meeting with President Roosevelt. He declared afterwards that 'we two Dutchmen had got on splendidly'.[7] But he was unable to persuade Roosevelt not to weaken the

Allied presence in the Middle East by the diversion of troops from Africa to northern Europe.

OPERATION OVERLORD

In April 1944 Smuts was in London again for the first official Commonwealth Prime Ministers' Conference. By now, preparations for Overlord had been completed and the south of England turned into 'one vast military camp'.[8] At the Conference, he expressed his grave misgivings at Russia's intentions in the Baltics and predicted that she would become a 'colossus without fetters'[9] who would spread the doctrine of communism across Europe and the world.

On 19 May, he was given the Freedom of Birmingham, the city at the heart of Britain's armaments manufacturing industry. He used the opportunity to press once again for a quick end to the war, and predicted that the post-war world would be one of 'social security for the common man'. Concerned as always about communism, he urged his working-class audience to follow the Russia of Tolstoy, and not of Karl Marx.[10]

According to Jannie, his father had become increasingly impatient at the delay in launching Operation Overlord across the English Channel. On the afternoon of 3 June, Churchill took Smuts along to the final planning meeting at General Eisenhower's headquarters outside Portsmouth where he (Smuts) was distressed to learn that the invasion might have to be postponed for a further twelve days because of unfavourable weather conditions. He urged the Allied commanders to be 'more audacious', prepared to sacrifice a few thousand additional men at the start for the greater benefit in the long run.[11]

As it turned out, Eisenhower – whom Smuts described admiringly as a 'big man'[12] – decided to launch Overlord in deteriorating weather conditions on 6 June, known forever as D-Day. On 16 June, six days after the invasion of France had been successfully concluded, Smuts was invited to accompany Churchill and Sir Alan Brooke to Normandy in the warship *Kelvin*. Landing in the Canadian sector, the party made its way by jeep to Montgomery's head-quarters near Bayeux.[13] The press was asked to keep Smuts's presence secret for fear of offending de Gaulle, who had not been invited.[14]

Two days earlier, Smuts had watched from his hotel window in London as the first V1 flying bombs fell on the British capital, an airborne assault that was to last for the next three months. Only days earlier, Stalin had embarked upon his promised westward offensive which, as Smuts had predicted, would put the Russians ahead of the Allies in establishing a presence in eastern Europe.

Smuts left London for South Africa on 21 June, stopping over in Italy for discussions with General Alexander and visits to South Africa's Sixth Armoured Division at Orvieto and SAAF personnel on the Adriatic coast. Briefed in person before leaving by the Danish atomic scientist, Niels Bohr, at Churchill's request, he carried home with him one of the war's great secrets – the imminent production of the atom bomb.

His visits to Britain, tiring though they were for a man of his age, had served as a huge morale booster. Although his inability to leave South Africa for long periods had precluded his playing another significant role in Allied war planning, he had been kept near the centre of events by Churchill and others. He had been consulted by kings, prime ministers, generals, business people, diplomats and experts from all walks of life. The fractious politics of South Africa, by contrast, must have seemed a long way off, and by comparison rather trivial.

DIFFICULTIES AT HOME

During his absences abroad, the government's political difficulties had multiplied despite the best efforts of his immensely hardworking deputy, JH Hofmeyr (back in the cabinet since the 'War Vote') who had been left in charge of 'domestic affairs'. As we have seen, Hofmeyr was much younger than Smuts and more liberal in racial outlook. At this time, there were several issues over which he and Smuts – whom he held still in awe – differed, but they were papered over in the greater national interest. While Smuts was away, the United Party had discovered, in Hancock's words, 'its inner disunity on almost every crucial issue except the war'.[15]

Political rights for Africans and Indians were now high on the national agenda. Dr AB Xuma had reinvigorated the African National Congress, which formed a Youth League in 1943 and launched a campaign to collect a million signatures for a petition demanding an end to the pass laws. On the Witwatersrand, thousands of Africans walked to work rather than pay increased bus fares and erected shanty towns on municipal land. A group of black

145

intellectuals drew up a Bill of Rights for Africans based on the right to self-determination set out in the Atlantic Charter formulated by Roosevelt and Churchill in 1941. Xuma sent the document to Smuts with a request for an interview, but the Prime Minister replied through his private secretary that he saw no point in discussing it.[16] A year later, acting Prime Minister Hofmeyr declined to accept a petition demanding an end to the pass laws and passed the buck to the minister of native affairs. At the UP Congress of 1944, Smuts reaffirmed his party's 'well-known standpoint of separateness in social intercourse, housing and field of employment between the colours'.[17]

In the Transvaal and Natal, dissatisfaction with the government had erupted over the 'Pegging Act', a temporary measure which restricted Indians from buying land in 'white' residential and business areas for the next three years. The Act was a response to political pressure from MPs in Natal, in particular, where Indian numbers had grown rapidly to reach near parity with whites. The SA Indian Congress appealed to Smuts, who was well aware of the international ramifications of the discriminatory legislation, to intervene. He agreed that the Act would be repealed and appointed a Board of Control comprising three whites and two Indians to monitor 'Indian penetration into white areas'.[18]

Adding to his concerns throughout most of the war years was the poor health of Isie, who had suffered a stroke in December 1942, shortly before her seventy-second birthday. Though she recovered quickly and resumed her work for the Gifts and Comforts Fund, she suffered another breakdown in health in 1944, from which she took many years to recover.[19]

REWORDING THE CHARTER

The parliamentary session of 1945 was notable chiefly for a furious row over the expulsion of civil servants who had refused to resign their membership of the secretive Afrikaner Broederbond. Like Hertzog before him, Smuts regarded the organisation as anti-South African and dangerous and had laid down that no Broeder would be permitted to hold a post in the civil service.[20] To the anger of the opposition, he made good on his promise.

Before the session ended, Smuts left on his last wartime visit to England, once again accompanied by Jannie. For those on board, the flight was nerve-wracking as the overweight York aircraft at first struggled to take off, was struck by lightning over East Africa and developed a crack in a tailfin, but Smuts displayed no sign of nervousness whatsoever.[21]

The reason for his journey to Britain was another meeting of Commonwealth prime ministers to discuss the proposed Charter of the United Nations, which had been drafted at a preparatory meeting at Dumbarton Oaks in September 1944. Having been instrumental in founding the League of Nations, he was determined that the new international organisation should not fail as the League had done.[22] He thought the proposed wording of the Charter was legalistic and uninspiring and took it upon himself to reword the Preamble to include phrases such as: 'We, the United Nations ... We declare our faith in basic human rights ... We believe in the practice of tolerance ... We believe in the enlargement of freedom ... We believe in nations living in peace.' [23] (His opening words were subsequently altered to read, 'We, the Peoples of the United Nations ...'[24]) He maintained that the Charter should reflect the values that had sustained the Allied nations in the war, which had been 'a moral struggle ... of faith in justice and the resolve to vindicate the fundamental rights of man.'[25]

The Commonwealth Prime Ministers approved Smuts's version, which was put forward at the San Francisco Conference and adopted with a few minor amendments. Ironically, Smuts's introduction of 'fundamental human rights' into the politics of the United Nations was soon to become a stick with which to beat him and South Africa.[26] In vigorously defending his government's racial policies at the UN, he was accused of undermining his own creation.

On 13 April, shortly before leaving London for the US, Smuts was shocked to hear of the death of Franklin Roosevelt, which he described as 'a knock-out blow' to hopes of post-war peace.[27] He had particularly admired the way in which Roosevelt had fought isolationism and adverse public opinion to bring America into the war on the Allied side.

AT THE UNITED NATIONS

Smuts viewed the San Francisco Conference, opened officially on 25 April by the new US president, Harry Truman, with scepticism and trepidation. He was dubious about the veto given to the Big Three powers at Yalta and

Smuts signs the UN Charter in San Francisco, 1945.

concerned about the belligerence of Russia. Described by Canadian prime minister, Mackenzie King, as a person 'who had a standing in the diplomatic world unsurpassed by any' and by Anthony Eden as 'the doyen of the Conference – quite unrivalled in intellectual attributes and unsurpassed in experience and authority', [28] the elderly South African leader was invited to speak early in the plenary session. On 1 May, a day after the suicide of Hitler, Smuts 'galvanised' the delegates in the San Francisco Opera House by claiming that: 'For the human race, the hour has struck. Mankind has arrived at the crisis of its fate, the fate of its future as a civilized world. Victory in the war must be crowned by "a halt to the pilgrimage of death".'[29]

He told the gathering that the difference between the League of Nations and the United Nations Organisation was that it was now recognised that force was necessary to maintain world peace. The combined forces of the Great Powers would be needed to guarantee the peace; therefore unity among the leading nations was essential.

The new Charter, he went on to say, should not be a legalistic document for the prevention of war: 'I would suggest that the Charter should contain at its very outset and in its Preamble, a declaration of human rights and of the common faith which has sustained the Allied peoples in their bitter and prolonged struggle for the vindication of those rights and this faith ... We have fought for justice and decency and for the fundamental freedoms and rights of man, which are basic to human advancement and progress and peace.'[30]

In Europe, the war was moving at last towards its end. On 27 April, the American and Russian forces had met each other on the Elbe in Central Europe. A day later, Italian patriots had captured Mussolini and, after a summary trial, executed him. Admiral Doenitz had taken command of German forces after Hitler's death. On 7 May, Germany surrendered, and the terms of the Armistice were signed. On VE Day, Smuts sent Churchill a cable congratulating him on the successful cessation of hostilities, to which Britain's war leader replied, 'Nothing in these past stirring days has brought me greater pleasure than your most kind message. Your presence beside me in the councils of the Empire and at the fronts in those long hard years has been to me a constant source of strength and inspiration for which I am most sincerely grateful.'[31]

In San Francisco, where Smuts had been elected as President of the General Assembly – charged with settling the Preamble to the Charter and trusteeship issues, progress was slow. Comparing the peace conferences at the end of both world wars – as only he could, having been present at both, he lamented the absence this time of dominating personalities such as Wilson, Lloyd George and Clemenceau.[32]

Besides the veto, the sticking points at the Conference were once again the territorial claims of the victorious nations: the US wished to retain its strategic bases in the Pacific; Russia demanded similar bases of her own; and Britain was set on resisting any interference in the affairs of her colonies. Smuts, for his part, was determined not to surrender South Africa's claim to South West Africa as a League of Nations 'C' class mandate.

While the delegates to the Conference haggled, Smuts left briefly to deliver a graduation address at Berkeley, and to unveil a memorial plaque to Franklin Roosevelt in Muir Wood, a 400-acre park of giant sequoia redwoods on the outskirts of San Francisco. Of the late President, he said: 'Here among the giant redwoods this great man will find fitting and congenial company. Here henceforth will be the company of Giants.'[33] On another occasion, he and Jannie took an 'unforgettable' round trip to Yosemite National Park in the Sierra Nevadas.[34]

On 25 June, after nine long weeks, the United Nations Charter was finally adopted. Smuts had prepared a long address to wind up the conference, but his contribution had to be shortened when President Truman decided to close the proceedings himself. Speaking at the closing plenary session, as 'an old veteran of the wars and peace conferences', Smuts described the Charter as 'a good, practical workmanlike plan for peace', but said that it needed to be supported by 'a total mobilisation of the human spirit and all the vast network of social and moral agencies which are the support of our civilisation'.[35] According to Mazower, he praised the United Kingdom as the greatest colonial power in the world: 'Men and women everywhere,' he stated, 'including dependent peoples, still unable to look after themselves, are thus drawn into the vast plan to prevent war.'[36]

Immediately after the Conference, Smuts was due to travel to Washington, at Truman's invitation, to address both the House of Representatives and the Senate, but the invitation was withdrawn after the Americans decided that this might compromise Truman and hamper the passage of the Charter through Congress. Instead, Smuts took up Mackenzie King's invitation to visit Ottawa, where he told a large audience at the Canadian Club that while the San Francisco Charter was far from perfect, it was at least 'a step forward'.[37] In his mind, it was, after all, little more than an improved version of the League of Nations model and not incompatible with his view of the world. There was no commitment to granting independence to colonies, the UN could emerge as a force for world order, and South Africa – as the Empire's agent on the African continent – could continue with its civilising role.

Travelling home via London – where he found Winston Churchill in the midst of an election campaign, then Italy and Cairo, Smuts arrived in South Africa on 16 July after a 27 000 mile journey, ready to tackle the demobilisation of the armed services and the country's transformation from a war- to a peace-time footing. He was soon to learn the stunning news that his friend Churchill had been ejected from office by the British people while at the Potsdam conference of the Great Powers. On 6 and 9 August, the first atomic bombs fell on Hiroshima and Nagasaki and nine days later Japan surrendered. To his immense relief, the war was over at last.

CHAPTER 17

A Year of Sadness

WEARY RESIGNATION

The post-war world turned out much as Smuts had predicted in his memorable 'Explosive Speech' in 1943. Most of Europe lay in ruins, while Russia had greatly enhanced her reach and influence: among the Big Three, only Stalin had emerged as a victor. Smuts had hoped the US would help maintain the equilibrium of power in Europe, but the Americans seemed uninterested in assuming the responsibility, more concerned about bringing their GIs home. He found it remarkable that the US should so quickly forget its wartime friendship with Britain, and regarded the sudden termination of Lend-Lease as 'the repudiation of a glorious alliance'.[1]

Elsewhere, he was concerned to note that Asian nations, incited by the Russians, were leading the attack on imperialism. America, as usual, was caught between its narrow strategic calculations and anti-colonial impulses. 'Equal rights for all' was now the cry, and Smuts foresaw difficulties ahead for South Africa and himself at upcoming meetings of the United Nations Organisation.

With weary resignation he once again took up his post-war responsibilities as South Africa's prime minister, writing to Margaret Gillett that he was 'back in the old harness pulling the old cart'.[2] Yet he continued to take the burdens of the world upon his shoulders. From 1942 to 1945, he had been away for two or three months each year, but in 1946 he was out of the country for much longer – at the Commonwealth Prime Ministers' Conference in London, the Peace Conference in Paris and the General Assembly of the UN. In his absence, the task of running the government fell as usual on JH Hofmeyr, whose formidable mother, Deborah, was a friend of Smuts but accused him of imposing an intolerable burden on her son.

In Paris, Smuts was the only delegate who had been present at Versailles a quarter of a century earlier. This time, he deliberately refrained from serving on committees, preferring to dispense advice privately to delegates from various countries. With his past experience in mind, he held out little hope of a successful outcome of the Conference, observing that the Slav and Western groups present differed on almost every issue – a cleavage that boded ill for the prospects of world peace. Speaking in Aberdeen, Scotland, he declared that far too much was expected of the Conference: the world was still too unsettled for hope of an early return to stability.[3]

Smuts's objective in attending the General Assembly of the UN himself was to press South Africa's claim to South West Africa and to rebut India's charge that his government was discriminating against Indians in Natal. While he understood the criticisms of the Indian representative, Mrs VL Pandit, Nehru's sister, he felt that coming from a country which had a caste system and where Muslim minorities had been brutally massacred, it was a case of the pot calling the kettle black. Although at times heated, Smuts's exchanges with Mrs Pandit were never personal; yet his argument that the social separation of races in South Africa violated no human rights under the Charter and was intended to avoid 'bloody affrays' like those in India and elsewhere fell on deaf ears.

Supported by the US, Mrs Pandit and her supporters won the day: South Africa was censured by the General Assembly and ordered to bring the treatment of its Indians into line with the UN Charter. Before Mrs Pandit left for the UN, Gandhi had said to her: 'I don't mind whether you come back having won your case or having suffered defeat, but you must come back as a friend of Field-Marshal Smuts.'[4] After the vote, Pandit made her way over to Smuts to ask his forgiveness if she had failed to match the high standard of behaviour set by Gandhi. Smuts is said to have replied, 'This vote will put me out of power in our next elections, but you will have gained nothing.'[5]

Such was the anti-segregationist feeling aroused against South Africa that Smuts found no support for his government's policies or for the retention of South West Africa. The vote by the UN, Mazower notes, was 'the first act of assertion by the colonial world against the principle of racial hierarchy and European rule'.[6] Though neither the Americans nor the British had wanted South Africa to be singled out for criticism, 'caught between competing international constituencies, they were unable to prevent it'.[7] Smuts had become the first victim of the new institution he had been instrumental in creating.

Also in New York at the time was the African National Congress president Dr AB Xuma, sent by the ANC to put the resolutions of the Native Representative Council before the General Assembly and to lobby against any incorporation of South West Africa into the Union of South Africa. Though Smuts met Xuma, he seemed puzzled by his presence in the US and suggested the two of them should 'sit down together and solve our problems' when back home.[8] Impressed by the manner in which India's representatives had raised the banner on behalf of South Africa's other races, Xuma forged links between the ANC and India which were to prove useful later.

Smuts left New York hurt and angry at his treatment, but his morale was improved en route home by the acclaim he received on speech-making visits to Holland, Belgium and Italy. His final stop-over was in Athens, where he was given a hero's welcome and feted by the Greek royal family. Back in South Africa, the opposition made much of the failure of his mission to the UN, which Malan described as an 'attack on our freedom as a nation and our sovereignty'.[9] Writing to a friend, Smuts complained that 'the world does not know us or understand us and we feel this deeply, even when we are conscious that we are much to blame'.[10] He was in no doubt, however, about the wider significance for South Africa of his dispute with Mrs Pandit: 'Colour queers my poor pitch everywhere,' he wrote to Margaret Gillett. 'But South Africans cannot understand. Colour bars are to them part of the divine order of things. But I sometimes wonder what our position in years to come will be when the whole world will be against us.'[11] By 'us', he still meant white South Africans.

FEELING HIS AGE

Despite being 76 years of age, and no longer in the best of health, Smuts drove himself as hard as ever, working for long hours on government business while continuing to climb Table Mountain regularly and take long walks in the mountains of the Cape and northern Transvaal for relaxation. Besides his prime ministerial responsibilities, his presence as party leader was required at an incessant round of official functions, conferences, social functions and rallies. He kept his health problems to himself, his family and close friends, confessing to Margaret Gillett that 'I am too much living at the end of my physical resources.'[12]

Dr AB Xuma, president-general of the African National Congress 1940–49. South African Library

With the war over, there were many pressing political issues to confront. Industrialisation during the war years had led to a rapid increase in black urbanisation, resulting in an acute shortage of housing and a proliferation of shanty towns and squatter camps outside cities. Encouraged by Communist Party activists, black trade unionism was on the rise. In August 1946, the Mineworkers' Union called 70 000 Africans out on a strike that was put down by the police with the loss of several lives. Union leaders and communists were arrested and tried.[13] At the same time, the Native Representatives Council met to demand the abolition of the pass laws, recognition of black trade unions and the repeal of banishment without trial. Despite the best efforts of the African representatives in Parliament, notably Margaret Ballinger and Dr Edgar Brookes, to keep open communications between the NRC and the government during Smuts's absences at the UN, the two sides were drifting far apart.

Smuts regarded the deterioration in relations between the NRC and his government in a serious light. He paid heed to Ballinger's and Brookes's suggestion that by recognising the permanence of Africans in 'white' areas, relaxing the pass laws and easing labour restrictions, he might buy time to nudge the white electorate towards some form of power-sharing. NRC leaders, including

Prof ZK Matthews, were called to an exploratory meeting at which the Prime Minister revealed that he was giving thought to increasing the size of the NRC and extending its legislative powers, as well as granting recognition to black trade unions. Many of these 'reforms' were already under consideration by the Fagan Commission into 'Native Laws' which had been appointed in 1946 with a remit to report back by 1948. The NRC considered Smuts's arguments but, in the absence of any immediate proposal to increase black parliamentary representation, declared them to be wanting. Smuts decided to await the Fagan Report before resuming the discussions.

Internal opposition to the United Party government from Africans, coloureds and Indians, as well as pro-Nationalist whites, began to mount just as South Africa's once-stellar international reputation began to wane. At the war's end, the Smuts government's grip on power seemed unassailable but despite an upturn in the country's macro-economic fortunes, it was not long before voter dissatisfaction began to manifest itself. Petrol was still rationed, there were shortages of accommodation, luxuries, meat and some foods, and returning soldiers were restless at the delays in demobilisation. The importation into South Africa of some 60 000 immigrants from Europe – recruited in an attempt to alleviate a critical shortage of skilled manpower – infuriated the Nationalists, who accused Smuts of attempting 'to plough the Afrikaner under'.[14] Overriding all was the racial question. As Smuts wrote to Margaret Gillett, 'I am anxious to try my hand at a solution. The danger is that by appearing pro-Native, I may run the risk to lose the general election next year and thus hand the Natives over to the other extreme.'[15]

ROYAL VISIT

The royal visit in early 1947 offered Smuts a welcome distraction from his domestic difficulties. At his invitation, King George VI and Queen Elizabeth and their two daughters spent two months in South Africa, travelling over 16 000 km to fulfil a punishing schedule of public functions. On the day of the King's arrival, he bestowed upon Smuts the Order of Merit, an honour never held by more than 24 people at one time.[16] Isie was not well enough to welcome the royals in Cape Town, so the visitors came specially to see her at Doornkloof for what proved to be a most convivial 'tea'. While in South

155

With the British royal family in the Drakensberg, 1947. AAI Fotostock SA/PA

Africa, the future Queen Elizabeth celebrated her twenty-first birthday and marked the occasion by broadcasting to the Commonwealth.

After the bleakness of the war years, the royal visit provided a rare and enjoyable spectacle for the public, and the visitors were greeted with friendliness and hospitality wherever they went. As expected, the opposition complained that the exercise was an expensive waste of public money, designed to further the government's political agenda. The Nationalist newspaper, *Die Transvaler*, edited by one HF Verwoerd, refused even to take notice of the royal family's visit – reporting for instance that there was traffic congestion in Johannesburg, without giving the reason why – which cannot have done much for its circulation figures.

Shortly before the arrival of the royals, Smuts was given an inkling of how voter sentiment was shifting when the UP's candidate in the Hottentots-Holland by election, the young Sir De Villiers Graaff, was defeated by his Nationalist opponent in what had hitherto been regarded as a safe UP seat. The government's defeat was attributed to remarks made by Hofmeyr, shortly before polling day, that 'Natives and Indians' would eventually be represented in Parliament by people of their own colour.[17] To the Nationalists, this was the ultimate heresy.

Smuts was now caught again in the dilemma to which he had become accustomed – damned if he did, and damned if he didn't. If his government moved in an illiberal direction, as it had done on the Indian question, it ran into strong criticism internationally, especially at the UN. If it eased up on racial policies, the Nationalists were quick to capitalise. The NP's twin bogeymen were the 'ultra-liberal' JH Hofmeyr, Smuts's heir apparent, and the communists, both of whom were held up as mortal dangers to white South Africa.[18] 'Apartheid' was the new slogan for a raft of NP policies intended to tighten segregation and balkanise the country into separate socio-economic units.

Notwithstanding his domestic concerns, Smuts left for London in late 1947, via Greece and Italy, to attend Princess Elizabeth's wedding, where he was seated next to Winston Churchill in Westminster Abbey. While in Britain, he received a warm message of thanks from an old friend, Dr Chaim Weizmann, about to become the first president of Israel. A few months later, on 14 May 1948, the state of Israel came into existence. Smuts, who had been pleased at the UN's partition of the Holy Land between Jews and Arabs, announced South Africa's *de facto* recognition of the new country on 24 May, his seventy-eighth birthday.

A STUNNING REJECTION

Nineteen forty-eight turned out to be a year of 'disappointment, disaster and sadness'.[19] It began with the assassination of Mahatma Gandhi, to whom Smuts paid tribute as 'one of the great men of my time … my acquaintance with him over a period of more than thirty years only deepened my high respect for him, however much we differed in our views and methods'. Despite much bloodshed, the battle that the Mahatma had waged to end the colour bar in the Empire had been won in almost every corner of the Commonwealth except South Africa, the country in which his campaign had begun.[20]

Mustering as much energy as he could, Smuts approached the forthcoming general election in May 1948 in an overconfident frame of mind. He thought that despite the electorate's impatience with restrictions and controls, his government's war record and comfortable parliamentary majority of 50 would be

157

Rooi gevaar: a cartoon by *Die Burger*'s DC Boonzaaier during the 1948 election. Museum Africa, Johannesburg

enough to ensure victory. Though urged to do so, he declined to reshuffle his cabinet of mostly elderly warhorses well past their sell-by date, or to permit a re-delimitation of seats in order to even out the disparity in numbers between rural and urban constituencies. Within the United Party itself, there were deep divisions over racial policy, many of its conservative members having been influenced by the NP's anti-Hofmeyr propaganda.

Malan's Nationalists fought a canny campaign, playing down the republican issue by promising to remain within the Commonwealth, and playing up the threat that the UP's 'liberal' policies posed to farmers and skilled workers, in particular. Though the party's anti-Smuts rhetoric bordered on the ludicrous, with its mouthpiece *Die Kruithoring* calling on patriots to 'Obliterate the red hordes. A vote for Jan Smuts is a vote for Joe Stalin',[21] its *swart gevaar* tactics and promise to introduce 'apartheid' resonated with white voters, fearful of what racial reform might entail. The NP was also able to exploit the natural desire for change on the part of voters who had grown tired of nine years of rule by the same party.

The result of the election – held two days after Smuts's birthday – came as a stunning shock to the Nationalists as much as Smuts himself, who lost his Standerton seat by 224 votes. Although the UP had gained a majority of votes, it had won only 65 seats against the NP's 70. Yet if each vote had enjoyed an equivalent value, Smuts would have won comfortably: in the most significant turnaround since Union, Malan's Nationalists had come to power with less than 40 per cent of the vote.

Smuts's cabinet colleague, Major Piet van der Byl, lamented years afterwards in sorrow more than anger that his long-time leader had never seemed to learn from experience.[22] As in 1924, he had blithely disregarded warnings of impending defeat. Worse still, Van der Byl suggests, because he had an important speaking engagement in the UK in June, and the prospect of a worldwide audience, Smuts had decided on a short session of Parliament before the election, dispensing with a Budget that could have brought tax relief to voters.[23] 'I strongly believe,' Van der Byl wrote, 'that no person over 75 should hold a commanding position. A better age would perhaps be 70.'[24]

The UP's entirely avoidable defeat at the polls left Smuts shaken and depressed. Like Winston Churchill, he felt that after all he had done for his country during the long years of war, his dismissal was deeply unfair and unjust. As his old friend and admirer, the British Conservative Leo Amery said in a message of commiseration, 'the proverbial ingratitude of democracy had been confirmed once more!'[25]

However, after recovering his composure, Smuts steadfastly resisted efforts to persuade him to retire from politics. Writing to Lady Daphne Moore, he acknowledged not only losing power but also forgoing 'the prospect of release, of some freedom at the end, and of quietly collecting my thoughts and gaining clarity in my own soul'. Explaining his determination to soldier on, he continued, 'But my defeat in South Africa leaves me now no choice. If I go out of public life, so much of what has been laboriously built up may be broken down again. I must defend my works – which means I must remain in the fighting line and continue to lead the Party. Hofmeyr has been too much under attack, and has been too severely wounded, to do this job – and I must continue in the leadership...'[26]

CHAPTER 18

Last Climb

CHANCELLOR OF CAMBRIDGE

Six months before he fell from power, Smuts was elected unanimously to the chancellorship of his alma mater, Cambridge University. This singular honour was one he valued above all the others he had received.[1] Soon after the May election, he left for England to attend his ceremonial installation.

Before departing, he had a delicate political issue to resolve. Election post-mortems had singled out Hofmeyr's liberal pronouncements as the proximate cause of the United Party's defeat. On 31 May, a group of ex-cabinet ministers met, without Smuts being present, and called upon Hofmeyr to resign as the party's deputy leader and executive chairman. Hofmeyr countered that it was up to the leader rather than him to decide. Smuts made up his mind immediately, announcing that he would continue to lead the party as it was he rather than Hofmeyr who had to take personal responsibility for the electoral defeat: 'If there is blame for the present failure, let it be mine.'[2]

In his inaugural address as Cambridge's Chancellor, he ignored his political travails and told students, 'We do not realise that we are in fact passing through one of the great secular revolutions of history, and that deeper forces are at work which – war or no war – may completely reshape our world, and are already in fact transforming our human scene …'[3]

He prefaced his reflections on the international situation with reminiscences about how, 57 years earlier, he had arrived 'as a young son of the veld' and found comradeship at Cambridge in one of the smaller colleges. Returning home, within a few years he and his people were at war with the British. Yet that war had not completely put out the light that Cambridge had kindled in him. Former enemies had learnt at long last to understand each other. One whose name should never be forgotten, he said, was Campbell-Bannerman,

Chancellor of Cambridge University, 1948: an honour Smuts valued above all the others. INPRA

a statesman whose generosity of spirit was needed in a world so much more dangerous than it was half a century before.[4] His own presence at the ceremony was a testament to the Liberal prime minister's wisdom.

Even the usually critical *Die Burger* approved of his performance: 'We may differ from him, but the honour which he has won for the Afrikaner does not leave us untouched. The thought expressed by General Smuts could in essence have come from Dr Malan,' the NP mouthpiece wrote.[5]

TWIN BLOWS

Smuts returned home via the University of Leiden in Holland, where he received a Doctorate of Laws, to a rousing reception from his supporters but another revolt against Hofmeyr in the Transvaal UP. By now, it was not only conservatives in the UP who thought that Hofmeyr's proper place was outside the party; liberals such as Leo Marquard believed that the deputy leader should leave the UP and establish his own political party – as like-minded 'Progressives' were to do a decade later. But Hofmeyr was hesitant to do so because he lacked a clearly defined political programme or sizeable constituency of his own.

Some Smuts loyalists, notably the University of Natal's principal, Dr EG Malherbe, felt that the UP should make overtures to Hertzog's heir, NC Havenga, leader of the Afrikaner Party, who had never been comfortable about his parliamentary alliance with DF Malan. Malherbe argued that the Afrikaner Party's nine seats would give the UP a parliamentary majority over the Nationalists, but Smuts refused to consider the idea: Havenga had flirted with the Ossewa Brandwag during the war and he was not prepared to work with 'a lot of Fascists'.[6] He was also not going to dispense with Hofmeyr, his loyal lieutenant who had given him staunch support during the war years.

Malherbe persisted, however, pointing out that Hofmeyr might not be the only one required to make a personal sacrifice for the sake of the country: Smuts himself might have to agree to serve under Havenga, as he had done under Hertzog many years earlier. Smuts discussed the prospect with Hofmeyr, who approved of the soundings with Havenga. Discussions were barely underway when, on 4 December 1948, Hofmeyr died suddenly from heart failure. He was only 54 years old.

Hofmeyr's death was a cruel blow for Smuts, who had experienced an even more devastating loss only weeks earlier, when – on 10 September – his beloved son Japie died from cerebral meningitis. Like his father, Japie Smuts had excelled at Cambridge, where he achieved a double first in the Engineering Tripos. In a letter to the Gilletts, Smuts poured out his sorrow: 'This date is a mark of calamity in my history. On it fifty years ago the Boer War was declared. On it at 12 30 this morning, Japie passed away, after an illness of less than 24 hours ... Japie was so much to us. Such a son, such a human, such a comrade – such a joy and pride of life. And some miserable microbe has robbed us of him.'[7] In another letter, to Lady Daphne Moore, he expressed concern for his wife. 'Isie has taken it calmly, but I think she is really dazed by the blow, as he was her favourite child,' he wrote.[8]

The loss of his eldest son caused Smuts to sympathise with even more feeling with Hofmeyr's elderly mother, who regarded him as primarily responsible for her bachelor son's untimely death from overwork. He visited Mrs Hofmeyr immediately after the funeral and listened in sorrowful silence to her recriminations, writing afterwards to her and the Gilletts that Hofmeyr was '... our ablest and most-high-minded public man … in a sense the conscience of South Africa. To me he was my right hand, and his going will add immensely to my labours – already as much as I can bear. He was only 54 and was my destined successor. The pity of it is that I should have had to bury him.'[9]

Smuts's reaction to setbacks that would have felled a younger and less driven man was to take even more upon his own shoulders and work harder than ever on party matters. Most of his ex-cabinet colleagues were not well-off financially and were struggling to re-establish themselves in business and the professions: so they had much less time for politics than he did. As it turned out, any alliance between Smuts and Havenga would not have kept the UP in power for long. In 1949, Malan introduced legislation to give South West Africa six seats in South Africa's parliament: they were all won by the NP, which freed Malan from any dependence on the Afrikaner Party.

RACIAL CLIMATE WORSENS

By 1949, the racial climate within the country had taken a turn for the worse. The new government had made clear its intention to check and eliminate any movement towards racial integration, such as mixed marriages. Further justification for segregation was found in the rioting that broke out between Zulus and Indians in Cato Manner in Durban and later in Newlands, Johannesburg – which resulted in the loss of over 100 lives. At the Prime Ministers' Conference in London in April, attended for the first time by Dr Malan, India was admitted as an independent republic within the Commonwealth, a concession that Smuts believed would create a highly undesirable precedent – especially for Nationalist-ruled South Africa.

After another brief visit to Cambridge in June, to preside over a graduation ceremony, Smuts returned to South Africa to fight against the government's patently anti-British inspired legislation to extend residential qualifications for immigrants from two to five years and to separate former dual-medium schools in the Transvaal into English- and Afrikaans-speaking institutions. He described 'this Broederbond Government' as 'a blight that has come over South Africa' and resolved to continue the fight against it.[10]

He was much amused by the ministry of defence's forgetfulness in having him replaced as titular head of the UDF. In October 1949, the embarrassed minister, FC Erasmus, who had not fought in the war, wrote him a curt, ill-mannered letter to say that his appointment had been terminated, without expressing a word of appreciation for his wartime leadership and service. Smuts replied equally curtly that he noted 'the termination of my appointment as commander-in-chief of the Union Defence Force *in the field*'.[11] In November, plagued by acute pain in a hip, he defied his family's wishes to fly to London to attend a dinner in honour of Dr Chaim Weizmann's seventy-fifth birthday. In toasting Weizmann's health, he compared him to Moses, who had led the Jews out of bondage into the Promised Land.

Soon after his return to South Africa, he was invited to address the huge throng gathered on a hill outside Pretoria on 16 December to celebrate the unveiling of the Voortrekker Monument. Smuts was the only surviving Boer general at the ceremony and the only politician present who had served in Paul Kruger's administration. He took the opportunity to remind the gathering that Kruger's last message to his people was to take the good from the past and use it for shaping their future. The past, he said, contained not only conflict but reconciliation. Union was a bridge built by Afrikaners and English-speakers for all South Africa's people, white and black. On this occasion, and at Stellenbosch where he had received a standing ovation two months previously, a younger generation of Afrikaners, conditioned into believing that he was anti-Afrikaner, were able, probably for the first time, to comprehend and appreciate the central role the youthful Smuts had played in the realisation of Boer independence.[12]

At this late stage in his long life, Smuts was finding that old friends meant more to him than books.[13] Still an inveterate letter-writer, he corresponded with wartime comrades such as Churchill's right-hand, General 'Pug' Ismay; with his respected adversary in East Africa, General Von Lettow-Vorbeck; with the palaeoanthropologist, Dr Robert Broom; and with various botanical friends, notably Mrs Bolus of the Cape Town Herbarium. Towards the end of 1949, he was particularly pleased to welcome back to South Africa, after an absence of ten years, his oldest and dearest English friends, the Gilletts, who spent Christmas with the Smuts family at Doornkloof.

He sat through the short parliamentary session in early 1950 in severe sciatic pain from a slipped disc. Once the session was over, he was faced with the usual round of political commitments, interspersed with some important personal milestones. On 30 April, he and Isie celebrated their fifty-third wedding anniversary. From Cape Town, he wrote to her at Doornkloof, 'I think with deep thankfulness of those fifty years of our most happy married life. How much have we experienced! What gains and what losses! Who could ever have dreamed that this would be our life's course? When I look back at it all today, it seems like a dream. And like a dream it has gone by incredibly fast. We have much to be thankful for, and for a history which we may regard with gratitude and pride.'[14]

His and Isie's life together, he reflected, had been an interweaving of tragedy and comedy, of good and evil, but withal worth living. He was hoping that their life together in the world to come would reveal a different pattern, 'provided he was not expected to wear a crown or twang a harp'.[15]

AT REST

Less than a month later – on 23 May, the day before he turned 80 – 300 000 people lined the streets of Johannesburg to watch him ride by in an open car to receive the Freedom of the City. Despite not being well, he inspected a guard of honour of ex-soldiers and in a short speech which contained a hint of pathos, he declared that 'he had served to the best of my ability with what strength God gave me'. At a grand banquet in the evening, guests listened to a recorded tribute by Winston Churchill, who said of his old wartime comrade, 'He is the man who raised the name of South Africa in peace and war to the highest rank of respect among the freedom-loving nations of the world. Let us pray that this may not be swept or cast away in the demoralisation which so often follows the greatest human triumphs.'[16]

Next day, 24 May, Smuts spoke at another birthday banquet in Pretoria in what was to be his last public appearance. On 29 May, he was struck down by a coronary thrombosis and confined by his doctors to bed at Doornkloof. He was not to know the exact nature of his illness, which was kept from the press and radio, but thereafter suffered a series of heart attacks which left him weak and exhausted. He asked constantly to visit his beloved bushveld, to which he was occasionally taken to enjoy the warm spring sunshine. He continued reading to the very end: at his bedside were *The Approach to Metaphysics* and the poems of Emily Brontë.

On Sunday 10 September, he felt well enough to be out on the lawn at Doornkloof, where he was photographed playing with some of his grand-children. On the next day, accompanied by Isie, he went on his last drive. After supper that evening, while being helped into bed by his daughters, Sylma and Louis, he slumped forward and lost consciousness.

In his grieving son Jannie's words, 'the *Oubaas* had climbed his last Great Mountain'.[17]

PART TWO

The Man

In 500 years of the College's history, of all its members past and present, three had been truly outstanding – John Milton, Charles Darwin and Jan Smuts.

Lord Todd, Master of Christ's College, Cambridge (1970)

Hobbies – walking, plants and mountains.

CHAPTER 19

Forged from Steel

Jan Smuts's trusted lieutenant, Leif Egeland, thought that his leader's outwardly simple yet inwardly complex, dynamic and forceful personality was beyond the capacity of any one biographer to portray: like a diamond, it had many facets, some of which shone more brilliantly than others.[1] Yet try to describe his personality one must – if only to explain to a modern reader what motivated this most cerebral and dedicated of South Africans. What sort of a person was Smuts? What was he like to meet? What was he most interested in? What gave him pleasure and amusement? Why, despite his introverted and reserved nature, did so many people revere and idolise him?

The answers to these questions will depend on the circumstances in which one encountered this Boer soldier, philosopher, politician, scientist and statesman. No one who met Smuts or worked for or against him was unaffected by the experience. Extravagant praise and adulation were heaped upon him, but so too were vitriol and hatred; no acclaim or blame, however, ever affected his (sometimes mistaken) belief that what he was doing was right for his country, and for humanity. Even his earliest biographer, who thought him arrogant, wrote of him, 'his reputation can stand on the firm foundations of his real qualities and achievements, and those foundations are of steel'.[2]

Physically, Smuts was of medium height, with a spare and wiry frame, fair (later silvery) hair, a goatee beard and piercing pale-blue eyes. As an orator, he was no spell-binder: his voice was high-pitched and he spoke Afrikaans and English with a distinctive Malmesbury 'brei'. He had no interest in fine clothes: when not in formal attire, military uniform or a business suit, he would be found in a khaki shirt and slacks.

His defining characteristic was, of course, his intellect. He possessed not only a daunting intelligence but a photographic memory to boot. His children used to tell how he could recap whole pages out of books from memory. A senior SAAF officer, Major General Kenneth van der Spuy, recalled an occasion in East Africa when a British colonel asked Smuts if it were true that if a few paragraphs of a book were read to him, he could repeat the words accurately. 'Of course,' Smuts replied, whereupon a book was chosen randomly and read out to him. After two and a half pages, he called 'stop' and repeated the whole of what had been read without a single error.[3]

No one knows what Smuts's IQ was, but it must have been very high – in a category somewhere between brilliant and genius. In this stratosphere, Nobel Prize winners and historical virtuosos such as Einstein, Milton, Newton and Kant, the source of most of humanity's advances may be found. In 1936, Einstein said of Smuts that he was one of only eleven men in the world who conceptually understood the theory of relativity.[4]

People as clever as Smuts are seldom fully understood or properly appreciated, and find themselves the butt of envy and hostility. Dr Edgar Brookes, the distinguished liberal politician, wrote that the petty attacks on Smuts by a section of the South African population reminded him of 'a crowd of malicious little birds pecking at a wounded eagle'.[5] 'Intellectually,' Brookes wrote in a centennial tribute to Smuts, 'he towered head and shoulders above his contemporaries; yet there was nothing mean or petty in his make-up'.[6]

In person, to those who did not know him well, Smuts could be most intimidating – especially if interrupted while working. Hancock recounts the experience of an Englishman who later became his friend. 'Smuts received me coldly, if not with mistrust. The lean unsmiling visage, the piercing blue-grey eyes, the quick impatient speech, the frigid bearing of the new State Attorney – all were disconcerting. This was no man to suffer fools gladly or at all.'[7]

Almost all of his political colleagues who worked with him over the years were in awe of his abilities, yet few felt close to him personally. Leslie Blackwell, QC, who served in Parliament under Smuts for 25 years after the Unionist Party had been absorbed into the SAP, could never make out whether his leader liked him or not. 'Did he like anyone in Parliament at all, except perhaps Deneys Reitz? Did he have any capacity for warm friendship?' asked Blackwell plaintively in his memoirs.[8] His much younger cabinet colleague, Harry Lawrence, said of Smuts: 'He was one of those men, who, realising how finite life is and how infinite the search, could waste no time on anything less absorbing than the pursuit of knowledge.'[9]

He could certainly be impatient with the foolish, yet to those closest to

Smuts he was a warm and friendly person with a strongly developed love of family, who lived simply and frugally. The worst that could be said of him, according to his son, was that he took life a little too seriously.[10] Like many extremely clever people, he was sometimes impatient with those less quick on the uptake, partially because he was a phenomenally busy person who was harried and lionised all his life. If he occasionally found it necessary to put the shutters up, it was often in sheer self-defence.[11] However, even members of his own family could be unnerved and tongue-tied in his presence. Visitors who wasted his time or asked interminable questions bored him and he would escape from their company as soon as it was politely possible to do so.

At Doornkloof, his impatience lessened as the years passed, but it was often tested by the number of people around him. Kathleen Mincher describes how, as the family grew and grandchildren started arriving, rooms were added to the house to accommodate everyone. Eventually there were 14 bedrooms in the house, sometimes filled by as many as 30 people, especially over weekends. If there was too much noise, Smuts might emerge from his study – 'like Nemesis', according to Isie – to complain that it was interfering with his work. His mood, according to Kathleen, was the barometer by which the atmosphere in the house was measured.[12]

Money was never of much interest to Smuts. What he managed to save went into the purchase of land, rather than stocks and shares. As long as he had sufficient property, he felt he could provide for his family's needs from his salary and a generous overdraft, without having to be too concerned about the admonitions of Isie, who managed his finances, or his bank manager. From time to time he would be given money by grateful organisations or well-wishers, but was scrupulous in turning these funds over to the public purse. Though never well-off, except for allowing his British friends the Gilletts to buy a house in Cape Town for his and his family's use during the parliamentary session, he refused to accept help from wealthy friends who wished to lessen his financial burden. Even when in debt, he would lend struggling friends sometimes large amounts of money, not much of which was ever repaid.[13] An ailing Emily Hobhouse, in old age, was one such beneficiary of his generosity.

Sarah Gertrude Millin, who knew Smuts well, wrote how he once confessed to her that he had little aesthetic feeling, and no sense of humour.[14] That was a charming admission, she said, but it did him an injustice. He may not have had much time in his busy life for art, music or the theatre, but he had a deep love of nature, and an ear for good poetry. He certainly had a sense of humour, though it was not often revealed. In private a good raconteur, like most South Africans he enjoyed telling 'Van der Merwe' stories.[15] His wit could be sharp: after one of his frequent absences from home, Isie remarked that she hoped to see more of him in the next life than she had in this one. To which he replied, 'It depends whether or not we end up at the same destination.'[16]

Jannie Smuts described his father as 'a perfect raconteur of stories and anecdotes on events and people. They covered almost every topic imaginable from the outer spaces of our expanding Universe to the commonplace non-entities of our daily life. On all these topics he was knowledgeable and lucid with a wealth of vision that enthralled both old and young.'[17]

What Smuts lacked, according to Millin, was a sense of fun.[18] The things which give ordinary people enjoyment – playing or watching sport, cards, dancing, hunting, racing, gambling, going to shows – simply didn't interest him. Kathleen Mincher recalls how her husband Paul was swinging a golf club on the lawn one morning while she and the 'Oubaas' were enjoying morning tea. Smuts turned to her and said, 'It must be wonderful, Kathleen, to be so simple-minded that one can enjoy a game of golf.'[19] Yet he loved exercise, climbing mountains until well into old age or striding for long distances across the veld. Shortly before his eightieth birthday, he told an interviewer that his rural background had been a sheet anchor to him throughout his life. 'My hobbies have always been walking, plants and mountains,' he said.[20]

The mountains were his refuge and source of inner strength. He was never happier than when climbing the peaks of the Cape, either on his own or with other climbers. On a mountain, according to his son, he was always warm, friendly and approachable.[21] During the first 35 of his 40 years in Parliament, he climbed Table Mountain almost every weekend, even in bad weather. Only once did he use the cableway – on the royal visit of 1947, when he descended in the cable car with the King and Queen.

The mountain was his cathedral, the place where he could leave below all the things that weighed on body and spirit, and find God. In one of his most inspired orations, delivered in honour of the fallen in the Great War at Maclear's Beacon on Table Mountain, he described the mountain as having great historic and spiritual meaning. 'It stands for us as the ladder of the soul, and in a curious way, the source of religion. From it came the Law, from it came the Gospel in the Sermon on the Mount. We may truly say that the highest religion is the Religion of the Mountain.'[22]

Botany was his other abiding passion. Interested in veld plants from an early age, he used the eight years in which he was in opposition to become recognised as an expert on South African grasses. His sorties into the countryside, armed with magnifying glass and clipping shears, took him across the African sub-continent to Lakes Tanganyika and Nyasa, the Victoria Falls and Zimbabwe, besides the bushveld of the Transvaal and mountains of the Cape. His interest in botany was both practical and intellectual. He not only read widely and collected books on the subject, but also saved specimens for his own private herbarium alongside his study at Doornkloof.

He was fortunate in having as a mentor and neighbour at Irene, Dr IB Pole Evans, who had studied plant pathology at Cambridge and whom he persuaded to give up his position as director of the botanical gardens at Kew and come to South Africa to improve the quality of highveld grasses. In the company of Pole-Evans and friends such as TC Robertson and CJJ van Rensburg, Smuts would spend day after day tramping across the veld in search of new specimens, with the purpose of improving – for the benefit of both man and beast – the quality of the country's pastures. More aware than ever of the importance of the ecology, on returning to government in the 1930s, he encouraged all forms of botanical research, and took the first legislative steps to conserve South Africa's vegetation, soil and water resources. (Chapter 23 deals more fully with Smuts's passionate interest in the natural world.)

Another of Smuts's outstanding qualities was his physical courage, whether climbing mountains, commanding his band of guerrilla fighters in the Anglo-Boer War, confronting mobs of striking miners, or standing up to thugs bent on harming him physically at political meetings. According to Piet Beukes, he was totally without fear – physical, or moral.[23] His bravery when leading his rag-tag commando through hundreds of kilometres of enemy territory became the stuff of legend, as did his disregard of danger when flying in wartime in unreliable aircraft in the most hazardous of weather and circumstances.

As we have seen, during the eruption of the labour militancy which engulfed the Rand in 1914, he and Botha intervened personally by driving in an open

173

A walk on Table Mountain with King George VI, 1947. Gallo Images/Getty Images/Keystone

car to the Carlton Hotel to negotiate with armed members of the strike committee. A year later, during the Boer rebellion, when his friend General de
la Rey was accidentally shot by the police, he and Botha again braved the
hostility of the crowd by attending the fallen Boer's funeral ceremony without
an escort.[24] At the time of the Rand Revolt of 1922, as prime minister, he disregarded warnings of impending danger and was driven into Johannesburg
amid a hail of bullets to see things for himself. Jannie Smuts recounts how
his father and party secretary Louis Esselen carried rifles with them in the car.
When they were shot at, Esselen returned the rifle fire for all he was worth,
calling on Smuts to shoot, but the Prime Minister just sat impassively. When
a striker's bullet punctured the back tyre and they had to pull up to change
the wheel, Smuts said to Esselen: 'You have kept on telling me to shoot, now
how many bullets have you left?' Esselen replied that he had used up all of his.

'A fine fix we might now be in,' Smuts retorted, 'if I had also used up all my ammunition.'[25] Smuts was described by his former Boer colleague, General Coen Brits, as the bravest man he had ever met.[26]

Another of Smuts's defining characteristics was his self-possession, which was often misconstrued as conceit or arrogance. Piet Beukes reckoned that one of the flaws in his character was that he was too sure of himself: 'He had that unwavering belief in the rightness of his cause and in his mastery of events.'[27] Yet, as is so often the case, a weakness can also be a strength. Alan Paton ascribed greatness to 'those masterminds, already having an outstanding intellect, who also possess the self-confidence of maturity to a sublime degree'.[28] It was precisely this quality in Smuts that commanded the confidence of others and enabled him to lead so effectively.

Kenneth Ingham, his perceptive biographer, attributes Smuts's self-belief to his superior mind and fundamentally religious sense of purpose. The latter might have been an onerous and often inhibiting burden to carry through life, but in later years he bore it more easily out of a deep-seated belief in his own rectitude.[29] As a politician, once he had thought through a problem and come up with an answer that was rational and satisfied his own conscience, he was often unable to understand why other less intelligent people might think differently. Their failure to do so, he told himself, could only be attributed to stupidity or outright hostility.[30]

After the death of Louis Botha, his mentor and sounding-board, Smuts had to take far-reaching political decisions on his own, frequently acting without consultation. Two notable cases in point were his impulsive decision in 1924, after his party had lost a by-election at Wakkerstroom, to call a general election. His colleagues warned him that the government was so unpopular that he risked not only losing the election, but his own Pretoria-West seat too. And they were proved right. In 1948 he once again disregarded the concerns of his caucus about party strategy, saying, 'I will not allow further discussion on this matter. There can be no questioning of my leadership. I will not allow the caucus to dictate to me.'[31]

In politics, as in life, Smuts was often a committee of one. Never shy of taking responsibility, the perfection which his conscience demanded meant that he was the only one allowed to measure himself. His friends and colleagues lacked the intellect to be of help; of his critics, he took no notice. Leif Egeland recalled suggesting to Smuts, after the royal wedding in 1947, that he should spend a few days in Britain relaxing with friends. 'No, no, my boy,' he replied, 'I must get back. While I'm away none of my ministers make decisions.'[32] As his longstanding parliamentary colleague, Major Piet van der Byl, wrote pointedly in his memoirs, older men who have great intellectual qualities and are fearless and powerful are inclined, when in command, to ignore advice and resent criticism or obstruction.[33]

Smuts was also not, according to his close associate Dr EG Malherbe, a good judge of character, being far too naïve and trusting of others.[34] Louis Botha was also of the opinion, noted Malherbe, that if Smuts had to choose between two men, he would as often as not pick the wrong one. As his reluctance to refresh his cabinet ahead of the 1948 election demonstrated, loyalty to old friends was often allowed to cloud his judgement.

As he grew older, his belief in his own abilities sometimes overshadowed his simplicity and humility. In international affairs, it led him – like Woodrow Wilson – to identify his own conscience with the conscience of mankind. And not surprisingly, given his exposure to royalty and the great and good, he succumbed occasionally to outbreaks of vanity.

He once confided to Queen Frederika of Greece that one of the reasons why World War II had happened was that he was not able to accept an offer from King George V to become Britain's prime minister after World War I.[35] And mention has been made of his suggestion to Lloyd George, during World War I, that he (Smuts) should take command of American forces in Europe. In 1946, on a visit to San Francisco, according to Piet Beukes, he let it be known that he would like to address a joint sitting of Congress, and was disappointed when no invitation was forthcoming.[36] There was also an occasion in Southampton after the end of World War II, when he was unhappy with the arrangements made for his reception. The mayor said afterwards that he had never met a more vain man; 'he even surpassed royalty'.[37]

Like most people, Smuts had contradictions in his makeup. As a white South African, he was bound by the limitations and prejudices imposed by his background and environment. While he treated people of all races with the utmost courtesy and respect, particularly those in his own household, he did not do enough as a political leader to reduce racism and discrimination. Despite his great intellect and high principles, he could not rid himself of the racial paternalism of the century in which he had been born, or balance the ideal values he preached to others with the demands of electoral politics in South Africa. Like others before him and since, he took refuge in the 'inevitability of gradualness'[38] instead, hoping that 'ampler shoulders and stronger brains of the future' might offer a solution to South Africa's racial dilemma.[39] In today's idiom, he kicked the can down the road – and South Africa, unfortunately, is the poorer for it.

Whatever present-day critics of Smuts, with the benefit of hindsight, might say of him, both friend and foe at the time agreed that his readiness to bear the burden of leadership throughout his long life, despite soul-tormenting personal challenges and setbacks, was simply astonishing. He always did what he believed was best for his fellow men, and never lost the desire or determination to be of service to his country.

CHAPTER 20

'A Refuge for Stoics'

Like most South Africans brought up on a farm, Smuts loved the land. A man with very few material wants in life, he nonetheless acquired several farms, not – according to his son Jannie – for speculative purposes, but in order to satisfy 'a possessive instinct'.[1] Not one to care much about money, he ploughed most of his earnings into land and animals, ignoring his wife's and bank manager's concerns about the state of his finances.[2]

After the Anglo-Boer War, when his legal practice was bringing in a good income, he invested most of it in land, as security for his and Isie's young family, then comprising a son and three daughters. In partnership with a friend, he bought two farms, Onderstepoort (now the home of veterinary education in South Africa) and Kameelfontein, near the Premier Mine. Both were sold a few years later. In the Western Transvaal, he took his old friend General Koos de la Rey's advice and bought three farms, Barberspan, Kromdraai and Welgevonden, on which he planted maize. Though their soil was good, these farms, according to his children, were rather bleak and uninviting.[3]

His next acquisitions were Buffelspan, near Rustenburg, and two farms on the Marico River, Wydhoek and Klipdrift, the latter two of which were sold in the 1930s when he needed money. In 1908, he bought the picturesque farm Doornkloof, near Pretoria, which became the family home for almost half a century. Two more farms were acquired in 1916 while he was away in East Africa: Rooikop and Droogegrond, in the bushveld north-east of Pretoria. Here he raised Afrikander beef cattle, with the help of an experienced manager. Rooikop was a particular favourite, and he would spend many weekends there, camping under the stars, studying bushveld grasses and taking long walks across the veld. In 1928, according to Jannie, his father possessed no fewer than ten farms, totalling some 25 000 morgen.[4] In 1945, having disposed of Barberspan and the two farms at Groot Marico, he donated the remainder of his properties by deed of trust to his children.

The 'Big House', Doornkloof: a wood-and-corrugated iron officers' mess transplanted from Kitchener's military headquarters at Middelburg. Smuts House Museum

Of all his acquisitions, Doornkloof, at Irene on the outskirts of Pretoria, was the one he treasured most. The farm lies in rocky and undulating dolomite countryside through which the headwater of the Limpopo, the Hennops River, runs. Green and verdant in summer, the terrain is dry and dusty in the winter months, though rich in tall highveld grasses. It was here that Smuts chose to acquire 2 000 morgen of the original farm from two of his relatives, and in 1908, to re-erect on the edge of the property a wood-and-corrugated iron officers' mess transplanted from Kitchener's military headquarters at Middelburg. Not having much money at the time, he intended the building – for which he paid a mere £300 – to be no more than a temporary home for the family, to be replaced in the fullness of time by a permanent brick and mortar house on the brow of the hill nearby. Reconstruction of the mess took a year to complete, at a cost of £1 000.

Seldom can any homestead have reflected more accurately the character of its inhabitants than the Smuts family's spacious but spartan home. The 'Groothuis' ('Big House'), as it became known, was large and rambling with several reception rooms and eventually no fewer than 14 bedrooms. Around three-quarters of it ran a narrow verandah or *stoep*. Jannie, who grew up there,

179

likened its architecture to a meccano set, because it was easy to dismantle the house's internal walls and alter its shape whenever necessary. The family grew so attached to the Big House that any thought of a more permanent structure was soon forgotten.[5]

By the time Doornkloof was acquired, the number of Smuts's surviving children had grown to four, all born in Sunnyside, Pretoria: Santa (who was to become the wife of Smuts's farm manager, Andries Weyers) in 1903; Cato (who married Bancroft Clark, a relative of the Gilletts in England) in 1904; Jacob Daniel (Japie) in 1906; and Sylma (who became Mrs Jack Coaton) in 1908. Another son, Jan Christian (Jannie) was born later in 1912 and a daughter, Louis (later Dr Louis McIldowie) in 1914. A much younger foster daughter, Kathleen (later Mrs Kay Mincher) was added to the family in the 1920s, and thereby hangs a tale.

In her book about growing up in the Smuts family, Kathleen (Kay) Mincher (née De Villiers) relates that her biological parents had died before she was old enough to remember them. As an infant, she had been brought to Doornkloof by her godmother, a friend of the Smutses, where she was 'adopted' as one of the family. Kay does not let on what later became apparent from some of her physical characteristics, and what she came to realise as she grew older: she was actually a Smuts herself – the daughter of Santa, born out of wedlock to an undisclosed father. In order to avoid gossip-mongering or political fall-out, Smuts and his wife had quietly taken her into the family and brought her up as one of their own. Kay was never formally adopted by her new parents. In later life, she spoke freely to her children about being a Smuts by blood;[6] her son Paul, in particular, bears a striking resemblance to his celebrated grandfather.

It must also be said that not all members of the greater Smuts family agree with this account of Kay's origins. Some adhere to the 'authorised' version and dismiss the alternative out of hand, but several sources within the Smuts family, including Kay's daughter Mary, are in no doubt about its veracity.

◆

The corrugated iron walls of Doornkloof's 'Big House', which Isie irreverently called 'Die Blikhuis' (tin shanty), were lined with wood and stood well above the ground on stone foundations. In summer, the dwelling was stiflingly hot, and in winter freezing cold; while swarms of wild bees made hives in the partitions between wood and iron. Although children and visitors grumbled (to themselves) about the unrelenting heat and cold, Smuts and his wife loved it. Their son Jannie described it as 'an ideal refuge for Stoics'.[7]

Since there were not many indigenous trees on Doornkloof, the Smutses planted thousands of non-indigenous blue-gums, wattles, pines and planes around the Big House. Though Isie was a keen gardener, Smuts preferred veld flowers and natural grasses to lawns and flower beds, and over time prevailed upon her to allow the veld to come up to the steps of the homestead. Only the bees and a variety of highveld birds, including cranes, ostriches and wild geese, disturbed an atmosphere of peace and tranquillity. Smuts much preferred Doornkloof to Groote Schuur, Libertas or any royal palaces abroad.

The couple's domestic tastes may be best described as 'severely simple'.[8] Smuts slept on a hard and uncomfortable mattress on the open stoep outside his bedroom. Next to his bed was an old kitchen chair which served as a table. The bedroom itself, to which he eventually repaired in later years to escape the cold, was little more than a converted passage and always kept fastidiously neat and tidy. The only people allowed to disarrange it were his grandchildren, who would clamber over the bed and sit on his tummy while he tried to read.[9] The walls of the room were covered with photographs of children and grandchildren.

Isie occupied her own separate room, which contained a large double bed in which the infant children were allowed to sleep until ready for their cots. The room had a door leading onto an enclosed *stoep* where the family spent most of their leisure time. Also on the *stoep* was a large boiler which provided water for the bathrooms and was lit on Sunday nights only. For the rest of the week, the family had to make do with cold baths or showers. In her book of reminiscences, Kay Mincher describes how, despite sometimes having eight blankets, she found it impossible to read in bed because her fingers were numb from the cold. Whenever the children complained, Smuts would say that the cold was good for them because it thickened the blood and made one healthy.

◆

The library at the heart of the house was out of bounds to one and all. Smuts House Museum

The Big House had a large living area which served as both sitting room and dining room; across the hall was another drawing room in which the Smut-ses entertained special visitors such as the royal family, who paid a visit to Doornkloof in 1947. In the main hall were two items of special note: a pair of enormous elephant tusks standing on an ebony base; and an oil painting of the pyramids by Winston Churchill.[10] Books and memorabilia were scattered everywhere. Sarah Gertrude Millin – who came to know the Smutses well – wrote that 'practically every single thing that, during the past quarter century, has entered the house, still seems to be there'.[11]

The floor of the house was covered in brown linoleum and as for furniture and fittings, the accent was on serviceability rather than style. According to Millin, 'nobody troubles about quality or beauty, except that Smuts troubles about his books. And nobody troubles what anybody does anywhere in the house as long as nobody troubles Smuts among his books. His library is invio-late …'[12]

Smuts's large and well-stocked library, formerly the officers' billiard room, lay at the heart of the house at the end of a long passage. Its shelves overflowed with more than 6 000 books on philosophy, botany, the sciences, law, religion, history, war and travel, all of which Smuts had read and from most of which he could quote extensively. According to Millin, 'The house may be full of people: relatives, connections, sick friends, children, the friends of children – the people Mrs Smuts invites in her large heart and out of old Boer tradition … [but] Smuts sits in his library by himself. He asks into it people who come on necessary business – the family do not obtrude.'[13] Leading off the study was another enclosed *stoep* housing cupboards containing Smuts's botanical specimens and a bed on which he rested in the afternoons.

In her book, Kay Mincher confirms that the study was out of bounds to one and all, and silence had to be kept outside it whenever the 'Oubaas' was at work. In the evenings, he would leave his books and come through to the living room where the family used to gather, to enjoy a cup of tea with them and listen to the radio news. Sometimes he would return to work, but often he would stay and play noisy games with the children.

Like so many brilliant people who find difficulty in relating to other less clever adults, Smuts simply adored children. According to Kay, whereas most people – even some family members – became so nervous in his presence that they either went into their shells or became garrulous and asked him stupid questions, with children it was different. He could spend hours playing games with them and never made them feel inadequate or inferior. They refreshed his spirit and helped to restore his faith in human nature.[14]

◆

In a letter to her mother after a three-week stay at Doornkloof with her husband, Lady Daphne Moore described her impressions: 'They [the Smutses] prefer this tin hovel, crawling with screaming children and cluttered up with every sort of junk. It's rather sweet of them. Henry is a bit bewildered by this household. … The din is incessant and terrific and apparently everyone likes this – bar us. … They are real darlings and quite the kindest people in the world bless them. Ouma is an everlasting source of joy and amusement and he is, of course, invariably enthralling.'[15]

As the family's matriarch, Isie (or Ouma) ministered to her husband's, children's and grandchildren's needs with an unswerving devotion. While Smuts

A fond grandfather: Smuts adored children.

was away for extended periods on official business, Ouma preferred to stay at home, even during parliamentary sessions, to look after their large family. Cultured and well-read herself, she had little time for the fashions and fripperies of the times, wore no make-up, and padded around the house in black stockings or bare feet in the most comfortable of clothes. She seldom wore a hat, even on official occasions. Though more sociable than her husband, like him she also loved to read; strewn around the house were hundreds of her books of fiction – from classics to potboilers. Her intellect was mostly kept hidden. At the breakfast table on one celebrated occasion, Hancock records, Smuts quoted a verse from the New Testament, I Corinthians 13, whereupon Ouma recited the whole chapter back to him in the original Greek.[16]

Accurately describing Smuts's attitude towards marriage, Kenneth Ingham says that for him, the world was divided into two spheres: 'In one, men shoul- dered their responsibilities seriously and courageously. In the other, women performed their humane and domestic tasks with warmth and cheerfulness and were ever ready to listen with intelligent solicitude to the problems which men faced in the great battle of life.'[17]

One of Ouma's chief hobbies was collecting press cuttings of all her hus- band's activities and speeches. She was keenly interested in his political career and more than anyone served as his guide, comforter and friend. In both World Wars, she organised a Gifts and Comforts Fund for South African soldiers, for which – as we have seen – she would hold work parties at Doornkloof and her official residences, Groote Schuur and Libertas. King George VI offered her the honour of a CBE, but she declined it on the grounds that there were other more deserving recipients.[18] As Crafford rightly observes, not a little of Smuts's success in life was due to Isie's self-effacing commitment and dedication.[19]

◆

For Smuts himself, Doornkloof was more than a home: it was an anchorage, a refuge where he could set aside his onerous political burdens and do what he loved best – commune with nature. Alone, or with his children, he would walk or ride for long distances over the rolling countryside, pausing only to examine a botanical specimen under the magnifying glass he always carried with him. On his walks through the bushveld, he discovered many new types of grass, which he delighted in showing off to anyone who expressed an inter- est. The children were never allowed to pick a wild flower or remove eggs from a nest as this would disturb nature. If Table Mountain in the Cape was Smuts's cherished 'cathedral', Doornkloof and the more remote Rooikop were the churches in which he chose to worship Mother Nature.

CHAPTER 21

At Ease with Women

It was no secret that Jan Smuts's deepest relationships were with women rather than his fellow men. 'I have a weakness for women, not in the sexual sense, but from some inner affinity and appeal,' he once confessed.[1] Writing to a woman he was to befriend in the 1940s, Lady Daphne Moore, he admitted, 'If I have to go through the list of my special friends in life, I find they are largely women … To me women are more interesting. I suppose it must be because I am fully a male type and the opposites attract as in electromagnetism.'[2] Like another famous general, the Duke of Wellington, Smuts was always more forthcoming with women than men – especially if they were young, brainy, and beautiful.

His closest political friendship, nonetheless, was with Louis Botha, eight years his senior and wholly dissimilar in character. He was aware of how different in temperament they were, saying, 'I deal with administration, Botha deals with people.'[3] He was far cleverer than Botha, but unlike the older man took no interest in idle pastimes and was inclined to be anti-social and withdrawn. Botha, who loved playing cards, was much more companionable and convivial. Smuts regarded his mentor as 'the greatest, cleanest, sweetest soul of all my days'.[4] In a lyrical tribute to Botha ten years after his death, he wrote. 'It was this blending of great power with extreme sensitiveness which made him a supreme friend. Great as soldier, greater as statesman, he was greatest as friend by right of his sheer humanity and sympathy.'[5]

Isie Smuts thought she had never seen a closer friendship than the one between Botha and her husband: 'They seemed to need each other in their work. They could not stay away from each other for long before one sent for the other, either for help or for advice,' she observed.[6] Socially, however, there was never much intimacy between the two comrades because their interests were so different. As a biographer of Botha wrote, 'each had his family, his domestic interests, his business to attend to. Botha, by way of recreation, liked a quiet game of bridge. To Smuts, such pleasures appeared an unimaginable waste of valuable time. It was his habit to pore over books and documents for hours at a stretch.[7] Though admiring of Botha's personality, Smuts would never have poured out his innermost feelings to him in the way he did to a variety of women.

◆

Piet Beukes, Rhodes scholar and distinguished Afrikaner journalist who came to know Smuts well, devoted an entire book – *The Romantic Smuts* – to the women who were his closest friends and confidantes. Beukes is in no doubt that Isie was always Smuts's real love and throughout their 53-year-long marriage the object of his most intimate affection.[8] Yet their married life was far from idyllic; it was to bring her much loneliness and loss, sadness and humiliation, as well as many periods of happiness and satisfaction when he was at home with her and the children.

Isie (later to become 'Ouma' to one and all) was a woman of extraordinary selflessness and fortitude, whose suffering during the latter stages of the Boer War can barely be imagined. Before being exiled to a Pietermaritzburg cottage, she had to live through the death from disease of their beloved infant son of 18 months, without having her husband there to comfort her.

During the Boer War, except for two brief meetings, she and Smuts were parted from each other for two years and two months. If she resented her husband always putting duty before family, she never betrayed it. As Beukes writes, 'if ever there was a woman who sacrificed everything that was near and dear to her in the interest of her husband, his task as a politician and a military commander, it was Isie Smuts'.[9] After the war, as her husband became nationally famous, and then world-famous, she had to hold the fort at Doornkloof and bring up their small children on her own.

◆

One of Smuts's remarkable characteristics was his fondness for putting his most intimate thoughts down on paper. During his long life he wrote some 23 000 letters to a wide circle of friends, which included Emily Hobhouse,

Smuts's closest confidante Margaret Clark-Gillett.
Alfred Gillett Trust

Olive Schreiner, Margaret Clark-Gillett, Alice Clark, Queen Frederika of Greece and Lady Daphne Moore.[10] Margaret Gillett was the person with whom he corresponded most frequently, writing as many as 2 000 letters to her over 40 years.[11] Although his letters to women often dealt with intimate, spiritual issues, his only real love letters were to Isie.[12] Written with great tenderness, they reveal the depth of his devotion and fidelity to his wife. He once described her as 'the one soul that I have ever truly loved or ever will be able to love'.[13] ·

Yet he could be strangely insensitive, on occasions, to Isie's feelings when women admirers – some of them young and unmarried – came to see him at home. He would often invite them to stay and invariably take them off to walk with him in the veld. If Isie was put out by this habit, she never showed it. The only time she revealed her hurt was when she eventually became aware of the vast correspondence between her husband and his women friends. In anger, she took her own letters to him and burned them – thereby denying them to posterity.[14]

Smuts's close friendship with Emily Hobhouse has been mentioned earlier. It was Emily who realised his exceptional qualities of leadership and brilliance of mind. She not only brought him to international attention by revealing, at an appropriate moment, their correspondence to *The Times* in London, but also introduced him to many of Britain's leading Liberal politicians. Addressing him as 'Oom Jannie', she wrote to him regularly until her death in 1926, freely dispensing advice and often intemperate criticism: why he should not allow Jopie Fourie to be shot, how to deal with Gandhi, why South Africa should not take Britain's part in the Great War, and so on – some of which he paid heed to, but mostly did not. He thought Emily 'a little mad', but always revered her for the selfless work she had done for the Boer cause. Isie, on the other hand, came to resent the passionate Englishwoman for some of the nasty things she said about her husband.[15]

◆

The author Olive Schreiner, though 15 years older than Smuts, was to become another of his most loyal and longstanding friends. Born in the Eastern Cape, this precocious, non-conformist free-thinker with no formal education became internationally famous for her novel, *The Story of An African Farm*, written at the age of 26. Strongly pro-Afrikaner, she became a campaigner for the equal treatment of women and an outspoken opponent of war. After Smuts had reviewed some of her writings, she wrote a letter to him suggesting they should meet 'to have a political fight'. He agreed to do so, and they immediately became friends.[16]

A supporter of the Boer cause, Olive also befriended Isie and during the Anglo-Boer War she would write to her once and sometimes twice a week while Smuts was on commando. In 1903, she went to stay with the Smutses in Sunnyside, Pretoria and remained in close touch over the next ten years. In 1913, an asthmatic Olive left South Africa to live in England and when Smuts arrived there in 1917, she attached herself to him as a fellow South African, despite her opposition to the war. Smuts took her with him to Cambridge on more than one occasion and also to France on wartime business. She and Emily Hobhouse, who in their different ways had cast him in the role of the world's saviour and lamented his backsliding when he failed to do as they suggested, bombarded him with advice on how to stop the war and bring peace to mankind.[17] In a foreword to one of Olive's books, Smuts described how, in 1917, she would 'literally fall to the ground before him and clasp his knees and beg him with tears in her eyes to stop the slaughter in the War'.[18]

◆

Emily Hobhouse's greatest gift to Smuts was the introduction to her secretary, Margaret Clark (later Gillett), granddaughter of the Radical Quaker, John Bright, one of Britain's most eminent political figures of the nineteenth century. An intelligent and attractive young woman, Margaret accompanied Emily by ship to South Africa in 1905. (Also on board was DF Malan, who gave the pair lessons in Afrikaans.) Emily took Margaret to stay with the Smuts family in Sunnyside, Pretoria, where the two Englishwomen were made to feel at home. A friendship was born between the 35-year old Smuts and the 23-year old Margaret, also an ex-Cambridge student, which was to endure for 45 years. Margaret and her friends and family were to influence and alter Smuts's life, thoughts and spiritual outlook.

Their attachment to each other grew in early 1906 when Smuts, by coincidence, found Margaret among the passengers on the German ship on which he was travelling to England to meet Campbell-Bannerman. On arrival at Dover, the Clarks – who had given support to the Boer cause – invited Smuts to stay with them for the weekend at their home in the village of Street, Somerset. On the Sunday, they took him to a Society of Friends (Quaker) meeting, at which the spirit moved him to express thanks for his new-found English friends. Beukes regards Smuts's association with the Clark family and subsequent engagement with the Quakers as the 'great turning point in his life'.[19]

The letters between Smuts and Margaret provide a rich source of information for historians seeking to trace the development of Smuts's thinking and understand his personality. The two exchanged opinions on poetry, literature, religion and politics and kept each other abreast of family developments. She would address him as 'My dear Oom Jannie' and he would call her 'My dear old Tante' ('aunt' in Afrikaans).[20] In Kenneth Ingham's view, in some respects Smuts was more at home writing to Margaret than to his wife. 'Isie shared more deeply the Afrikaner side of his nature. Margaret ... linked him most firmly with the wider world beyond South Africa.'[21]

In 1908, Margaret wrote to tell him of her engagement to a banker, Arthur

Gillett, only three years younger than Smuts. He wrote immediately to Gillett to congratulate him on acquiring, as a wife, 'a woman with a fine mind and a finer character'. Wishing them happiness, he continued: 'For some years now I have known her most intimately, indeed I do not know that I have a dearer friend in the world.'[22] ('Intimately' obviously had a more innocent connotation then than it does today.) After their marriage, the Gilletts moved to Oxford, where Smuts was a frequent house guest when he came to Britain during World War I. From 1919 until his death 31 years later, Margaret wrote a letter to Smuts every weekend, and he would respond as often as he could. Their remarkable correspondence has been preserved intact to this day. In Beukes' judgement, besides Isie, Margaret was the woman who had the longest-lasting and most significant influence on Smuts.[23]

In 1928, concerned at the lack of a Cape home for Smuts, Isie and the children, the wealthy and generous Gilletts bought a house for the family in Bowwood Road, Claremont, within easy reach of Table Mountain. The house, named Tsalta ('at last' spelt backwards) gave Smuts the privacy he had not always enjoyed at his previous headquarters, the Civil Service Club, in the heart of the city.

◆

A devoted male friend of Smuts and recipient of many of his letters was a lonely old Cambridge don, HJ Wolstenholme, with whom he struck up an unlikely friendship in 1892. This reclusive teacher of German had lost his Congregationalist faith and taken refuge in his books on philosophy, sociology and economics. Long after Smuts had left Cambridge, the pair kept up a correspondence – half a dozen or more long letters a year from each – until Wolstenholme's death in 1917. Theirs was an attraction of opposites: Smuts, young, energetic and idealistic; Wolstenholme, middle-aged, world-weary and disillusioned about a universe he considered purposeless and morally indifferent.[24] The older man provided a useful sounding board for Smuts's metaphysical musings and took it upon himself for the rest of his life to send Smuts the latest books from England on politics, philosophy and other esoteric subjects of mutual interest.

◆

Margaret Clark was not the only member of her family to form a close bond with Smuts. Her sister, Alice, who met him on his first visit to the Clarks in 1906, had since spent many years in a sanatorium fighting tuberculosis. The two met again when Smuts came to England in 1917. Alice was a highly intelligent woman, a graduate of the London School of Economics and author of a book on working women in the seventeenth century. She was a pacifist, suffragette and deeply religious. She also developed what can only be described as a crush on the man she affectionately called 'Oom Jannie'.

Hancock describes Alice as 'a beautiful woman with a rare sensitivity to beauty, a lover of little things as well as of great causes, a clear thinker … with a genius both for sympathetic and critical understanding'.[25] Alone in a hotel suite during the last two years of the War, indifferent to the adulation of those around him, Smuts would ask Alice up to London for weekends, where the two would go walking in Richmond Park and on the Epsom Downs. In between her visits, they would correspond regularly. Later Alice moved to London to be closer to Smuts and medical treatment. The existence of their relationship was never kept secret from Isie.

Smuts was sufficiently impressed by Alice's intellect to give her a copy of the manuscript which later became his book *Holism and Evolution*. Whereas his friend Wolstenholme had given up reading his copy after the first 50 pages, Alice read the whole of hers and responded with criticisms based on the insights of her Quaker beliefs. As Hancock observes, at last Smuts had found someone who could really understand his philosophical quest, and its place in the activities of his life.[26] Alice was one of the few people with whom he was able to discuss his relationship with God, the issue he was to grapple with throughout his life.

Although their correspondence continued after the war, the relationship was to end after Smuts became prime minister and put down the Rand Revolt – in which hundreds were killed or wounded – by the use of force. As a Quaker and friend of the working class, Alice felt deeply conflicted, and their letters and visits ceased. She devoted the rest of her life to looking after her aged parents and engaging in charitable work until her death in 1936.

◆

Princess Frederika of Greece.

Smuts's extraordinary ability to charm attractive and brilliant women was most evident in the last ten years of his life, when he struck up close friendships with Princess Frederika of Greece and Lady Daphne Moore from Kenya. It was World War II that brought the three of them together. In 1941, the Greek King, his son Crown Prince Paul and daughter-in-law Crown Princess

193

Frederika and their two small children had to flee Athens to Egypt ahead of the advancing German forces. The King and Queen decided to settle in London, but Smuts was asked if Paul and Frederika and family and their entourage could stay out of harm's way in South Africa. The 24-year-old princess, a highly intelligent and pretty mother of two, was a granddaughter of the Kaiser and had four brothers in the German army. Her husband Paul decided to station himself in Egypt, but over the next two years made regular visits to his wife and family in South Africa.

Frederika and her two children and maids were housed at first in Government House, Westbrooke, which caught fire one night and forced them to take shelter in the adjacent – and at the time, unoccupied – Groote Schuur. Smuts gave them permission to stay until they could find other accommodation. They were later installed at neighbouring Highstead, official residence of the minister of native affairs, Major Piet van der Byl.

Smuts and Frederika were attracted to each other immediately. He thought 'she was a real good German who hated Hitler and all his works and thoughts and longed for a peace that would finish Nazism but spare her people'.[27] She read *Holism and Evolution* and was captivated by his theory of wholeness, which – he explained to her – embraced the tenets of Greek philosophy as well as Christianity.

Whenever they were both in the Cape, she and Smuts would see each other almost every day. He would take her to the seaside or walking in his beloved mountains and discuss the conduct of the war in Europe and the coming peace.[28] He also tried, as best he could, to prepare her for her future role as queen of Greece, advising her to learn to speak Greek properly (she and Paul conversed in German, but wrote to each other in English) if she wished to win over her people. On three occasions, he allowed her to accompany him in military aircraft on flights to see Crown Prince Paul her husband in Egypt.

Lonely without her husband, Frederika attached herself closely to the Smuts family, visiting them often in Pretoria, where she stayed in the official residence Libertas, rather than at Doornkloof which was far less comfortable. If she and Smuts were apart for longer than a week, they would write each other long letters on matters of religion, philosophy and monarchy, a correspondence that continued long after her return to Athens in 1943.

Fortunately for Smuts, Isie liked 'Freddie' and enjoyed having the young

Greek children around her. As Hancock observes dryly, by this time she had become used to his habit of bringing attractive women into their home. This young woman, at least, 'had a husband with whom she was deeply in love'.[29] Not surprisingly, however, the friendship between the by now elderly Smuts and the foreign princess in her twenties set tongues wagging furiously. As Beukes, a government information officer at the time, recounts, rumours ran wild at public gatherings, cocktail parties, private dinners and receptions.[30] Visitors to South Africa found local society much more interested in gossip about what the smitten *Oubaas* and his little princess were up to than in news of the war 'up North'. Smuts's enemies, of course, made a meal of it, suggesting that once again the prime minister was kow-towing to royalty to the detriment of his own family and people.

Smuts, for his part, took no notice. His sublime indifference to scandal-mongering – and his lack of sensitivity to his wife's feelings – was never more evident than when Isie was given an honorary doctorate by Wits University and he, immensely proud of her honour, invited Frederika to the ceremony. As Hancock records, it was fortunate that the Crown Princess decided at the last minute that she ought not to accept the invitation: 'If she had accepted it, she and Smuts would have become inevitably the focal point of everybody's attention, and Ouma would have been humiliated.'[31]

In Smuts's defence, he was bearing the burden of being the war leader of a bitterly divided nation and needed some diversion from his onerous duties. In Hancock's view, Frederika brought him 'refreshment of spirit' when he most needed it. He was able to enjoy, in old age, the company of an exceptionally attractive and intelligent young woman, eager to receive – across a gap of nearly 50 years – the gift of the wisdom he had gathered in his long spiritual and political odyssey.[32]

After the war ended, Smuts was instrumental in persuading Churchill (who had always been suspicious of Frederika because she was German) and delegates to the Peace Conference in Paris to restore the Greek king to his throne. When King George died suddenly in 1947, Paul became king and Frederika queen, thanks in large measure to her relationship with Smuts.[33]

When Smuts was unexpectedly ejected from office in the 1948 election, Queen Frederika invited him to visit her in Athens where he received the freedom of the city and had a street named after him. After his serious heart attack on his eightieth birthday, she made plans to come and see him at Doornk-loof, but two days before she was due to leave for South Africa, he died. She expressed her sorrow by composing an English sonnet in his honour.[34]

Not long after Smuts's death, however, Frederika sent an envoy to South Africa to retrieve all the many letters she had written to him during the previous nine years and which he had carefully preserved in his study at Doornkloof. When Beukes subsequently asked for her help in his researches into Holism, she responded politely, but 'flatly refused' to send him any of her letters to Smuts or allow him to fly to Athens to read them there. No one knows the whereabouts of this correspondence today, which enables us only to speculate about the true nature of Smuts's intriguing 'royal' relationship.

◆

Lady Daphne Moore, wife of Sir Henry Moore, the British Governor of Kenya and later Governor-General of Ceylon, became Smuts's closest woman friend during the last nine years of his life. The two met in Nairobi during one of Smuts's stopovers en route to London on the York aircraft that Winston Churchill had given him. As Beukes, who came to know Lady Moore well, relates, Smuts was intrigued from the moment he learnt that this beautiful and obviously intelligent 47-year-old had been born in Britstown, South Africa.[35]

Beukes poses the question why Smuts should have chosen Lady Moore as a special friend and confidante when he was already engaged in regular correspondence with Crown Princess Frederika and Margaret Clark-Gillett.[36] He concludes that it was because of her intellect and interests as much as her proficiency as a letter writer. Smuts brought the Moores to South Africa to stay at Groote Schuur and Doornkloof and took them to the Kruger National Park on holiday. After one long stay at Irene, Daphne wrote and told her mother that even Princess Frederika had eventually succumbed to the charms of the 'Big House', despite its 'disorder and noise and aesthetic horrors and the bitter cold of the Highveld which seeped in through the wood and tin'.[37]

Lady Moore kept a diary in which she recorded impressions of her stay with other guests at Groote Schuur during the parliamentary session of 1943.[38] In it, she was less than complimentary about the Greek royal family, recording

Smuts with Lady Daphne Moore. Museum Africa, Johannesburg

how members of the Smuts family felt the visitors were 'sponging' off 'Oom Jannie'. Despite the Crown Princess being her rival for Smuts's attention, she thought Frederika and her husband were 'very natural and charming and although there is no doubt that Oom Jannie is very partial to the Princess, one can't blame him for she is most attractive, small and curly, clever and only 25. She is exceedingly self-centred and most of her conversation is about herself, her feelings and opinions but she is very much in love with her 40-year old husband and he with her.'[39]

For the next few years up to his death in 1950, the paths of Smuts, Daphne and Frederika were to cross frequently. When they did not, they kept in touch by letter. He was to write lyrically about the comfort of his memories of them, being 'often greater/richer than the presence itself'.[40] In February 1947, Daphne wrote to Smuts to thank him for two letters 'written in solitude which were some of the loveliest I have seen from you even though one of them was mostly about Frederika'.[41]

That Daphne Moore did not entirely approve of Smuts's closeness to Frederika was apparent from a letter she wrote him after she discovered that

197

Frederika was to accompany him to the wedding of Princess Elizabeth and Prince Philip in London in 1947. She warned him about the 'renewed talk' this would cause in England, South Africa and Greece,[42] but he took no notice. He met Queen Frederika in Athens and she accompanied him to London for the royal wedding. Daphne wrote her last letter to Smuts in March 1949.[43] A year later she wrote to Isie to ask about Smuts's health, saying she would like to visit Doornkloof to see them both again, but the visit never took place. The letters between them remain, in Beukes's words, 'a permanent reminder of the friendship between Smuts and a remarkable woman who became his dearest friend in the last years of his eventful life'.[44]

◆

There were several other women to whom Smuts became close at various times. Ethel Brown, his walking companion at Cambridge, has already been mentioned. Dr Hilda Clark, sister of Margaret and Alice, visited him on several occasions in the UK and South Africa, though they never wrote much to each other. Florence Lamont, the beautiful wife of American banker Tom Lamont became – along with her husband – among his 'special friends' and the three exchanged long letters over many years. He also took a grandfatherly interest in the young daughters of Lady Moore, Jo and Deidre, having them to stay at Groote Schuur and taking them mountaineering while they were at Oxford and Rhodes universities respectively.

After examining the many thousands of letters that Smuts wrote to his women friends, Piet Beukes concludes that the warrior-statesman was deeply romantic at heart – and proud of it.[45] Though frequently apart from Isie for long periods, however, he remained faithful and loving to her throughout their long marriage. While physically attracted to other women, his relationships with them – rather like those of his hero, Goethe – were platonic and overwhelmingly intellectual in nature. They were carried on mainly in writing, and enabled him to reveal a much softer side of his character – one he preferred to keep hidden from his fellow men.

CHAPTER 22

Finding Order in Complexity

Spirituality was the element of Smuts's character that distinguished him from most of his peers. Nurtured from his earliest days as a herd-boy on the family farm, his interest in matters of the spirit was to guide, uplift and sometimes perplex him throughout his life. His family hoped he would become a minister in the Dutch Reformed Church, but at Stellenbosch his strict Calvinist views were tempered by his introduction to the poetry of Shelley and Goethe, and later the works of Keats, Milton and Shakespeare. His new-found proficiency in Greek, on the other hand, enabled him to read the New Testament in its original form.

It took his study of the American poet, Walt Whitman, a kindred seeker after universal truths, while at Cambridge to free Smuts from many preconceptions, especially puritanical notions of sin and guilt.[1] Like him, Whitman had been deeply influenced as a child by the beauty of his natural surroundings. His world-view took account of Nature as well as God and expressed his poetic belief in the fundamental unity of all existence. The American's powerful and rhythmical verse was deeply personal, centred on himself as an exemplar of the general human personality, determined to discover the many possibilities that lay within every human being. It was this interest in the wonder of human personality that excited the young Smuts, who regarded Whitman as the foremost example of the integrated personality that he so admired.[2] He nonetheless admitted in the first chapter of his book on Whitman that he could just as well have written about another of his role-models, Johann Wolfgang Goethe: it was not so much the person who mattered as Man in general, and the make-up of the individual.[3] Whitman's ability to reconcile the contradictory impulses within his personality helped Smuts to synthesise his own love of nature with his religious beliefs, within a Universe that formed 'an ordered and harmonious Whole'.[4]

In his book on Whitman, Smuts set out to demonstrate a method of

While working for long hours on government business Smuts continued to take long walks in the mountains of the Cape and northern Transvaal for relaxation.

analysing personality. Scientists, he felt, were too easily satisfied with the study of origins and tended to explain human morality by reference to principles prevalent in the animal world. Psychologists, by contrast, held to the opposite fallacy: they regarded mind as a separate and superior entity, quite independent of the natural world. Smuts believed that the two approaches had to be synthesised: every person had to be viewed as a whole.

In studying Whitman, the young Smuts was really examining his own character; and through analysing Whitman's personality he was exploring his own core intellectual and philosophical beliefs.[5] At this stage in his life, he fell under the spell of another ground-breaking thinker, Charles Darwin, father of the theory of evolution. He found Darwin's belief in a world of continuous growth and development, via the forces of variation and natural selection toward ever higher forms, in many respects similar to his own.

In *On the Origin of Species* Darwin wrote: 'It is interesting to contemplate a tangled bank, clothed with many plants of many kinds, with birds singing in the bushes, with various insects flitting about and with worms crawling through the damp earth, and to reflect that these elaborately constructed forms, so different from each other, and dependent upon each other in so complex a manner have all been produced by laws acting around us. … There is a grandeur in this view of life, with its several powers, having been originally breathed by the Creator into new forms or into one; and that, whilst this planet had gone cycling on according to the fixed law of gravity, from so simple a beginning endless forms most beautiful and most wonderful have been and are being evolved.'[6]

Smuts loved this passage. In *Holism and Evolution*, he was to write: 'I am free to confess that there are few passages in the great literature of the world which affect me more deeply than these concluding words of Darwin's great book. They have a force and a beauty out of all proportion to the simple unadorned phrasing. They are the expression of a great selfless soul, who sought truth utterly and fearlessly, and was in the end vouchsafed a vision of the truth which perhaps has never been surpassed in its fullness and grandeur.'[7]

◆

As a young man, Smuts was to have his religious faith tested to the utmost during the decade from 1896 to 1906, when he was caught up in the maelstrom of the Boer-British struggle, the ruin of the land, the hatred and sorrows of war, and the grievous death of his infant son. He had to bear the loss of many close comrades, killed on commando beside him, and often stared death in the face himself. After the humiliation of the Boers' defeat at the hands of the British, he had to endure the triumphalism of his new masters, Milner and the mining magnates. Yet, while the conflicts of the Anglo-Boer War and its aftermath touched the depths of his soul, it also led to the most significant change in his life: his development from Boer fighter and thinker to greater, fuller and richer South African. 'I learnt to bow my head to the inevitable,' he was to acknowledge years later.[8]

The transformation in Smuts's philosophical outlook appears to have been due in large measure to the benign influence of the Society of Friends, otherwise known as the Quakers. Piet Beukes, in his study *The Holistic Smuts*, maintains that it was his fortuitous encounter with the Quakers in the English village of Street in Somerset in 1906 which revealed his true destiny to him. Unsure after the Anglo-Boer War whether to be 'an embittered Afrikaner or a co-operative South African',[9] he discovered in the gentle and undogmatic Friends, the spiritual home of Emily Hobhouse and the pro-Boer Clark family, a haven where the main forces in his life – his religion, his interest in the writings of poets, scientists and philosophers, and his concerns for humanity – coalesced. In his mid-thirties, Smuts came upon his own true mission in life from which he never looked back – to be a synthesiser of ideas and a reconciler of men. For the rest of his days, he maintained an association with the Quakers, adopting their form of silent worship even if unable entirely to accept their pacifist beliefs.

Smuts wrote later of the effect on any life of 'a moral awakening': 'It is then that the still small voice of the inner life comes to the fore, and conscience and duty take over to bring moderation, self-control, tranquillity of the soul and finally that peace of God which passes all understanding. It is then that a person learns to be himself with perfect honesty, integrity and sincerity.'[10] In analysing Smuts's character, Beukes observes that breaking away from any race or group to embrace a wider loyalty entails sacrifice, character and discipline – not to mention a willingness to suffer insults and misrepresentation – and is a difficult path which only exceptional characters can tread. It is these rare people, he asserts, who are the freest, most enlightened and most dependable in the great conflicts and crises of life.[11] One of his earliest bio-graphers, N Levi, wrote the following assessment of Smuts way back in 1917: 'His is a clear-cut personality, in spite of the antimony [sic] that seems to exist between the different parts. … So you will discover in Smuts a contempt for amateurs and theorists, a strong predilection for materialism, coupled with a genuine belief in pure science. He is surely the most practical idealist, the most martial metaphysician that ever lived. He indulges in day-dreams, but rises in the dead of night to turn them into facts. The subtle lawyer within him has not made him a legalist. Chockfull of sentiment, he knows no sentimen-tality. In Parliament, he once spoke of conscientious objectors as "the salt of the earth". Outside, he peppers them.'[12]

Alan Paton, biographer of Hofmeyr and not a devotee of Smuts, summed up the latter's character as succinctly as only he could. 'Many a life,' Paton wrote, 'is tragic because a man does not know what he is. He is a man of affairs, but wishes he had been a poet. He is carnal, but wishes he had been religious. Religious, he wishes he had been carnal. So bound by the one and desiring the other, he is nothing at all. But Smuts combined and contained them all … he possessed them, and was not possessed by them. He was, as we say, the master of himself.'[13]

◆

After being unable to find a publisher in England for his treatise on Walt Whitman, Smuts only returned to his examination of 'wholeness' in 1910, as a diversion from the stresses of Union-making in a polarised South Africa. He sent the manuscript of *An Inquiry into the Whole* to his old friend in Cam-bridge, HJ Wolstenholme, who did not think highly of it, and advised him to regard it as no more than a rough draft requiring revision if it were ever to be published. Wolstenholme urged his former student to write history and prac-tise politics,[14] but Smuts remained convinced that politics and philosophy could go hand in hand.

Another 14 years went by before Smuts returned to what he had written. He had lost the premiership to Hertzog and for once had some time for deep reflec-tion. In the interim, some aspects of his concept of 'wholeness' had changed. Beginning in the summer of 1924, he spent eight months quietly in his study, unaided by any stenographer, re-writing a manuscript of *Holism and Evolution* in his untidy longhand. Even then, he could not focus exclusively on the task, being continually interrupted by party and parliamentary duties. Completed in late 1925 and published less than a year later, the book eventually ran to three editions in England as well as reprints in America and Germany.

For all its poetic language, *Holism and Evolution* is not – as Jannie Smuts says with filial understatement – a book for casual or easy reading.[15] His political colleagues Leslie Blackwell and Deneys Reitz compared notes and confessed to having read ten and three pages respectively.[16] Smuts's fundamental premise was that we live in a universe in which every living thing – atoms, cells, plants, animals and humans – forms a whole. Each whole consists of more than its parts and combines with others to form an even greater whole. Whole-making is real, organic, evolutionary and creative. It gives rise to a progressive scale of wholes, from simple matter through plants and animals to human beings and upwards to personality and the spiritual world. This progression of wholes, rising tier upon tier, makes up the structure of the universe.

Smuts asserted that there were several stages in the process of whole-making: from the physical and material to the living plant world; from the animate field of birds and beasts to the conscious world of man; from human associations to communities and states; and finally to the world of truth, beauty and goodness which underpinned order in the Universe. As whole-making went higher, it came nearer to the ideal of perfection, to the ultimate whole – the end of all creation.[17]

In advancing this fundamentally optimistic thesis, he was seeking to impose some pattern upon the amazing complexity of the world around him. There had to be some guiding laws in nature and science, he reasoned, if only they could be found. As a scientist himself, he thought science's most notable contribution to the field of ideas was the notion of creative evolution. The universe is not ready-made and complete, he believed, but in a state of constant, creative flux, growing and developing just as a human being does. 'Wholes have no stuff; they are arrangements. Science has come round to the view that the world consists of patterns, and I construe that to be that the world consists of wholes,' he wrote.[18]

◆

Smuts's theory is not far removed from the teleology of Teilhard de Chardin or the philosophy of Aristotle, where everything has its specific end or purpose. It has echoes of St Thomas Aquinas, who saw a progression of 'partial wholes' as leading upward to God.[19] Yet Smuts went further than these eminent thinkers, and even beyond Immanuel Kant, who attributed the ideal of perfect knowledge to the Supreme Being alone. Smuts argued that Man has the power of 'intuitive understanding', a *sensus communis* or sixth sense, which enables him to comprehend the Whole.[20]

An essential element in shaping the progress of any organism, Smuts asserted, is the freedom to be itself: the freedom that shapes and moulds any organism is a vital element in the process of growth and development. 'Freedom broadens out into a world of opportunities. The animal finds that it is no longer imprisoned in its cell like the plant; it begins to move about. Gradually it learns the lessons of direction and self-direction. The great Experiment of life assumes ever-widening degrees of freedom, until finally at the human stage freedom takes conscious control of itself and begins to create the free ethical world of the Spirit.'[21]

This view of the world is in no sense Panglossian: observing the afflictions of old friends, he once wrote, 'I firmly believe that the universe is good and friendly, but it has very dark patches and the dark places are often close by the bright ones. But what is the use of moralising when one is face to face with such human agony? One … can but look on in dumb sympathy, very much as a dog stands by its dead master.'[22] He knew only too well that the universe could inflict unimaginable pain, evil and terror, but believed that no man could make himself whole and free except by perpetual combat with these realities. 'Hence the greatest men are usually the least happy in the ordinary sense. But here again the Whole exerts its wholesome, beneficent influence and as a compensation they know a blessedness which is unintelligible and unrealisable to smaller natures.'[23] He was speaking, of course, from personal experience.

Smuts's philosophy of holism gave him, as Hancock says, a sense of realism, proportion and purpose. Combining both the time-scale of modern science, expressed in evolutionary theory, and the doctrine of God's sovereignty, which he had imbibed from his early youth, it enabled him to link the physical world with the metaphysical, to approach a comprehension of the Universe and locate man's place within in it. It did not, unfortunately, provide him with a practical solution to South Africa's apparently intractable racial problems, as we shall see in Chapter 24.

The marvel of human personality always fascinated Smuts, who placed it at the very pinnacle of the upward progression of Wholes. He viewed a 'rounded' personality, tested and tempered in the fire of life and imbued with energy and creativity, as the supreme achievement of the evolutionary process. In 1938, concerned about the impending conflict in Europe, he wrote: 'I cannot get away from the conviction – borne in upon me by a lifetime of thought and active participation in affairs – that the way of reform, the way of salvation lies through the fostering, the purification, the enrichment of the human personality. There the Divine Light shines most clearly in the dark world.'[24]

◆

In emphasising the need for the synthesis of spirit and body, Smuts often referred admiringly to Jesus Christ's ethical contribution to the evolution of personality. Through the teachings of Jesus, he claimed, the legalistic Roman concept of the person had become suffused with the dignity and inalienable rights of human beings as children of God.[25] Although in later life his views on the divinity of Christ gave rise to some disagreement among those close to him, Smuts always regarded Jesus as a figure of the greatest historic importance – the supreme expression of human personality. Writing to a friend in New York, he described Jesus as 'the outstanding miracle of our human story. And the more one gathers experience of life and sees the pitiable lot of mankind, the more one is drawn to the Figure and the message He delivered and stands for in our human story.'[26]

Few people had read and studied the Bible in its original Greek more meticulously than Smuts, whose copy of the New Testament had been with him on commando and lay beside his bed always. According to Jannie Smuts, he was intrigued by the extreme brevity of Jesus's life and confessed that he could never decide how much of the New Testament was fact and how much the product of faith, piety and tradition.[27] Being responsible himself for issues of war and peace, he wrestled with the humility of Jesus and his pacifist prescriptions. Yet at the times of the greatest stress in his life, he turned unfailingly for comfort to Christ's example. In a letter to the Gilletts during some of the darkest days of World War II, he wrote that the Galilean, if not divine, was the nearest to Godlike that mankind could become.[28]

The apostasy that his son detected is at odds with the view of Piet Beukes, who made a close study of Smuts's metaphysical beliefs in *The Holistic Smuts – A Study in Personality*. In the book, Beukes takes other biographers to task for failing to fully appreciate the role which religion played in Smuts's make-up. Obviously a believer himself, Beukes goes to some length to make the case that Smuts never strayed far from the tenets of orthodox Christianity, but the evidence he produces is not conclusive. Even in hindsight, it is not clear what Smuts really believed about the divinity of Jesus.

◆

As with his politics, Smuts's religious beliefs gave rise to public controversy – and drew criticism from his enemies. His enthusiastic advocacy of evolutionary theory led to charges by religious leaders of a narrower persuasion that he denied the existence of God. The truth was much more complex. Although his belief in God had moved beyond anthromorphism, he always avowed his faith and trust in a supreme, holistic Deity, whose laws governed all of Creation. If this was no longer the conventional religious doctrine he had grown up with, it was one that remained real and practical to him.

The astute and perceptive Alan Paton thought that the religious Smuts was in thrall to the Creation rather than the Creator. Fascinated by the human past as well as the future of humanity, 'Smuts had a faith that the Universe was good, and headed towards a good end', Paton wrote.[29]

In seeking to evaluate Smuts's contribution to the debate about religion and philosophy, Beukes makes mention of a lively exchange of opinion between Smuts and his fellow Afrikaner friend, Dr FC Kolbe, who had courted the enmity of his own family by breaking with his Protestant past and becoming a Catholic priest.[30] Kolbe was the only South African in whom Smuts ever confided about philosophy, religion and other matters of the spirit. The monsignor acknowledged that *Holism and Evolution* was a study in scientific philosophy, not an exercise in metaphysics or philosophy, but he disagreed with Smuts's acceptance of Kant's celebrated argument that from the facts of nature no inference of God is justified. Kolbe argued that if a person believed in a Divine Being, he should acknowledge it – whether in matters of science or philosophy.

Smuts accepted the criticism as valid, but pointed out that within the limited purview of his book, he had not touched upon the application of holism to religion. In 1948, after his defeat at the polls, he wrote to a German academic saying that he would dearly like to revise his thoughts on holism in order to resolve the confusion that prevailed in science, philosophy, religion, and to build a 'philosophical bridge between the material and spiritual worlds'. Sadly, the demands of politics upon the limited time of an old man of 78 meant that this hope was never realised.[31]

◆

In their assessments of Smuts's religious outlook, both Beukes and Ingham allude to the extent to which he came to regard himself as the conscience of his people, and in later life as the wiser conscience of mankind. From his earliest days, he had an unwavering belief in his mastery of events and, like Woodrow Wilson in years to come, in the rightness of his cause.[32] Yet it was holism, Ingham suggests, that freed Smuts from his Calvinist origins and enabled him to combine the life of the intellect with the activism he had always craved.[33] In order to justify his philosophy in action, he donned the formal dress of a statesman or the uniform of a soldier as a substitute for the robe of the *predikant*, a role for which he had once been destined.

The closest Smuts came to recanting any of his core beliefs came late in his life, immediately after the crushing loss of his eldest son, Japie. Pouring out his anguish to the Gilletts, he wrote, 'We can understand the aged going, who has had their chance for good or evil. But this senseless thing is almost unpardonable and looks like a blasphemy on the Universe. Through it all runs this strand of the accidental, the unaccountable, the outrageous, the unforgiveable … The only excuse I can offer for the universe is that we do not understand, that the mystery is greater than our limited outlook can explain, and that humility rather than violent remonstrance becomes us.'[34]

Yet he never yielded to despair, for he had others to think of. On learning of Japie's death, at what must have been one of the lowest points of his life, his instinctive recourse was to call for spiritual help from his local DRC pastor, Ds Johan Reyneke, with whom he had often discussed holism and religion. In his book-lined study at Doornkloof, he and Reyneke knelt down and prayed to the God in whom each, in his own way, devoutly believed.[35]

CHAPTER 23

'Our Wisest Ecologist'

From his student days, Smuts was intrigued by the existence of the human personality within a seemingly impersonal cosmos. At Cambridge, he puzzled over whether science or personality was sovereign in the universe, and oscillated between the two views.[1] *Holism and Evolution*, as we have seen, was his ambitious attempt to forge an overarching unity between the sciences of matter, life and mind. The study of science being a fairly new discipline at the time of *Holism*'s publication, the book gave Smuts an international – though not universally acknowledged – reputation as a philosopher of science.

Political defeat in the 1924 election and release from the burdens of the premiership allowed him the time he craved to develop his scientific interests, most notably in the botanical field. In the annual six-month-long parliamentary recesses, he was able to travel widely across sub-Saharan Africa, studying at first hand the region's flora, fauna and palaeontology.

Geology was a subject which had fascinated him from boyhood, when he first wondered how the great mountains of the Cape had come into existence. Inspired by his experience of the Great Rift Valley during war service in East Africa, he was particularly attracted to Wegener's theory of continental drift, which posited Gondwanaland as the mother lode from which the other southern hemisphere land masses – South America, Madagascar, India and Australasia – had broken away.[2]

Although insistent that the Wegener thesis was still unproven, he thought it provided a useful foundation for scientific study in the southern hemisphere. It confirmed his belief that Africa occupied a key position among the continents and that South Africa might provide the scientific world with fresh perspectives, besides helping to shift the focus of evolutionary science away from the northern hemisphere, where it had its roots.[3]

Although Europe was the home of the modern scientific spirit and possessor of most of the world's scientific manpower and resources, 'northerners' were apt to follow a north south axis of investigation, whereas – Smuts argued – an east west axis might be just as rewarding. It would also put South Africa at the very centre of important scientific explorations.[4]

The theory of continental drift, he suggested, helped to explain the geological and biological similarities between continents now divided by the oceans. It was possible, for instance, that the Cape Floral kingdom, so different from other flora in southern Africa, might have originated in temperate Northern Europe and been driven south by the onset of the last Great Ice Age. On the other hand, the Cape flora displayed similarities to the flora of other countries in the southern hemisphere: the quite remarkable wealth of endemic forms in the south-western Cape might have come from the remains of a land stretching into the southern ocean as far as Antarctica.[5] All these discoveries provided exciting research opportunities for scientists to explore, he claimed.

◆

His interest in hominids was excited by Professor Raymond Dart's discovery in 1924 of the Taung skull, from *Australopithecus africanus*, an infant creature 'neither ape nor man but somewhere in between' and thought to be the elusive 'missing link'. As president of the South African Association for the Advancement of Science, he wrote to congratulate Dart on his important discovery: 'Your great keenness and zealous interest in anthropology have led to what may well prove an epoch-making discovery not only of far-reaching importance from an anthropological point of view, but is also well-calculated to concentrate attention on South Africa as the great field for scientific discovery which it undoubtedly is.'[6] In an address to the Association on 'Science from the South African Point of View' in 1925, he predicted that South Africa might yet become the Mecca of human palaeontology.

His suggestion proved prophetic when, 22 years after Dart's discovery of the Taung skull – which had been derisively dismissed by many leading scientists overseas – his old friend Dr Robert Broom discovered the complete skull of an adult australopithecine. It had been Smuts who had influenced Broom to give up his medical practice and become a researcher at the Transvaal Museum. Broom's discovery helped to make South Africa a world leader in the field of palaeoanthropology, a status that endures to this day.

Smuts in the veld with his close friend and neighbour, botanist Dr IB Pole Evans.

Smuts also brought several eminent foreign scientists to South Africa, notably the French climatologist and anthropologist, Abbé Henri Breuil, to study South Africa's pre-history. He became friendly with local pre-historians including C van Riet Lowe whom he persuaded to give up engineering and found a department of archaeology at Witwatersrand University.[7]

◆

After visiting Oxford in November 1929 as the Rhodes Memorial Lecturer, Smuts was much in demand as a speaker across the United Kingdom and North America. Having spent two months lecturing abroad, he returned to South Africa to be offered the rare distinction of the presidency of the British Association for the Advancement of Science in 1931 – its centenary year. Nationalist-supporting newspapers, to whom the honour meant little, referred to him derisively as 'Professor Jan Smuts of Oxford'.[8]

His presidential address to the British Association was entitled 'The Scientific World-Picture of Today' and attempted to provide an answer to the question: 'How has value become a reality?'[9] He suggested that man was a picture-making animal, who made comprehensive images of his particular experiences and beliefs. These pictures deserved to be called scientific because of the disciplined observation they embodied. Physical science needed to dig down below the level of things observed to account for the facts of observation, he argued.

Though unable to refute scientifically the eventual confrontation between cosmic disintegration and organic evolution, he refused to accept that 'our origin is thus accidental, our position is exceptional and our fate sealed, with the inevitable running down of the solar system'. To that prospect, he offered a defiant answer: 'The human spirit is not a pathetic, wandering phantom of the universe, but is at home, and meets with spiritual hospitality and response everywhere. Our deepest thoughts and emotions are but responses to stimuli which come to us not from an alien, but from an essentially friendly and kindred universe.' In Hancock's words, this was magnificent, but it was not true science. Yet decades later, Smuts's words were being applauded by scientists for their interpretive insights. One distinguished physicist described his address as 'a living contribution to thought which deserves to become an indispensable part of the education of every man of science'.[10]

◆

On the sea-voyage back to South Africa in the company of Professor van Riet Lowe, Smuts read Louis Leakey's book on East African prehistory and immediately became interested in the subject of climatic oscillations and their effect upon early man. Eighteen months later, he presented his thoughts on Climate and Man in Africa to a meeting of the SA Association for the Advancement of Science in Durban. His hypothesis that the Pleistocene scheme of climatic change was applicable in Europe as well as Africa was described by the eminent archaeologist John Goodwin as 'a landmark in the history of both geology and climatology in their relation to human history'.[11]

◆

His favourite hobby, which grew into a passion from 1924 onward, was the study of botany. 'Botany to me,' he wrote, 'is what bridge or patience is to card players. Of course it is also much more.' Besides mountain climbing, his best-loved form of exercise was tramping long distances across the veld,

With colleagues at Dongola. When the Nationalists came into power they reversed Smuts's proclamation of the area as a national park. The much smaller Mapungubwe is all that remains.

magnifying glass in hand, collecting specimens of plants and grasses for his botanical press. It was the grasses of the highveld around Doornkloof that excited him most. He did not care nearly as much for trees or exotic flowers, and had little interest in animals, except for his pedigreed cattle. Having grown up in the Cape, he encountered on the Transvaal highveld an entirely different floral region, one in which he was surrounded on all sides by grassland savannah.[12] 'Give me the grasses, the rolling veld, the Bushveld Savannah, with bush and trees dotting the endless grass scene in all its variety of shade and tone, with scents and sounds of birds and insects added, and shy animals stealing through the grass cover. That is the grass pattern of life and there is no fascination like it,' he was to write later.[13]

As a neophyte botanist, he was fortunate in having as his neighbour at Irene Dr IB Pole Evans, the chief plant pathologist of the Department of Agriculture, and in Cape Town the botanist Rudolf Marloth, who, along with Dr Harriet Bolus of the Cape Town herbarium, helped him to identify and arrange the plants he so avidly collected. As usual, he steeped himself in the history and bibliography of botany, reading botanical works from England and Germany as well the writings of palaeo-botanists such as Dr Marie Stopes.[14]

He was a quick learner. In 1924, he confounded the experts by discovering on Doornkloof a supposedly unidentified grass which was given the name Smuts fingergrass (*Digitaria smutsii*).[15] It was considered a new species at first, but was shown much later to be identical to a previously discovered grass, *Digitaria eriantha*. His researches in the botanical field were enhanced by his quite phenomenal memory. In 1927, two American botanists who had climbed Kilimanjaro told him of a grass they had come across, whose name they had forgotten, growing on the mountainside next to the snowline. Smuts at once named three grasses which he remembered having found back in 1916.[16]

During the years from 1924 to 1932 his researches took him as far afield as Tanganyika, Nyasaland, the Victoria Falls, the Zimbabwe Ruins, Portuguese East Africa and across most of the mountain ranges of the Transvaal and Cape.[17] Some of these areas, according to his son, had not been visited by collectors before, so the specimens he brought back aroused great interest.

Shortly before his death in 1950, he contributed a foreword to two books, *Wild Flowers of the Cape of Good Hope* and *The Grasses and Pastures of South Africa,* written at great speed and without having the necessary reference books at hand.[18] In the latter he wrote: 'In general, I may say that people do not realise the importance of grasses for human life. We literally live on grasses. All the important cereals which sustain human life, such as wheat, rice, maize, millet, kaffir corn, are grasses. ... Meat also, through animals, is a product of grasses. Directly and indirectly, therefore, all life is grass, and not merely like grass, as the poets say. And when we consider how small this globe is, and how rapidly the human race is expanding and over-occupying it, we begin to realise to what an extent the whole future of the human race on this globe is dependent on the progress we may make in the development of our grass resources through conservation and research into new and improved forms.'

Written shortly before his eightieth birthday, those words, according to Beukes, came from the core of his spiritual-intellectual being and were his last message to mankind.[19]

◆

According to Dr Pole Evans, Smuts was the first South African political leader to understand the vital role that grasses play in the life of a country, and he went out of his way – at agricultural shows and on other public occasions – to emphasise the importance of the natural veld and the urgent need to prevent soil erosion.[20] He encouraged all branches of botanical research and played a role in the establishment of the National Herbarium in Pretoria and the Botanical Survey, which mapped the country's vegetation. He established Grass and Pasture Research Stations in various parts of the country, the Low Temperature Research Station for the study and promotion of fruit for export and Horticultural Research Stations in the Cape and Transvaal to further the interests of fruit growers.

Professor JFV Phillips, former chair of Botany at Wits and author of hundreds of scientific papers, described Smuts as the wisest ecologist he would ever know – because of his unique understanding not only of the philosophy and science of ecology, but also of its practical application to all aspects of life.[21] On their walks through the veld, he would impress upon Phillips that ecology is more than the study of the details of plants, animals and men, but an approach to learning more about the art and science of life, and to appreciating both philosophy and religion better. Like holism, ecology was at the core of Smuts's thought, his inner life, his politics and his relationship with the Deity.

CHAPTER 24

An Uncertain Trumpet

Historicism – the notion that each individual or society should be judged in terms of the norms and values prevailing at the time – is commonly advanced as the reason, and justification, for Smuts's segregationist beliefs and policies. While that may well be true, it does not fully explain why so far-sighted a thinker did not do more to illuminate the way forward for his white compatriots. Dr Edgar Brookes, one of the wisest academics and politicians of his time, thought that historians of the twenty-first century would regard Smuts's greatest shortcoming as his failure ever to face the question of colour fairly and squarely. Although always respectful and courteous to people of colour, never making them the pawns of an ideology as his opponents did, he gave too little and what little he gave was mostly too late. 'He never rallied his followers to a clear lead. The trumpet gave forth an uncertain sound and none made himself ready for battle,' wrote Brookes.[1]

Dr Bernard Friedman, once a member of the United Party, was much more trenchant in his criticism of Smuts, the political leader – and scornful of his holistic philosophy. He noted that instead of blending the various elements of South Africa's multi-ethnic make-up into an all-embracing whole, Smuts – by insisting that white unity must come first and the 'native question' be left for later – brought a dichotomy into his earliest holistic enterprise, namely the creation of Union.[2] In the field of practical politics, holism gave him no special insight, inspiration or guidance, Friedman observed.

Nor could Professor Keith Hancock, pre-eminent biographer of Smuts, resolve the contradiction between his subject's holistic philosophy, with its emphasis on the supreme worth of the individual, and its application to South African politics. 'The biographer cannot find any short cut to its solution; in particular, he cannot identify any particular scheme of race relations as the proper counterpart of the *Inquiry into the Whole*. As a philosopher, Smuts employed the cosmological time scale; as a politician he had to

217

reckon time from one election to the next and sometimes from one day to the next.'[3]

Piet Beukes, who revered Smuts and worked for him, ascribed his employer's views to a duality in his character: 'For all his high ideals, great intellect and the supreme value he placed on human personality, he was bound by his environment and the limitations, indeed restrictions, of his background as a South African.'[4] Hindsight enables us to put it more plainly today: as a politician, and even as a statesman, Smuts was simply unable to balance ideal values with the social practices and imperatives of his time.

Like Winston Churchill, he was a man of contradictions and inconsistencies, which make his character both elusive and more fascinating. Churchill was a firm believer in democracy – except when it applied to India. Smuts propounded unity between races, but left the 'natives' out of proper consideration. Both men were products of the Victorian era, in which whites in general regarded themselves as superior to all other races on earth. In colonial South Africa, Smuts was brought up in a deeply conservative environment where the master–servant relationship was taken for granted and never questioned. His earliest encounter with other races was with 'coloured' workers on the family farm. Growing up in the Western Cape in the 1890s, he had little direct contact with Africans. And like most whites, he feared that if he and his countrymen were not united, strong and vigilant, they would simply be overrun by an 'overwhelming majority of prolific barbarism'.[5] This fear and apprehension was fuelled by years of experience of racial conflict along the Cape's eastern frontier.

In Smuts's view, Europeans and Africans were separate and there could, and should, be no intermingling between them. As Ingham put it, relations between the black and white races were regarded as more of a threat to be averted than a problem to be resolved.[6] Although Smuts tempered many of his views in later life, his belief in keeping the races apart never wavered.

He was not unaware, of course, of the inconsistency between his ideals and political policies, but could not imagine how to resolve it. 'When I consider the political future of natives in South Africa, I must say that I look into the shadows and darkness, and then I feel inclined to shift the intolerable burden of solving that sphinx problem to the ampler shoulders and stronger brains of the future. Sufficient unto the day etc. My feeling is that stronger forces are at work which will transform Afrikaner attitudes to the natives.'[7] This was wishful thinking, as history was to prove.

◆

As we have seen, it was at Stellenbosch, and later at Cambridge, that he first expressed his thoughts publicly on the colour question. The European population in South Africa ought to stand together, he asserted, because 'the race struggle is destined to assume a magnitude on the African continent such as the world has never seen …'[8] Returning to the Cape from Cambridge, he took an undogmatic, empiricist approach to the 'native' policy that had developed in the Colony over the years. That policy was based largely on Rhodes's Glen Grey Act, which laid down the rules for African land holding, introduced a limited form of self-government in the Cape and imposed a tax on any African who did not work for three months in the year.

Smuts's own instincts were paternalistic and pragmatic rather than authoritarian; it was the duty of the whites who held political power, he would argue, to exercise that power in 'a spirit of responsibility, and prudence'.[9] It seemed unquestionable that the majority of black people were 'raw, barbarous and uncivilised' and therefore had to be treated differently. Whites had an obligation to bring blacks to 'a state of civilisation through systematic work and practical education'.[10]

He foresaw that a future South Africa faced two fundamental problems: white disunity, and white policy towards other races. As Hancock writes, the need to fuse or consolidate the two 'Teutonic peoples' seemed to him self-evident. But some of his youthful language was apocalyptic and betrays the extent of his fear. 'At the southern corner of a vast continent, peopled by over 100 000 000 barbarians, about half a million whites have taken up a position, with a view not only to working out their own destiny, but also of using that position as a basis for lifting up and opening up that vast dead-weight of immemorial barbarism and animal savagery to the light and blessing of ordered civilisation.'[11]

It should be remembered that in the Western world at this time the existence of black inequality was barely questioned. Racial segregation was common while a universal or common franchise was almost unknown. In the US, even

219

Abraham Lincoln had felt obliged to separate the issue of black suffrage from that of slavery. During his 1858 senatorial campaign against Stephen Douglas, he said the following: 'I am not, nor ever have been in favor of bringing about in any way the social and political equality of the white and black races, that I am not nor ever have been in favor of making voters or jurors of negroes, nor of qualifying them to hold office, nor to intermarry with white people; and I will say in addition to this that there is a physical difference between the white and black races which I believe will forever forbid the two races living together on terms of social and political equality. And in as much as they cannot so live, while they do remain together there must be the position of superior and inferior, and I as much as any other man am in favor of having the superior position assigned to the white race.'[12] Smuts and others were still echoing these views 50 years later.

In most parts of the world, the vote was limited to those who owned property or assets, which meant a minority of the population. In Britain, from where the Cape took its lead, male citizens only became fully enfranchised in 1918 (when Smuts was in his forties) and women a decade later. Yet as early as 1853, the Cape Colony had adopted a constitution as liberal as any in the British Empire. It extended the franchise to all men, white, 'coloured' or 'native' who owned property worth £25. Every citizen who qualified to vote was eligible for election to Parliament, yet very few Africans who qualified for the vote were able or felt inclined to register. The northern colonies, by contrast, had a strict colour bar in their constitutions, which excluded everyone who was not 'European' from the franchise.

◆

It was Milner rather than Smuts who first tackled the 'native question' in the Transvaal. His Lagden Commission, set up in 1903-05, gave the stamp of approval to territorial separateness and proposed that black squatters should be removed from their holdings on white farms and given rights in the 'native reserves'. It also recommended the abolition of the Cape franchise and the setting aside of a limited number of seats for black representatives in each colonial parliament.

Milner's successor, Lord Selborne, a strong believer in economic upliftment and an opponent of pass laws and industrial colour bar, asserted in a magisterial memorandum to Smuts and Botha in 1908 that 'the black man is absolutely incapable of rivalling the white ... No one can have any experience of the two races without feeling the intrinsic superiority of the white man.'[13] Like Smuts, Selborne did not believe in politics for blacks and poured scorn on their 'futile' participation in Cape elections. As Hancock comments laconically, 'The doctrine of separateness, as now defined under Lord Milner's auspices, could get along quite comfortably with *baasskap*.'[14]

As a Transvaal politician, Smuts was preoccupied before and after the Anglo-Boer War with the improvement of relations between Boers and Britons. It was only when embarking on constitution-making for the proposed Union that he was obliged to think more deeply about the colour question. He began a protracted correspondence with John X Merriman in the Cape, who agreed that South Africa should become united under the Crown, but disagreed on the franchise question. Merriman wished to extend the Cape's limited non-racial franchise to every province of the Union. Smuts knew that a non-racial vote would be out of the question in three of the four provinces. The best he could do, he explained to liberal friends in Britain, was to allow the franchise provision in the four colonies to be left undisturbed, entrenched in the new constitution and reconsidered only after the Union had become established.

◆

The ink on signatures to the Union constitution had scarcely dried before the Botha government began to press for a uniform Native policy throughout South Africa, based on territorial separation. The Natives Land Act of 1913, the first stage in such a policy, made it illegal for black people to purchase land outside the existing reserves – which comprised less than eight per cent of the country's land area. The Act created an anomaly in the Cape, where blacks who qualified for the franchise could not, in law, be relegated to their own areas. Yet the day would come, the advocates of separatism warned, when blacks in the Cape would outnumber whites: it was necessary therefore to get rid of the non-racial franchise.

In these early days of Union, Smuts had little to say about native policy, having more than enough to occupy him as minister of mines, defence, interior and, for a short while, finance. As minister of the interior, however, it fell to him to engage with MK Gandhi on the rights of immigrant Indians. Gandhi was primarily concerned with the laws affecting his own race, and refrained from crusading for complete and immediate equality for South Africa's Indian population, or for the rights of the black majority. He was to be a thorn in Smuts's flesh throughout his stay in South Africa – and indeed after his departure for England in 1914. Much later, Smuts was to write a letter to Gandhi which helped to explain his attitude to Indians (and perhaps blacks, also): 'When I was, about the same time as you, studying in England, I had no race prejudice or colour prejudice against your people. In fact had we known each other we would have been friends. Why is it that we now have become rivals with conflicting interests? ... How will you solve the difficulty about the fundamental differences of our cultures? Let alone the question of superiority, there is no doubt that your civilization is different from ours. Ours may not be overwhelmed by yours. That is why we have to go in for legislation which must in effect put disabilities on you.'[15]

◆

Though involved, as minister of mines and labour, in policies affecting black people, Smuts took no part in parliamentary debates about native policy until he became prime minister in 1919. However, two years earlier, he had expressed his thoughts on race at some length to an audience at the Savoy Hotel in London, where he argued that the Commonwealth, and South Africa in particular, had a 'civilising mission' to perform in Africa.[16] Pointing to the United States, which also had a racial problem but where the ratio of whites to blacks was inversely proportionate, he explained that in South Africa a small white population had been trying for more than two centuries to secure a footing in Africa. Two fundamental axioms defined white–black relations: no intermixing of blood between the two colours, and whites basing their conduct towards blacks on the 'granite bedrock of the Christian moral code'.

A practice had grown up in his country, he explained, of creating 'parallel institutions' for whites and blacks. 'Instead of mixing up black and white in the old haphazard way, which instead of uplifting the black degraded the white, we are now trying to lay down a policy of keeping them apart in our institutions. It may be that on those parallel lines we may yet be able to solve a problem which may otherwise be insoluble ...'[17] In the chair, and leading the applause of an audience whose knowledge of South Africa was limited, was none other than Lord Selborne.

◆

His awareness of the centrality of the colour question, and reluctance to delegate, caused Smuts, in 1919, to add the portfolio of native affairs to his already onerous responsibilities as prime minister. He was aware that Botha had done his best to deliver on the underlying promise in the Native Land Act to make more land available for black occupation, but Parliament had refused to make the extra land available. Yet MPs also repudiated Hertzog's demand that the Cape franchise be abolished before blacks anywhere in the Union could be given more territory.

A series of strikes and protests in 1919, as well as a warning to Smuts from the Bishop of Pretoria that his policy was drifting dangerously, had an outcome in the Native Affairs Act of 1920, which established a three-member Native Affairs Commission (NAC) with wide powers to make recommendations, introduced Native Councils for the first time, and authorised the governor-general to convene conferences of chiefs and other black representative bodies. The lack of representation for 'natives', the new prime minister asserted, was the main cause of a growing estrangement between black and white which boded ill for the country's future. His own simple motto was 'one step at a time'.[18]

The legislation satisfied neither the SA Native National Congress (later the ANC), in favour of consultation but hoping for representation in the sovereign legislature, nor Creswell's Labourites and Hertzog's Nationalists, who demanded the total separation of black and white. It was hailed by radicals and liberals in Britain, however, as a 'significant advance' and 'the beginning of a new epoch in the relations of the white and native races'.[19]

Concerned with the impact of industrialisation on African tribal life, Smuts urged the NAC to make a study of the problem which took two years to complete. The outcome was the Native (Urban Areas) Bill of 1923 which provided for the establishment of 'native' villages and townships. The legislation bore the stamp of authoritarian and paternalistic planning: it made consultation with Native Advisory Boards mandatory and gave municipalities control over the comings and goings of blacks in urban areas. Yet it was a step forward. Buoyed by its favourable reception, an upbeat Prime Minister declared in a Christmas message, 'White and black both have a proper place in South Africa. Both have their human rights, and let us in a fair and humble spirit approach the difficulties which arise out of them and labour to make this land a home in which both races can live together in peace and friendship and work out their salvation in fairness and justice.'[20]

◆

Not a session of Parliament went by, however, without angry rumblings from Hertzog, Creswell and others: segregation, they insisted, was a matter of life and death for white civilisation. Any legislation which gave black people more land or accommodation on the fringes of cities and towns was denounced as the thin end of the wedge; soon natives would be demanding the vote! Segregationist policies proved to be a powerful vote winner in the 1924 election and were primarily responsible for Smuts's defeat at the hands of the Hertzog-Creswell Pact.

Prime Minister Hertzog, like Smuts before him, took on the portfolio of native affairs that he had held in the Botha government twelve years earlier. After marking time for more than a year, he announced that Africans had to be given the rest of the land promised to them in 1913. In 1926 he tabled four bills on 'native policy' which gave a resentful Smuts an opportunity to go onto the attack. In a 7 000-word memorandum on behalf of his party, Smuts condemned the proposal to provide more land for Africans because it would result in territorial intermingling. He rejected the idea of removing blacks from white farms as it would increase congestion and force rural Africans into the cities. Opportunistically, he attacked the plan to give Africans seven white representatives in the House of Assembly, because it might affect the balance of power between the white parties, but had to tread more carefully around the proposal to extend the voting rights of coloureds because opposing the measure might cost the SAP votes in the Cape. His attitude, as Ingham suggests, was less liberal than reactionary.[21]

The closest he and Hertzog came to a bi-partisan racial policy came at a series of wide-ranging talks between them in 1928, at which Smuts somewhat uncharacteristically called for a common franchise for the whole country – to apply to black and white alike – based on property and educational qualifications set high enough to ensure that the bulk of the black population would be excluded. Hertzog promised to consider the proposals but at their next meeting told Smuts that the northern provinces would not stand for it. Smuts had given the same answer to Merriman 20 years earlier.[22]

◆

Race was the predominant issue in the *swart gevaar* election of 1929. Knowing he had no hope of winning the two-thirds majority required to alter the franchise provisions in the Union constitution, Hertzog nonetheless tabled two Bills which made provision for the representation of natives and coloureds in Parliament, by whites. The pivotal proposal was the abolition of the Cape Native franchise. By introducing the bills, Hertzog hoped to dramatise the 'peril' facing white voters – from which only Nationalist policies could rescue them. By fighting the bills clause by clause and calling for a national convention or commission to address the country's socio-economic and political complexities, Smuts was able to create the impression that it was his party which stood for justice and fair treatment for blacks,[23] but Nationalist leaders denounced him as 'the man who put himself forward as the apostle of a black Kaffir state ... extending from the Cape to Egypt'.[24] Lacking an effective counter to this crude propaganda, the SAP managed to win the larger share of the national vote but fell well short of a parliamentary majority.

Beaten not so much by his opponents as by the electoral system, Smuts took himself off to Oxford for a series of Rhodes Memorial Lectures, in which he urged the British to follow Rhodes's example of encouraging European settlement across Africa as a means of promoting the cause of civilisation – without injustice to the African, 'a child-type, with a happy-go-lucky disposition, but with no incentive to improvement'.[25] In South Africa, he suggested, the way forward was a policy of 'parallel institutions', as pioneered by Rhodes, based on 'white settlement to supply the steel framework and stimulus for enduring civilisation, and indigenous native institutions to express the specifically African character of the natives in their future development and civilisation'.[26] His own government had extended Rhodes's system to cover the whole Union. He did concede, however, that Africans who had become 'civilised and Europeanised' were entitled to the political rights of citizenship, but the tone of his lectures was paternalistic and, though well-received by his audience, drew mixed reactions in both Britain and South Africa.[27]

On returning home, Smuts became a member of the parliamentary select committee appointed by Hertzog to examine his native bills once again. Stung by liberal criticism of his views, Smuts approached the committee's deliberations in a more flexible frame of mind. Writing to Margaret Gillett, he indicated that his thoughts were turning towards accepting Hertzog's proposals for the Cape, but removing the colour bar in the South Africa Act (so that blacks could sit in Parliament) and adopting a provision that would enable Africans with educational qualifications to continue voting with whites. But the committee's deliberations stalled and native policy was deferred to a future session of Parliament, by which time a realignment of white political forces was under way.

◆

Differences over racial policy continued to be an issue of contention between Hertzog and Smuts and their respective supporters in the lengthy negotiations over Coalition and Fusion. Hertzog remained determined to remove black voters from the common roll and extend white control over the country's political structure. Smuts, who had consistently defended the Cape's century-old franchise, was insistent that it would be a mistake to alter the Union constitution or to attempt any single, comprehensive solution to the country's complex socio-political and racial circumstances. Hertzog's settlement, he predicted, would be the 'beginning of a new unsettlement'.[28] Yet Smuts was growing increasingly out of tune with right-wing sentiment in his own party as hardliners, such as Heaton Nicholls from Natal and Col Stallard from the Transvaal, began to do Hertzog's work for him. Though no liberal himself, Smuts found himself defending black franchise rights and voting against SAP reactionaries in the select committee of Parliament.

Fusion greatly increased Hertzog's political authority over Smuts within

the new United Party. Sensing there was much latent support within the former SAP for his amended native bills, Hertzog put them before Parliament in
1935, and again in 1936. He now proposed that Cape Natives be placed on a
separate roll, but given three white representatives in the House of Assembly,
as well as a Native Representative Council and more land under a Native Trust
and Land Bill. At the Joint Session of both Houses of Parliament, a troubled
Smuts voted in favour of proposals, leaving it to his lieutenant JH Hofmeyr to
lead liberal opposition to the legislation. 168 members voted in favour of the
Bills, and only 11 against them. Col Stallard voted against because Hertzog, in
his view, was being far too 'liberal'.

Smuts defended his abandonment of a cherished principle by referring to
'a tide of reaction' that those who felt as he did were powerless to resist.[29]
Although the legislation was not ideal, he contended, it contained 'the elements of justice and fair play, and the promise of fruitfulness for the future'
and provided a base from which to work for black advancement in years to
come. Of his own decision, he had this to say, 'Of course, I could have died in
the last ditch, so to say. I could have said "I fight to the bitter end for the Cape
Native Franchise" but what would have been the result? It would not have
been I that died, but the Natives, metaphorically speaking.'[30]

Many theories have been advanced for Smuts's *volte-face* in the historic
1936 debate. Bernard Friedman argues that Hofmeyr's defiant speech,
which – echoing Smuts's recent high-minded address at St Andrew's University – affirmed liberal values and called for courage in defence of freedom
and justice, was the one his leader should have made.[31] Why, it was wondered, had the principled Smuts made such a fateful surrender?[32] The answer
lies, surely, in Smuts's evolutionary approach to politics – and his instinct for
compromise. Realising that the opposition of the deputy leader to Hertzog's
legislation could split the United Party and leave him in the political wilderness at a time of rising European tension, he did what most conflicted party
politicians do – put expediency before principle.

◆

Not many years later, the uneasy alliance between Hertzog and Smuts fell
apart over the second of the two issues that had always divided them: South

Africa's obligation to the British Empire in the event of war. For Smuts, the international dangers outweighed the domestic; for Hertzog, it was the other way round.[33] On becoming prime minister again, Smuts inherited Hertzog's racial policies. His ministers chose not to further enforce segregation, but rather to let it run down – largely because a shortage of labour made the new laws impractical for a rapidly industrialising economy. Another reason for the slowing of segregation was the presence in Parliament of three highly effective Native Representatives – Messrs Brookes and Molteno and Mrs Margaret Ballinger – who saw to it that African demands were kept on the table. A relaxation of the application of the pass laws in 1942, however, led inevitably to a strong Nationalist counter-attack which failed to dislodge the United Party in the 1943 election.

Smuts's major pronouncement on colour policy during the war was a speech to the Institute of Race Relations in Cape Town 1942, where he took as his theme South Africa's economic development and its social consequences. Rather surprisingly, he refuted the theory that whites and blacks could live in separate territorial compartments: 'The whole trend both in this country and throughout Africa has been in the opposite direction … Isolation has gone and segregation has fallen on evil days … You might as well try to sweep the ocean back with a broom.'[34]

Social policy, he argued, had to be extended to all races. As to what was to distinguish him from the future architects of apartheid, he declared, 'When people ask me what the population of South Africa is I never say two millions. I think it is an outrage to say it is two millions. This country has a population of over ten millions, and that outlook which treats the African and the Native as not counting, is making the ghastliest mistake possible. If he is not much more, he is the beast of burden; he is the worker and you need him. He is carrying this country on his back.'[35]

Yet, as the historian Saul Dubow points out, on this occasion Smuts was less concerned with conceding segregation's shortcomings than with reinforcing the notion of white 'trusteeship', a concept which harked back to the time of Cecil Rhodes and had since been endorsed by the League of Nations.[36]

Conscious of his responsibilities to the country's black population, Smuts nevertheless went out of his way to invite constructive criticism from the Native Representatives in Parliament, who took up his invitation with alacrity. But in so doing, he gave his critics rods for his back.[37] His reactionary opponents accused him of promoting indiscriminate integration, while liberals accused him of failing to practise what he preached. In response to a formidable list of demands from Margaret Ballinger and her colleagues, the government extended social pensions to all races and substantially increased expenditure on black education, health and housing – subjecting the country's wartime economy to additional strain.

◆

By the end of World War II, however, a weary and disillusioned Smuts had become concerned at the widening breach between his government and the NRC, which had issued a ringing Declaration of Rights demanding equality between Africans and Europeans in law, politics and society. In 1946, an NRC resolution passed in Smuts's absence at the Paris Peace Conference, complained about the government's 'continuation of a policy of Fascism which is the antithesis of the letter and spirit of the Atlantic Charter and the United Nations Charter'.[38] The resolution brought the NRC into line with the African National Congress and the Indian National Congress and increased international criticism of Smuts. He gave vent to his frustration in a letter to his friends, the Moores, who had first-hand experience of living in Africa. 'The world,' he wrote, 'is reeling between the two poles of White and Colour.'[39] His own duty, he believed, was to keep South Africa steady, but on what basis, and how? On one hand, he was a humanist and the author of the Preamble to the Charter; on the other, he was a South African of European descent, proud of his civilisation and determined to maintain it. For that, he had been branded a hypocrite at the UN.[40]

Lady Moore replied to him by saying there was no possibility of compromise on the colour question: 'The trouble is that the subject is one which is difficult to be logical about because of the underlying fear, repulsion or whatever it is that the white man feels for the black and which to you in South Africa, with generations of colour-strife in your blood, is an essential element of your characters of which you are almost unaware ... English-people with their copy-book maxims and their smug humanitarian theories, cannot understand the instinct inherited from forebears who have had to fight black races for their very existence ... How can you have a practical compromise?' she asked.[41]

◆

How does one explain the contradiction between Smuts's belief in segregation and political inequality and his plea, at the end of the war, for the worldwide recognition of 'human rights'? Pretoria academics Christof Heyns and Willem Gravett provide the most likely explanation: Smuts's concern for human rights had grown out of his experience of the Anglo-Boer War and two World Wars. In his mind, human rights meant basic needs such as security, safety, freedom of expression and freedom of religion – values whose violation had led to devastating wars. It never meant that human rights were synonymous with political or racial equality.[42]

It was inconceivable to Smuts, Heyns and Gravett suggest, that the framers of the UN Charter could ever have intended to make political equality a fundamental human right: 'To do so would have meant the end of progress in countries where the "less progressive races" constituted the majority.'[43] That is why Smuts argued vigorously with Mrs Pandit at the UN that South Africa had not violated any fundamental rights within the Charter. It also explains why he advocated, along with Australia, the adoption of a clause in the Charter to ensure that the UN could not interfere in the domestic affairs of member states. His concern was not so much to protect individuals from their own governments, but to keep peoples safe from harm by other states.

The truth of the matter is that after World War II the elderly Smuts still held to the outdated nineteenth-century notion that the promotion of 'freedom' meant entrenching the values of Western Christian civilisation, in which the stronger, more advanced nations had a duty to look after the weak. What had changed over the course of his long public life was not his ideas, but the postwar international world around him.

◆

A practical compromise on race was always to elude Smuts, as it would any other politician of the mid-twentieth century. He returned from representing

Professor ZK Matthews.
Drum Social Histories/Baileys African History Archive/Africa Media Online

South Africa at the UN to find that relations between his government and the NRC had reached deadlock. Trying to retrieve the situation, he indicated in talks with Professor ZK Matthews and others in 1947 that he was thinking of substantially increasing the political rights of Africans, but still held out no promise of Africans being elected to Parliament.[44] The NRC was unimpressed, and decided to suspend negotiations until after the 1948 election. They were never to resume.

Smuts's final attempt to chart a way forward before the approaching election was to endorse, on behalf of his party, the report of the Native Laws Commission, chaired by Advocate Henry Fagan. The Fagan Report's main findings were that the separation of South Africans was a self-deceiving dream, that the migratory system was obsolete, and that black South Africans had to be accepted as a permanent part of the urban population. Four days later, the Nationalists produced their own pro-segregation blueprint, the Sauer Report, which they used to fight and win the 1948 election.

◆

The British politician Enoch Powell once lamented that all political lives, unless they are cut off in mid-stream at a happy juncture, end in failure because that is the nature of politics and of human affairs.[45] Smuts's political

231

life was no exception. His failure was not only in allowing power to slip from his hands in 1948, when he could have prevented it. It was also – as one who set himself higher standards than other men – in failing to address more boldly the one issue he had tried to avoid for much of his political life and which came to cast a shadow upon his once stellar reputation.

CHAPTER 25

Counsellor to Kings

Discussing his newly published biography of Woodrow Wilson, the American writer A Scott Berg argues that one cannot understand the United States in the twentieth century without understanding its twenty-eighth president.[1] The same could be said of South Africa and Smuts. There are uncanny resemblances between Wilson and South Africa's foremost figure of those times. Both were child prodigies, raised in simple, religious homes (Wilson's Protestant, Smuts's Calvinist), whose adult lives were infused with a sense of morality and piety and whose intellectual vitality could not disguise a deep-rooted ambition to make history as much as teach it.

They were both men of the South, who grew up in segregated societies which had suffered defeat in civil wars that had ended in devastation and humiliation. Each was a devout Christian, deeply aware of race, who thought that separation would be in the best interests of whites and blacks and saw no iniquity in racial segregation. Wilson, says Berg, felt 'as right as he was righteous' and hoped to 'make the humble doctrine of service to humanity a cardinal and guiding principle of world politics'.[2] Smuts thought likewise.

In her much-acclaimed book, *Peacemakers – Six Months that Changed the World*, Canadian historian Margaret Macmillan also draws attention to the similarities between Wilson and Smuts.[3] Both were idealistic thinkers, she writes, having 'a fondness for dealing with the great questions, deep religious and ethical convictions; and a desire to make the world a better place … Both were sober and restrained on the surface, yet passionate and sensitive underneath. Both combined vast self-righteousness with huge ambition and were quick to see the inconsistencies in others while remaining blind to their own.'[4] Mark Mazower describes both men as 'instinctive moralists, idealizing the power of communal ethics over the selfish pursuit of state or sectional interests, convinced above all that the sources of conflict vanished when men of lofty judgment approached things as a whole'.[5]

Smuts and US President Woodrow Wilson during World War I. Museum Africa, Johannesburg

Scott Berg says of Wilson, 'Beholden to nobody, he had risen to his position through brainpower. Wedding the complexity of his intellect with the simplicity of his faith, placing principles before politics, he followed his conscience, never first checking public opinion. He spoke only for himself, and he found much of the nation agreeing with what he had to say.'[6] The former president of Princeton University, an intellectual like Smuts, had succeeded in transforming an inward-looking country with limited defensive capabilities into a competent military power. But like Smuts, he divided opinion among his countrymen, many of whom found him too high-minded and had no liking for his Utopian scheme for a new and better post-war world order. It was said of Wilson that once he had emerged with a decision on an issue, particularly one which mobilised his aspirations for high achievement, 'his mind snapped shut. In such cases, he felt that his decision was the only possible one, morally as well as intellectually.' However, where the idealistic Wilson differed from Smuts was his inability to agree to practical solutions or to compromise with those who disagreed with him.[7]

During World War I, Smuts found in Wilson a kindred spirit: 'It is this moral idealism and this vision of a better world which had up-borne us through the dark night of this war,' he said of the American. 'It is for us to labour in the re-making of that world to better ends, to plan its international reorganisation on lines of international freedom and justice, and to re-establish among the classes and nations that goodwill which is the only sure foundation for any international system.'[8] With a self-confidence startling in retrospect, Smuts took it upon himself to put Wilson's 'rather nebulous ideas'[9] for a League of Nations into coherent form. In December 1918, five weeks after the Armistice was signed, he wrote for the Imperial war cabinet what an impressed Lloyd George described as 'one of the most able state papers he had ever read'.[10] It was published under the title 'The League of Nations – A Practical Suggestion' and sent to Wilson, who liked what he saw, particularly the author's suggestion that establishing the League should be the first task of the Paris Peace Conference. He described Smuts as 'a brick'[11] and incorporated many of his ideas – including the notion of 'mandates' for former German colonies – into his own proposals for the League. Having his system of mandates accepted by the American was a triumph for Smuts, as Wilson might never have accepted the concept if it had come from another source.[12]

Smuts seems to have been mildly amused at having his ideas appropriated by the American president. Writing to Margaret Gillett in January 1919, he expressed his satisfaction 'with the way things were going. The League of Nations is making headway rapidly. Lloyd George says Wilson talks of the scheme as if he is the author of it, and may yet give it to the world as his own special creation. Who minds as long as the work is done.'[13]

Smuts's enthusiasm for Wilson began to wane sharply, however, during the drawn-out peace negotiations in Paris, when he failed in his repeated attempts to persuade either the American or Lloyd George that imposing harsh terms upon a defeated Germany would be foolishly short-sighted and counterproductive.[14] After warning the President that there would be terrible disillusionment if 'people came to think that we are not concluding a Wilson peace, that we are not keeping our promises to the world or faith with the public,' he wrote despairingly to Alice Clark,[15] '... I get no support from Wilson. I do not even know whether he really agrees with me.'[16] He expressed his disappointment in both Wilson and Lloyd George, 'who are smaller men than I should ever have thought'. As Ingham observes, although Wilson shared Smuts's qualities of 'idealism, intellect and a preacher's fervour', in this

235

instance he happened to be preaching what Smuts believed to be a heretical doctrine.[17]

Nonetheless, when a disillusioned and ailing Wilson left office, having failed to win the US Senate's support for the League of Nations, Smuts wrote in a widely syndicated article in the *New York Evening Post* that the Covenant of the League which Wilson had fought for and protected was 'one of the great creative documents of human history'.[18] Predicting that Americans would one day rank the outgoing president alongside Washington and Lincoln, he asserted that hundreds of years hence Wilson's name 'will be one of the greatest in history'[19] – a judgement that posterity has not entirely vindicated.

Wilson's death in 1924 greatly saddened Smuts, who wrote that 'this heroic figure will stand out ever more clearly and his work will be recognised as among America's greatest contributions to the world'.[20] His assessment of Wilson's seminal contribution to US foreign policy has been echoed many times since, by Henry Kissinger among others.[21]

◆

Though they did not always see eye to eye, Great Britain's most eminent statesman of the early twentieth century, David Lloyd George, also held Smuts in special regard. Their first encounter occurred in 1906 during Smuts's démarche on behalf of the Transvaal to members of Campbell-Bannerman's cabinet. They were to meet again on Smuts's triumphal arrival in London in 1917, when the British prime minister – aware of the 'Boer General's' capabilities (and propaganda value) brought him into the British war cabinet and began to deploy him, in preference to his own ministers, on a variety of delicate assignments.

He described Smuts as the 'gifted and versatile Dutchman, who could be safely trusted to examine into the intricacies of any of our multifarious problems and unravel and smooth them out'.[22] Smuts's detailed memorandum to the cabinet on how Britain should conduct the war, and Lloyd George's dissatisfaction with his own generals, led to the visitor being offered the command of British forces in Palestine, an offer that he turned down regretfully.

Hancock puts his finger on the similarities between Smuts and Lloyd George: 'Both men had the gift of envisaging the problems of war comprehensively, not just as a heap of bits and pieces ... Lloyd George, like Smuts, was audacious, experimental, resilient. Both men possessed the gift of coming fresh to the work of each successive day ... [but] whereas Smuts was never content unless he could see his day-to-day tasks in deep perspective, Lloyd George was intent upon the immediate foreground. Smuts, so Merriman had said, was a "ruthless philosopher". Nobody had ever accused Lloyd George of being philosophical.'[23]

However, the intellectual and temperamental differences between the two were bound to surface sooner or later, as they did at the Paris Conference. With a discontented and vengeful electorate to satisfy, Lloyd George was intent upon exacting reparations from the losers. Smuts, by this time no longer a member of the war cabinet, had set his sights upon a peace that would endure. Refusing to be intimidated by any of the Big Four in Paris – Wilson, Lloyd George, Clemenceau and Orlando (of Italy) – and supported only by John Maynard Keynes, he succeeded in having the British prime minister call the war cabinet and Dominion leaders together to consider Germany's response to the Allies' peace terms. But when Lloyd George, having been given the necessary authority, refused to alter the terms, a furious Smuts found himself alone in his opposition. His relationship with Lloyd George was never to recover.

◆

Smuts and John Maynard Keynes, the twentieth century's most eminent economist, became friends and allies in the run-up to the Paris Conference in 1919. Both were visionary thinkers who understood that mankind had somehow to be saved from the excesses and barbarities of warfare. They believed that a peace settlement required two things: an economic and financial plan to resurrect the European economy, and the creation of a new dispute-resolving international order. Keynes was as appalled as Smuts at the extent of reparations demanded by the victorious Allies. He insisted that if compensation was set too high, it would hurt not only the German economy, but that of Europe and the world as well.

He and Smuts would commiserate with one another over their inability to persuade Allied leaders to their way of thinking. In a letter, Smuts described how the two of them would often sit together after a good dinner and 'rail against the world and the current flood'.[24] He would then tell Keynes that there was 'nothing for it but to pray like the old Griqua chief whose tribe was beset by grave danger, "Lord, save Thy people. Lord, we are lost unless Thou savest us. Lord, this is no work for children. It is not enough this time to send Thy Son. Lord, Thou must come Thyself." And then we laugh, and behind the laughter is Hoover's terrible picture of 30 million people who must die unless there is some great intervention,' Smuts wrote despairingly.[25]

Smuts strongly urged Keynes to launch a full frontal attack on the provisions of the Paris Treaty, but in a letter of farewell before leaving for home, he had second thoughts and suggested that it might be better to be constructive rather than destructive.[26] Keynes took no notice. His seminal book *The Economic Consequences of the Peace* had a seismic effect on the Versailles Treaty, giving succour to the Germans, pleasing the isolationists in the US, and damaging international confidence generally.

◆

Smuts's rapport with Winston Churchill was close and long-lasting: the pair kept in touch with each other for almost 50 years. 'Between these two friends,' Jannie Smuts recalled, 'there existed a warmth of feeling and mutual admiration that was touching to behold. In public, it was "Prime Minister" and "Field Marshal", but otherwise it was simply "Winston" and "Jan".'[27] Given their contrasting characters, the relationship was an attraction of opposites: Churchill was a Falstaffian figure who took no exercise, smoked and drank a lot, worked late into the night and only reached his desk in mid-morning; Smuts was ascetic, a non-smoker and occasional drinker who loved walking and going to bed and rising early. He was said to be the only person who could cut Churchill short during one of the British war leader's late-night soliloquies and declare that he was off to sleep.

Like Lloyd George, Churchill was a member of the Liberal Party cabinet canvassed by Smuts in 1906, but the two only became close after World War I when Churchill, who had lost his cabinet seat in the aftermath of Gallipoli, returned to centre stage as secretary of state for war, with special responsibility for the Royal Air Force. Here, his respect and admiration for Smuts's

Smuts and son Jannie with Winston and Clementine Churchill during World War II.
Museum Africa, Johannesburg

capabilities were nurtured. After the war, the two men embarked on an irregular correspondence in which genuine concern for each other's political fortunes was intermixed with generous doses of flattery. After Smuts had dodged bullets in the miners' strike of 1922, Churchill sent him the following telegram: 'Warmest congratulations your escape. Urge you to take greatest care of yourself. Your life is invaluable South Africa and British Empire.'[28] In the same year, after Churchill had lost his parliamentary seat in Dundee, Smuts's cable of sympathy ended, 'But perhaps it is as well that you get a short spell of rest after the very heavy labours you have had to bear recently. I trust you will soon be all right and all the better to do the great work which is still before you.'[29]

Churchill sent Smuts a copy of his new book on World War I, ending his accompanying letter with the words, 'Your friendship is always much cherished by me.'[30] Smuts laid it on with a trowel in reply: 'I envy you the great gift of being a man of action and a great writer at the same time. Julius Caesar was that rare combination. And although you are not as Francophobe as he was, your book will stand comparison with the Gallic War!'[31]

239

World War II brought Churchill and Smuts even closer together. In the run-up to the war, both men in their different ways had sought to alert the British people to the storm-clouds building up over the European continent. In his rectoral address at St Andrew's University in 1934, Smuts warned presciently that Nazism and Fascism were beginning to threaten the essential freedoms that were so dear to Britons. Churchill spent most of the 1930s – as historian Lawrence James puts it – persistently and rightly crying wolf over Hitler, because 'he had understood the nature of the beast and its diet from the start'.[32] At the first meeting of his cabinet after the momentous war vote in the South African parliament, Smuts received from Churchill the following telegram: 'From First Lord of the Admiralty to General Smuts. I rejoice to feel that we are once again on commando together.'[33]

Throughout the war, Churchill consulted Smuts regularly on military strategy and the appointment of key personnel. 'When Smuts came to England,' wrote John Colville, Churchill's private secretary, 'Churchill would drop all else and listen attentively to the accented words of wisdom, spoken in high staccato tones, which poured from the South African patriarch on all the issues of present and future policy ... There were few of Churchill's colleagues in the British Government whose views carried the same weight.'[34] Lord Moran, Churchill's acerbic personal physician, wrote that 'He [Smuts] is the only man who has any influence with the PM, indeed he is the only ally I have in pressing counsels of common sense on the PM. Smuts sees so clearly that Winston is irreplaceable that he may make an effort to persuade him to be sensible.'[35] A cabinet member, Harold Macmillan, declared that it was very good for Churchill to have a colleague older than himself whom he could not browbeat.[36]

In his War Diaries, Churchill's right-hand Lord Alanbrooke writes how Smuts came closer than anyone to realising how close the British war leader was to a breakdown in late 1943.[37] After a dinner in Egypt, Smuts drew Alanbrooke aside to say he was 'not at all happy with the condition of the PM'. Churchill was working too hard, exhausting himself and then having to rely on drink to stimulate him. He was in doubt whether Churchill would be able to stay the course. Alanbrooke harboured the same fear himself – which proved, in the end, to be unfounded.

After the war, Churchill and Smuts were to suffer similarly unexpected and stunning rejection by their respective electorates. Churchill's loss of the premiership in 1945 came as a rude shock to Smuts, who regarded the new Labour government as lacking in sufficient experience and understanding of international affairs. Writing to Margaret Clark, he observed that Britain had lost a leader who really was not conservative, 'but a great human, with vast experience and a great breadth of sympathies. ... to be so decisively rejected in the very hour of victory by the people whom he saved by his courage and stupendous exertions is truly the unkindest cut of all.'[38]

Smuts went on to predict a similar destiny for himself, 'I know my fate from what happened after the last war. Rejection and repudiation will once more close the chapter and end the glory. It will break no hearts ... Nothing can add or subtract from what is done and finished. And I shall face whatever may come with no wry face.'[39] He remained true to his word. His High Commissioner in London, Leif Egeland, recalls a luncheon in Cambridge less than two weeks after his unexpected defeat at the hands of Dr Malan, when, after conferring an honorary degree upon a visibly depressed Churchill, a relaxed Smuts teased his old wartime colleague, saying, 'Look at him, there he sits. They kicked us out. It's good for us old fogeys to be kicked out. But I call him Demogorgon [a primal Greek god] – he marched with destiny; let us never forget it.'[40]

◆

Another world figure with whom Smuts had a long-lasting friendship was Dr Chaim Weizmann, founder and first president of Israel. Along with Lloyd George and Arthur Balfour, Smuts had been the driving force behind the Balfour Declaration of 1917 that Palestine would one day offer a home to the Jewish people. Smuts had supported the proposal because of its biblical implications and because of his understanding, as an Afrikaner, of the longings of an oppressed people. In 1922, he described the plan for a Jewish homeland as 'one of the outstanding results of the Great War, and one of the greatest acts of reparation in the history of the World'.[41]

In 1930, after the publication of a White Paper in Britain which Zionists regarded as a departure from the Declaration, at Weizmann's request Smuts took matters up with Ramsay MacDonald, as well as his predecessor Lloyd

George. Failing to obtain satisfaction from MacDonald, who denied that there had been any backtracking, he gave a copy of their correspondence to the press to ensure that the British government could not renege on its promise. In South Africa, he rallied the United Party to oppose, unanimously but unavailingly, the Hertzog government's legislation to curb Jewish immigration.

In a letter to Weizmann in 1944, Smuts commiserated with him over the inability of the Jews to establish their homeland, saying that Arab pressure was forcing the British government to move slowly. In May 1947, he responded to a 'sad letter' from Weizmann by saying that much as he (Smuts) longed for an undivided Palestine, partition seemed to be the only way out.

After the UN approved a partition plan a few months later, Weizmann wrote in a letter to Smuts: 'At this milestone in Jewish history, I think with feelings of deepest gratitude of your noble friendship and unwavering support throughout the years from 1917 onward for the cause of my people. May God bless you and guard you. Affectionately.'[42] To which Smuts replied, 'I was deeply moved by your kind wire from New York on the passing of the partition motion. ... My service in the cause has been small, but it has been wholehearted all the way, and in all weathers.'[43] On the eve of his election defeat in 1948, Smuts announced South Africa's recognition of the state of Israel – among the first countries in the world to do so.

Four months later, against the wishes of his family, an ailing Smuts journeyed by air to London to speak at a dinner in honour of Weizmann, and launch an appeal for funds to plant a forest in Israel to be named after him. He paid tribute to 'Chaim Weizmann, the scientist, the great Zionist, the indomitable leader who, after his people had been all but wiped out in the greatest purge of history, assembled the remnants, led them back to the ancient homeland in the face of the heaviest opposition, and welded them once more into a sovereign state among the nations. Surely his achievement bears comparison to Moses.'[44]

◆

France held Smuts in much lower regard, however. The French could never understand why Britain let a Commonwealth politician interfere in the affairs of Europe. In 1917, when Lloyd George sent Smuts secretly to confer with an Austrian emissary in Switzerland, Georges Clemenceau was heard to say, 'Lloyd George is a fool, and an extra fool for sending Smuts, who doesn't even know where Austria is.'[45] French resentment of Smuts deepened at the Paris Peace Conference, where Clemenceau was hell-bent on destroying the German economy and altering the balance of power in Europe in his country's favour. Smuts's prescription for European peace was exactly the opposite: he argued that European prosperity could only be achieved by rebuilding Germany and reviving its economy. Clemenceau referred scornfully to Smuts as 'le saboteur du Traité de Versailles'[46] and regarded him as a traitor to the French cause.

Smuts's view of the French was no less jaundiced. Writing to the new British prime minister, Bonar Law, after Versailles, he expressed a fear that Britain might lean over too far in favour of France: 'French policy was for centuries the curse of Europe and it was only the rise of Germany in the first place that changed her attitude. Now Germany is down and out, and France is once more the leader of the Continent with all the old bad instincts fully alive in her.'[47] He predicted a revived France would pose a threat to the British Empire and suggested that 'we should keep a sharp look-out in that direction'. In 1942 he told King George VI: 'We can never trust the French, for they can never forget that they were masters of Europe for over 200 years.'[48]

As a member of Churchill's inner circle of advisers in World War II, Smuts came into contact with the France's de facto leader in exile, the notoriously prickly General Charles de Gaulle. Relations between de Gaulle, the British and the Americans were always fractious and Smuts, who believed that Allied unity was vital, took it upon himself to act as intermediary, writing to de Gaulle in 1942 to say that he welcomed the opportunity of making contact again, and pointing out that petty trivialities ought not to be allowed to impede co-operation between the Allies.[49] He assured de Gaulle of Churchill's goodwill and suggested a meeting between the two to clear the air: 'Between two such men as you and Mr Churchill there should in this crisis be the utmost frankness and mutual confidence and any little differences should be thrashed out in personal exchanges.'[50]

Yet there were times Smuts could not conceal his exasperation with the French. When he saw France giving the Germans free passage through Tunis to supply Rommel's Afrika Korps, he wrote, 'If God would only send them a women, another Joan of Arc, for her men have failed her.'[51] In late 1943, he really put his foot in it – as far as the French were concerned – in his 'Explosive' speech to the Empire Parliamentary Association. Thinking he was addressing a closed meeting, he gave this pessimistic assessment of France's future. 'A nation that has once been overtaken by a catastrophe such as she has suffered, reaching to the foundations of her nationhood, will not easily resume her old place again. We are dealing with one of the greatest and most-far-reaching catastrophes in history, the like of which I have not read of. The upward climb will be a bitter and a long one. France has gone, and will be gone in our day and perhaps for many a day.'[52] When these remarks were reported in the British press, there was understandable fury across the Channel.

◆

For a South African brought up in humble rural surroundings, Smuts was flattered – as Nelson Mandela was to be many years later – to be courted and lionised by the crowned heads of Britain and Europe. On his first visit to London during World War I, he felt out of place and resisted invitations from the great and the good, preferring the company of the Gilletts and the Clarks in the English countryside. But time mellowed him and enhanced his ability to mix with all kinds of men and women, 'including those in high stations'.[53] In 1918, King George V confided in his diary that 'He is a very agreeable and interesting man.'[54] The King was so impressed with Smuts's capabilities as a member of the war cabinet that, in 1921, he asked him to draft the speech from the Throne at the opening of the Irish Parliament. Thereafter, Smuts was a frequent weekend visitor to Windsor Castle and other royal palaces. Even when leader of the opposition in South Africa and no longer prime minister, he would always be invited, whenever he visited London, to Windsor or Sandringham by King George V and Queen Mary.

He often took the liberty of writing personal letters to the King and Queen and, in the midst of a crisis in the MacDonald cabinet in the early 1930s, George V once again called on him for counsel. Smuts wrote afterwards, 'it shows what faith the dear old King has in me and how much he likes to look to me for help and advice'.[55] The King made notes in his diary after all of

Smuts's visits, and refers on several occasions to long and interesting talks between them about 'the Empire'.[56]

Smuts was to become even more of a friend to King George VI, Queen Elizabeth and their two daughters. Once again, it was war that brought them together. Like his father, the King frequently called on Smuts for advice and invited him to spend weekends with the royal family when in Britain. Years later, the late and much lamented KwaZulu-Natal historian and raconteur, David Rattray, a friend of the royal family, would often recount how the elderly Queen Mother had sung to him, in passable Afrikaans, some of the words of *Sarie Marais*, the song that Smuts had taught her at Balmoral – and that was to be played at her funeral. Churchill thus had little difficulty in persuading George VI to make Smuts a British Field Marshal. The honour pleased Smuts, but not as much as it delighted Nationalist newspapers in South Africa, who never failed to use the title ironically in order to demonstrate that 'Field Marshal Smuts' was more British than Afrikaner.

Smuts's invitation to the royal family to visit South Africa in 1947 had a twofold purpose – to give the King a holiday break after the strains of the war years and to consolidate his own support among English-speaking voters ahead of the forthcoming general election. The King, for his part, was keen to help Smuts dampen the secessionist agitation of DF Malan and his colleagues. On 21 February 1947, George VI opened the South African parliament, the first time in the history of the Commonwealth that the monarch had opened a parliament outside Britain. The King took advantage of the occasion to invest Smuts with another rare honour – membership of the 24-strong Order of Merit.

Britain was not the only country whose royal family felt indebted to Smuts. As we have seen, in mid-1941, George VI's cousin, King George II of the Hellenes and a large entourage of relatives, including his son and daughter-in-law, Paul and Frederika, were given shelter in South Africa as refugees from the Nazi invasion of Greece. Smuts appointed a member of his cabinet, Major Piet van der Byl, to look after the King, who eventually made his headquarters in London and thereafter in Egypt. The forward-looking Smuts believed that the preservation and restoration of the monarchy in Greece was important not only for that country's post-war stability, but also for the 'vital Mediterranean interests of the British Commonwealth'.[57] At the war's end, it was largely at Smuts's urging that the monarchy was restored in Greece.

Among royalty and in the upper echelons of European society during World War II, the by now elderly Smuts was known as 'a wise old bird',[58] a staunch friend to Britain and British interests. On meeting him for the first time in Cairo in 1942, Lord Alanbrooke wrote of the experience: 'Smuts I look upon as one of the biggest of nature's gentlemen that I have ever seen. A wonderful clear grasp of all things coupled with the most exceptional charm. Interested in all matters, and gifted with the most marvellous judgment.'[59]

That helps to explain why Smuts, the statesman, was called upon as a counsellor by commoners and kings.

CHAPTER 26

Envoi

The historian Hermann Giliomee, in his fine book *The Last Afrikaner Leaders*, poses some of the questions that biographers have to answer when evaluating the quality of political leaders. What was in their minds when they made policy? What role did vision play in their thinking? And how should we, with the advantage of hindsight, assess their achievements today?[1]

In his notably unstarry-eyed account of Jan Smuts's life, published in the 1980s, the distinguished British historian of Africa, Kenneth Ingham, concluded that when writing about Smuts it would be wrong to over-emphasise his segregationist views.[2] Race, in the first half of the twentieth century, even in African society, was not as sensitive an issue or thought to be the problem it would later become. In *Long Walk to Freedom*, Nelson Mandela refers to his excitement at being able to listen to Smuts at a graduation ceremony at Fort Hare in 1939. He found Smuts a 'sympathetic figure', whose accent in English was almost as poor as his own: 'I cared more that he had helped to found the League of Nations, promoting freedom around the world, than the fact that he had repressed freedom at home. ... Along with my fellow classmates, I heartily applauded him, cheering Smuts' call to do battle for the freedom of Europe, forgetting that we did not have that freedom here in our own land.'[3]

Smuts's paternalistic attitude was far from unusual in his day: many members of his own political party showed far less sympathy for other races than he. To the technically advanced 'Europeans' of those times, it seemed inconceivable that Africans in general should be accepted as equals. It took several decades – and two World Wars – before attitudes began to change.

Even today, the assumption that history is a narrative of human progress in which some races have progressed further than others is still widely held. As the historian of Empire, Lawrence James, observes, Western notions of superiority have still not vanished entirely; they permeate the sermons preached to the 'Third World' on human rights, and form the basis of the disparaging modern concept of the 'failed state'.[4]

Where Smuts can be faulted is in not making provision – in his philosophy and political outlook – for cultivated Africans of the likes of DDT Jabavu, ZK Matthews and many others, who met and often superseded the levels of education and 'civilised' standards he was always so anxious to maintain. Reluctant though his acceptance of Hertzog's scrapping of the non-racial franchise in 1936 might have been, it deprived him of the backing of educated Africans, the one group who might have supported his notion of a qualified franchise that would have kept the vote in responsible hands. Here was the hole at the heart of holism that Smuts was never able to fill.

Yet both he (and Hertzog, for that matter) accepted that black Africans were citizens of an undivided South Africa, who had to be accommodated within one overarching political framework. If the gradualist in him gave no indication of where segregation might lead South Africa, he foresaw that Nationalist-style apartheid would endanger rather than safeguard the future of whites. In his heart of hearts, he knew that JH Hofmeyr and not DF Malan was right, which is why he resolutely defended his lieutenant against the reactionaries in his own ranks. His confidant, Dr Ernie Malherbe, believed that Smuts wished for 'a new orientation' after the 1948 election, but was too old and tired to take on the tremendous task of building a new, more forward-looking political party.[5] To adapt one of Smuts's favourite aphorisms, by then the dogs had barked, and the caravan moved on.

After Smuts's death, his once-powerful United Party gradually and hesitantly moved away from old-fashioned segregation. Though standing always for 'white leadership', the UP advocated an extension of black political rights and the incorporation of all races into the economy. A confrontation over Verwoerd's plan to link the granting of more land to Africans (under the 1936 legislation) to the independence of the reserves in 1959 caused eleven MPs (out of 53) to walk out of the UP and form their own party. The Progressive Party in due course proposed a similar form of the qualified franchise that Smuts had dangled before Hertzog some 30 years earlier, a policy which found little favour with white voters. With the rump of the UP failing to offer any convincing alternative to apartheid, Smuts's old party continued to drift into irrelevance, until it disbanded in 1977. Whether he could or would have saved it had he been younger, is one of those tantalising political questions that will always be open to conjecture.

◆

South Africa has been fortunate, at critical times in its relatively short history, to have produced a handful of inspirational leaders who have not only directed the country's affairs with dedication and skill, but made their mark on the wider world also. After the Anglo-Boer War, it was the Afrikaner generals Botha, Smuts and eventually Hertzog who sought to persuade their white compatriots to set aside deep-rooted animosities and build a nation. Almost a century later, Nelson Mandela, Thabo Mbeki and others seized the opportunity provided by a faltering apartheid regime to negotiate a political settlement with their own historic foes.

These nation-building exercises, a little less than a century apart, required political leadership of the highest order. They brought out the talents of four exceptional individuals, two of whom influenced South Africa's political and economic development more than anyone else. Smuts was called upon by his comrade-in-arms, Botha, to run the government of the fledgling Union of South Africa. In time, he not only directed the fortunes of the Union, but became a statesman of world renown. Less than a century later, Mandela made the much younger Mbeki his prime minister and de facto chief executive. Besides putting his imprint firmly upon post-apartheid South Africa, Mbeki set about regenerating the entire continent of Africa. Like Smuts, he was instrumental both in determining the kind of nation the new South Africa would become and in defining the role he believed the country should play on the African continent and in international affairs. Like Smuts, he leaves a legacy that will endure – for good or ill – long after his departure from the political stage.

While their differences in background, temperament and achievements defy comparison, Smuts and Mbeki have another overriding feature in common. Neither is remembered with much affection by the majority of South Africans today. Smuts's views on race make him anathema to the current post-apartheid generation. For entirely different reasons, Mbeki – ignominiously forced out of office and into retirement – is also looked upon with disfavour by the ruling regime and its followers. His legacy to the country is a leadership vacuum that shows no sign of being filled.

There are other curious similarities between these two once powerful individuals. Besides being standard-bearers for far more popular personalities – Louis Botha in Smuts's case and Nelson Mandela in Mbeki's, in forging a political settlement both men had to fight the militants within their own ranks who fiercely resented having to lay down arms. Lionised for a time around the world for their achievements, both spent long periods out of the country trying to solve the problems of others, only to be accused by their opponents of neglecting their obligations at home. They each took their eyes off their domestic constituencies and were caught by surprise when ejected from office. In the result, neither of these founding figures is honoured as much as he might have been in the South Africa of today.

◆

In Smuts's case, it remains extraordinary, even in retrospect, that he was thought by so many of his countrymen to be less than a true Afrikaner – a man who did not have the interests of his own people at heart. So great was the bitterness felt by many Boers at his rapprochement with the British at a time when the wounds of the Anglo-Boer War were still raw, that for most of the second half of his life he was a figure of hate for many of his erstwhile admirers. He was charged with forsaking his language and culture in order to achieve the fame and glory that his own country could not give him. It also rankled that when in power, he never associated himself closely with the struggle for recognition of the Afrikaans language.[6]

These critics could never comprehend, or, if they did, readily subscribe to his Olympian philosophy that mankind's evolution lay along the paths of healing, holiness and 'wholeness' – the gradual progression of disparate parts into a greater whole. This translated, in practical political terms, into Afrikaner–English unity, freedom and economic security for the Union within the Empire, and recognition of South Africa's independent status in the wider world. His opponents, led initially by Hertzog and then by Malan, began from a much more inward-looking premise, and their minds and his were never really to meet.

His intellectualism and forbidding public persona did not help either.

The obelisk on Smuts Koppie, Doornkloof.

Political popularity is more than a matter of abstract theorising and appeals to the better nature of voters: it requires an ability to touch hearts and minds. Smuts was able to reach out to English-speakers, thousands of whom followed him into two world wars, but to one section of Afrikanerdom only. After the Anglo-Boer War, he could never persuade the more diehard of his countrymen to his side. Unlike Hertzog, who saw his fellow Afrikaners as a group whose primary task was to establish its own identity, Smuts wished the Afrikaner to become part of a much larger entity – the diverse British Empire – which embraced many races and creeds.

Yet the great paradox of his life was that – as Leif Egeland pointed out – it was precisely because Smuts was an Afrikaner and a Boer soldier that he built up such a formidable reputation worldwide. On his many visits abroad, and in his personal life, he kept alive the image of the Boer general, 'one of the most romantic and bravest figures in history'.[7] While many of his countrymen derided him for being an Englishman at heart, in Britain and around the world 'General Smuts' was respected and revered for being a true and patriotic Afrikaner – the finest example of his tribe.

251

Notes

PREFACE

1. William Hazlitt, Characteristics, in the manner of Rochefoucauld's Maxims, 158 (1823).

PROLOGUE

1 Sir Louis Blom-Cooper, 'Jan Christiaan Smuts (1870–1950): Middle Templar extraordinary', in *Advocate*, August 2013, p 40.
2 Winston Churchill, quoted by Lord Moran in *Diaries*, p 317.
3 Alan Paton, quoted by Sir Louis Blom-Cooper, 'Jan Christiaan Smuts', p 40.
4 Piet Beukes, *The Holistic Smuts: A Study in Personality*, p 41.
5 Alan Paton, *The Forum*, September 1952, quoted by Beukes, Ibid, p 38.
6 Emerson, *Essays, History*.
7 Winston Churchill, House of Commons, 26 June 1952.

CHAPTER I
'TOTSIENS, OUBAAS'

1 *Rand Daily Mail*, 12 September 1950.
2 Ibid.
3 DF Malan, *Rand Daily Mail*, 13 September 1950.
4 Clement Attlee, *The Times*, 12 September 1950.
5 Winston Churchill, *Rand Daily Mail*, 14 September 1950.
6 *Die Transvaler*, quoted in *Rand Daily Mail*, 13 September 1950.
7 *The Star*, 14 September 1950.
8 Pika Zulu, *Rand Daily Mail*, 13 September 1950.
9 *Rand Daily Mail*, 14 September 1950.
10 Ds Johan Reyneke, *Rand Daily Mail*, 16 September 1950.

11 *Rand Daily Mail*, 16 September 1950.
12 *The Times* (London), 12 September 1950.
13 *Rand Daily Mail*, 12 September 1950.
14 *The Star*, 12 September 1950.

CHAPTER 2
A QUEER FELLOW

1 Although he later became known as Jan Christian Smuts, his second name was spelt 'Christiaan' with two a's, according to his entry in the baptismal register.
2 FS Crafford, *Jan Smuts: A Biography*, p 5.
3 JC Smuts, *Jan Christian Smuts*, p 12.
4 WK Hancock, *Smuts: The Sanguine Years 1870–1919*, p 11.
5 Ibid, p 10.
6 Ibid, p 13.
7 Ibid, p 15.
8 Smuts, *Jan Christian Smuts*, p 19.
9 Crafford, *Jan Smuts*, p 11.
10 Piet Beukes, *The Romantic Smuts*, p 19.
11 Hancock, *Smuts: The Sanguine Years*, p 16.
12 Beukes, *The Romantic Smuts*, p 20.
13 Smuts was never to meet Rhodes in person. This meeting was their only, indirect, contact.
14 Piet Meiring, *Smuts the Patriot*, p 17.
15 Trewhella Cameron, *Jan Smuts: An Illustrated Biography*, p 21.
16 Ibid.
17 Hancock, *Smuts: The Sanguine Years*, p 42.
18 Ibid, p 50.
19 Meiring, *Smuts the Patriot*, p 22.
20 Hancock, *Smuts: The Sanguine Years*, pp 43–44.
21 Ibid, p 44.
22 Meiring, *Smuts the Patriot*, p 23.

23 Ibid, p 21.
24 It was eventually published in 1973 by Wayne State University Press, Detroit, in the form of a photocopied manuscript.

CHAPTER 3
BURSTING WITH IDEALISM

1 FS Crafford, *Jan Smuts: A Biography,* p 14.
2 O Geyser, *Jan Smuts and his International Contemporaries*, p 6.
3 Piet Meiring, *Smuts the Patriot*, p 26.
4 WK Hancock, *Smuts: The Sanguine Years 1870–1919*, p 58.
5 Kenneth Ingham, *Jan Christian Smuts: The Conscience of a South African,* p 16.
6 JC Smuts, *Jan Christian Smuts*, p 37.
7 Crafford, Jan Smuts, p 29.
8 Charles van Onselen, *The Fox and the Flies*, p 162.
9 Crafford, *Jan Smuts*, p 28.
10 Meiring, *Smuts the Patriot*, p 38.
11 HC Armstrong, *Grey Steel: JC Smuts – A Study in Arrogance,* p 73.
12 Walter Nimocks, *Milner's Young Men*, p 12.
13 Ibid, p 9.
14 Nimocks, Milner's Young Men, p 18
15 Trewhella Cameron, *Jan Smuts: An Illustrated Biography*, p 27.
16 Crafford, *Jan Smuts*, p 37.
17 Ibid, p 36.
18 Ibid, p 37.

CHAPTER 4
BOER STRATEGIST

1 Also called the 'South African War', the 'Second Anglo-Boer War' or, in Afrikaans, 'Die Tweede Vryheidsoorlog'.
2 Martin Meredith, *Diamonds, Gold and War: The Making of South Africa,* p 417.
3 WK Hancock; *Smuts: The Sanguine Years 1870–1919*, p 110.

4 FS Crafford, *Jan Smuts: A Biography,* p 39.
5 Kenneth Ingham, *Jan Christian Smuts: The Conscience of a South African*, p 34.
6 Crafford, *Jan Smuts*, p 40.
7 Hancock, *Smuts: The Sanguine Years,* p 107.
8 JC Smuts, *Jan Christian Smuts,* p 51.
9 Ibid, p 50.
10 Arthur G Barlow, *Almost in Confidence*, p 85.
11 Meredith, *Diamonds, Gold and War,* p 434.
12 Ibid, p 435.
13 Smuts, *Jan Christian Smuts*, p 53.
14 Ibid, p 57.
15 Ibid, p 58.
16 Ibid, p 62.
17 Thomas Pakenham, *The Boer War,* p 473.
18 Ibid, p 235.
19 Hancock, *Smuts: The Sanguine Years,* p 125.
20 Ibid, p 126.
21 Trewhella Cameron, *Jan Smuts: An Illustrated Biography,* p 37.

CHAPTER 5
FIGHTING THE BRITISH

1 FS Crafford, *Jan Smuts: A Biography,* p 46.
2 JC Smuts, *Jan Christian Smuts*, p 66.
3 Thomas Pakenham, *The Boer War,* p 522.
4 Deneys Reitz, *Commando: A Boer Journal of the Boer War*, p 210.
5 Reitz, *Commando*, p 221.
6 Hancock, *Smuts: The Sanguine Years,* p 139.
7 Reitz, *Commando*, p 223.
8 Pakenham, *The Boer War*, p 523.
9 Reitz, *Commando*, p 230.
10 Pakenham, *The Boer War*, p 525.
11 Hancock, *Smuts: The Sanguine Years,* p 140.
12 Ibid.
13 Reitz, *Commando*, p 299.
14 Piet Meiring, *Smuts the Patriot*, p 47.
15 Reitz, *Commando*, p 240.
16 Crafford, *Jan Smuts*, p 55.

17 Hancock, *Smuts: The Sanguine Years*, p 142.
18 Ibid.
19 Ibid, p 143.
20 Meredith, *Diamonds, Gold and War*, p 459.
21 Crafford, *Jan Smuts*, p 57.
22 Reitz, *Commando*, p 320.
23 Hancock, *Smuts: The Sanguine Years*, p 151.
24 Crafford, *Jan Smuts*, p 61.
25 Trewhella Cameron, *Jan Smuts: An Illustrated Biography*, p 43.

CHAPTER 6
AFTERMATH

1 HC Armstrong, *Grey Steel: JC Smuts – A Study in Arrogance*, p 149.
2 Mark Mazower, *No Enchanted Palace: The End of Empire and the Ideological Origins of the United Nations*, p 20.
3 RW Johnson, *South Africa: The First Man, The Last Nation*, p 106.
4 Piet Beukes, *The Romantic Smuts*, p 35.
5 Ibid, p 29.
6 Armstrong, *Grey Steel*, p 158.
7 Ibid, p 159.
8 Smuts, *Jan Christian Smuts*, p 96.
9 Antony Lentin, *Jan Smuts: Man of Courage and Vision*, p 21.
10 WK Hancock, *Smuts: The Sanguine Years*, p 215.
11 Lentin, *Jan Smuts*, p 21.
12 Piet Beukes, *The Holistic Smuts: A Study in Personality*, p 142.
13 Hancock, *Smuts: The Sanguine Years*, p 228.

CHAPTER 7
NATION BUILDER

1 Piet Beukes, *The Holistic Smuts: A Study in Personality*, p 145.
2 *The Star*, Johannesburg, quoted by Beukes, Ibid, p 144.
3 FS Crafford, *Jan Smuts: A Biography*, p 73.
4 WK Hancock, *Smuts: The Sanguine Years 1870–1919*, p 233.
5 Crafford, *Jan Smuts*, p 76.
6 Piet Meiring, *Smuts the Patriot*, p 67.
7 Ibid, p 71.
8 Hancock, *Smuts: The Sanguine Years*, p 231.
9 GHL le May, quoted by O Geyser, *Jan Smuts and his International Contemporaries*, p 67.
10 Basil Williams, *Botha, Smuts and South Africa*, p 57.
11 Hancock, *Smuts: The Sanguine Years*, p 250.
12 Ibid, p 247.
13 Martin Meredith, *Diamonds, Gold and War: The Making of South Africa*, p 512.
14 Ibid, p 513.
15 Hancock, *Smuts: The Sanguine Years*, p 221.
16 Bernard Friedman, *Smuts: A Reappraisal*, p 20.
17 Hancock, *Smuts: The Sanguine Years*, p 256.
18 Ibid, p 253.
19 Ibid.
20 Ibid, p 233.
21 HC Armstrong, *Grey Steel*, p 211.
22 Friedman, *Smuts*, p 33.
23 Crafford, *Jan Smuts*, p 85.
24 Hermann Giliomee, *The Afrikaners: Biography of a People*, p 276.
25 Crafford, *Jan Smuts*, p 87.
26 Meredith, *Diamonds, Gold and War*, p 515.
27 Hermann Giliomee & Bernard Mbenga, *New History of South Africa*, p 231.
28 Hancock, *Smuts: The Sanguine Years*, p 280.
29 Meredith, *Diamonds, Gold and War*, p 517.
30 Ibid.
31 Ibid.
32 Ibid, p 519.
33 Sarah Gertrude Millin, *General Smuts*, p 251.

CHAPTER 8
REBELLION

1 FS Crafford, *Jan Smuts: A Biography*, p 95.
2 Sarah Gertrude Millin, *General Smuts*, p 260.
3 WK Hancock, *Smuts: The Sanguine Years 1870–1919*, p 243.
4 Ibid, p 357.
5 Ibid, p 358.
6 He was to exchange the ministries of mines and the interior for finance in 1912–13.
7 Millin, *General Smuts*, p 237.
8 Crafford, *Jan Smuts*, p 77.
9 Hancock, *Smuts: The Sanguine Years*, p 324.
10 O Geyser, *Jan Smuts and his International Contemporaries*, p 120.
11 Ibid, p 132.
12 Hancock, *Smuts: The Sanguine Years*, p 345.
13 Ibid, p 364.
14 Crafford, *Jan Smuts*, p 103.
15 Ibid.
16 According to Crafford (Ibid, p 105), four of the deportees returned to South Africa in due course. One actually became a party organiser for Smuts's SAP; another became a leading member of the Chamber of Mines; a third went into government service; and a fourth became an MP.
17 Ibid.
18 Hancock, *Smuts: The Sanguine Years*, p 380.
19 Crafford, *Smuts*, p 107.
20 Ibid, p 381.
21 Hermann Giliomee & Bernard Mbenga, *New History of South Africa*, p 237.
22 Bill Nasson, *WWI and the People Of South Africa*, p 80.
23 Hancock, *Smuts: The Sanguine Years*, p 383
24 Giliomee & Mbenga, *New History of South Africa*, p 239.
25 Piet Meiring, *Smuts the Patriot*, p 84.
26 Basil Williams, *Botha, Smuts and South Africa*, p 92.
27 Ibid.

CHAPTER 9
ON BRITAIN'S SIDE

1 WK Hancock, *Smuts: The Sanguine Years 1870–1919*, p 378.
2 Gerald L'Ange, *Urgent Imperial Service. South African Forces in German South West Africa 1914–1915*, p 3.
3 Ibid, p 4.
4 JC Smuts, *Jan Christian Smuts*, p 156.
5 David Williams, *Springboks, Troepies and Cadres: Stories of the South African Army 1912–2012*, p 4.
6 Hancock, *Smuts: The Sanguine Years*, p 400.
7 Bill Nasson, 'Jan Smuts, His Different Dominion, and the Great War', Smuts Memorial Lecture, Cape Town, 12 September 2014.
8 L'Ange, *Urgent Imperial Service*, p 333.
9 Ibid, p 330.
10 Hermann Giliomee & Bernard Mbenga, *New History of South Africa*, p 240.
11 Hancock, *Smuts: The Sanguine Years*, p 401.
12 Smuts, *Jan Christian Smuts*, p 159.
13 Hancock, *Smuts, The Sanguine Years*, p 402.
14 Sarah Gertrude Millin, *General Smuts*, p 334.
15 Kenneth Ingham, *Jan Christian Smuts: The Conscience of a South African*, p 84.
16 Lawrence James, *Churchill and Empire: Portrait of an Imperialist*, p 92.
17 Ross Anderson , quoted by David Williams, *Springboks, Troepies and Cadres*, p 20.
18 FS Crafford, *Jan Smuts: A Biography*, p 125.
19 Ibid, p 124.
20 HC Armstrong; *Grey Steel: JC Smuts – A Study in Arrogance*, p 261.
21 Ibid, p 263.
22 Hancock, *Smuts: The Sanguine Years*, p 414.
23 Ingham, *Jan Christian Smuts*, p 84.
24 Crafford, *Jan Smuts*, p 130.
25 Ibid, p 131.

26 Nasson, see note 7.
27 Ibid.
28 Hancock, *Smuts: The Sanguine Years*, p 421.
29 Ingham, *Jan Christian Smuts*, p 86.
30 Crafford, *Jan Smuts*, p 125.
31 Von Lettow-Vorbeck successfully evaded capture for the duration of the war. On 13 November, two days after the Armistice was signed in Europe, he agreed to a ceasefire and surrendered his army on 23 November 1918.
32 Hancock, *Smuts: The Sanguine Years*, pp 412, 416.
33 Ibid, p 419.
34 Ross Anderson, quoted by David Williams, *Springboks, Troepies and Cadres*, p 26.
35 Piet Meiring, *Smuts the Patriot*, p 86.
36 Crafford, *Jan Smuts*, p 133.

CHAPTER 10
'ON SERVICE FOR HUMANITY'

1 FS Crafford, *Jan Smuts: A Biography*, p 134.
2 Ibid.
3 Hancock, *Smuts, The Sanguine Years*, p 438.
4 Kenneth Ingham, *Jan Christian Smuts: The Conscience of a South African*, p 90.
5 Trewhella Cameron, *Jan Smuts*, p 77.
6 Antony Lentin, *Jan Smuts: Man of Courage and Vision*, p 37
7 Joan Joseph, *South African Statesman Jan Christiaan Smuts*, p 127.
8 Antony Lentin, *Jan Smuts*, p 34.
9 O Geyser, *Jan Smuts and his International Contemporaries*, p 79.
10 WK Hancock, *Smuts, The Sanguine Years*, p 430.
11 Ibid, p 431.
12 Ibid.
13 Crafford, *Jan Smuts: A Biography*, p 137.
14 Hancock, *Smuts, The Sanguine Years*, p 432.
15 Ibid, p 433.
16 Ibid, p 435.
17 Ibid, p 436.
18 Ibid, p 437.
19 Crafford, *Jan Smuts*, p 147.
20 Geyser, *Jan Smuts and his International Contemporaries*, p 85.
21 Crafford, *Jan Smuts*, p 151.
22 Ibid, p 146.
23 Hancock, *Smuts: The Sanguine Years*, p 456.
24 Ibid, p 477.
25 Crafford, p 158
26 FP Walters, *A History of the League of Nations*, vol 1, p 27.
27 Mark Mazower, *No Enchanted Palace: The End of Empire and the Ideological Origins of the United Nations*, p 20.

CHAPTER 11
LOSING THE PEACE

1 WK Hancock, *Smuts: The Sanguine Years 1870–1919*, p 507.
2 Antony Lentin, *Jan Smuts: Man of Courage and Vision*, p 60.
3 Ibid, p 62.
4 Hancock, *Smuts: The Sanguine Years*, p 517.
5 Margaret MacMillan, *Peacemakers – Six Months that Changed the World*, p 190.
6 Frank Welsh, *A History of South Africa*, p 387.
7 Lentin, *Jan Smuts: Man of Courage and Vision*, p 77.
8 Hancock, *Smuts: The Sanguine Years*, p 512.
9 Ibid, p 528.
10 Hancock & Van der Poel, *Selections from the Smuts Papers*, Vol IV, p 218.
11 Ibid, p 221.
12 Hancock, *Smuts: The Sanguine Years*, p 532.
13 HC Armstrong, *Grey Steel: JC Smuts – A Study in Arrogance*, p 315.
14 Joan Joseph, *South African Statesman Jan Christiaan Smuts*, p 137.
15 Ibid, p 138.
16 Hancock, *Smuts: The Sanguine Years*, p 555.
17 Ibid, p 557.

18 Hancock & Van der Poel, *Selections from the Smuts Papers*, Vol IV, p 288.

CHAPTER 12
A RELUCTANT PRIME MINISTER

1   JC Smuts, *Jan Christian Smuts,* p 244.
2   Ibid.
3   Kenneth Ingham, *Jan Christian Smuts: The Conscience of a South African,* p 118.
4   Trewhella Cameron, *Jan Smuts: An Illustrated Biography,* p 83.
5   FS Crafford, *Jan Smuts: A Biography,* p 187.
6   Ibid, p 83.
7   WK Hancock, *Smuts: The Sanguine Years 1870–1919,* p 558.
8   Smuts, *Jan Christian Smuts,* p 248.
9   Crafford, *Jan Smuts,* p 188.
10 Ingham, *Jan Christian Smuts,* p 122.
11 Smuts, *Jan Christian Smuts,* p 248.
12 Crafford, *Jan Smuts,* p 198.
13 TRH Davenport, *South Africa: A Modern History,* p 252.
14 Ingham, *Jan Christian Smuts,* p 126.
15 WK Hancock, *Smuts: The Fields of Force 1919–1950,* p 38.
16 Ibid, p 41.
17 Mark Mazower, *No Enchanted Palace: The End of Empire and the Ideological Origins of the United Nations,* p 34.
18 Hancock, *Smuts: The Fields of Force,* pp 41–42.
19 Ingham, *Jan Christian Smuts,* p 127.
20 O Geyser, *Jan Smuts and his International Contemporaries,* p 150.
21 Smuts, *Jan Christian Smuts,* p 252.
22 Ingham, *Jan Christian Smuts,* p 128.
23 Antony Lentin, *Jan Smuts: Man of Courage and Vision,* p 126.
24 Hancock, *Smuts: The Fields of Force,* p 44.
25 Cameron, *Jan Smuts,* p 87.
26 Ibid, p 59.
27 Crafford, *Jan Smuts,* p 217.
28 Ibid, p 220.
29 Hancock, *Smuts: The Fields of Force,* p 84.
30 Ibid, p 135.
31 Ibid, p 155.
32 Ibid, p 156.
33 Crafford, *Jan Smuts,* p 233.
34 Cameron, *Jan Smuts,* p 96.
35 Crafford, *Jan Smuts,* p 234.
36 Cameron, *Jan Smuts,* p 97.

CHAPTER 13
MODEL OF RESTRAINT

1   WK Hancock, *Smuts: The Fields of Force 1919–1950,* p 189.
2   http://en.wikipedia.org.wiki/Jan Smuts.
3   Hancock, *Smuts: The Fields of Force,* p 191.
4   Roy Campbell, from 'The Wayzgoose' (1928).
5   JC Smuts, *Jan Christian Smuts,* p 288.
6   Ibid, p 290.
7   FS Crafford, *Jan Smuts: A Biography,* p 237.
8   Trewhella Cameron, *Jan Smuts: An Illustrated Biography,* p 110.
9   Hancock, *Smuts: The Fields of Force,* p 199.
10 Crafford, *Jan Smuts,* p 242.
11 Hancock, *Smuts: The Fields of Force,* p 200.
12 Hermann Giliomee & Bernard Mbenga, *New History of South Africa,* p 252.
13 Hancock, *Smuts: The Fields of Force,* p 209.
14 Cameron, *Jan Smuts,* p 113.
15 Kenneth Ingham, *Jan Christian Smuts,* p 170.
16 Hancock, *Smuts: The Fields of Force,* p 238.
17 Lindie Koorts, *DF Malan and the Rise of Afrikaner Nationalism,* p 242.
18 Cameron, *Jan Smuts,* p 115.
19 Ibid.
20 Ibid.
21 Ibid.
22 *Cape Times,* quoted by Kenneth Ingham, *Jan Christian Smuts,* p 164.
23 Smuts, *Jan Christian Smuts,* p 298.
24 Crafford, *Jan Smuts,* p 259.
25 Smuts, *Jan Christian Smuts,* p 314.
26 Ibid, p 314.

27 Hancock, *Smuts: The Fields of Force*, p 234.
28 'Climate and Man in Africa', *South African Journal of Science*, vol 29, 1932.
29 Ibid, p 236.

CHAPTER 14
ACHIEVING THE UNTHINKABLE

1 Trewhella Cameron, *Jan Smuts: An Illustrated Biography*, p 118.
2 Hermann Giliomee, *The Afrikaners: Biography of a People*, p 336.
3 WK Hancock, *Smuts: The Fields of Force 1919–1950*, p 237.
4 Ibid.
5 JC Smuts, *Jan Christian Smuts*, p 341.
6 Quoted by Basil Williams, *Botha, Smuts and South Africa*, p 147.
7 Hermann Giliomee & Bernard Mbenga, *New History of South Africa*, p 285.
8 Kenneth Ingham, *Jan Christian Smuts: The Conscience of a South African*, p 182.
9 Hancock, *Smuts: The Fields of Force*, p 286.
10 Giliomee, *The Afrikaners*, p 346.
11 Basil Williams, *Botha, Smuts and South Africa*, p 134.
12 Smuts, *Jan Christian Smuts*, p 354.
13 Ibid, p 357.
14 Ibid, p 362.
15 Ibid, p 364.
16 FS Crafford, *Jan Smuts: A Biography*, p 277.
17 Cameron, *Jan Smuts*, p 130.
18 Hancock, *Smuts: The Fields of Force*, p 259.
19 Ibid, p 231.
20 Ingham, *Jan Christian Smuts*, p 188.
21 Cameron, *Jan Smuts*, p 131.
22 JC Smuts, *Jan Smuts*, p 372
23 Cameron, *Jan Smuts*, p 135.
24 Crafford, *Jan Smuts*, p 282.

CHAPTER 15
WAR LEADER

1 WK Hancock, *Smuts – The Fields of*

Force 1919–1950, p 329.
2 Ibid, p 331.
3 Ibid.
4 Ibid, p 333.
5 Hermann Giliomee & Bernard Mbenga: *New History of South Africa*, p 295.
6 Ibid, p 301.
7 Hancock, *Smuts: The Fields of Force 1919–1950*, p 338.
8 FS Crafford, *Jan Smuts: A Biography*, p 288.
9 Lindie Koorts, *DF Malan and the Rise of Afrikaner Nationalism*, p 350.
10 Giliomee & Mbenga, *New History of South Africa*, p 301.
11 Crafford, *Jan Smuts*, p 306.
12 Trewhella Cameron, *Jan Smuts: An Illustrated Biography*, pp 142–3.
13 Ibid, p 143.
14 Kenneth Ingham, *Jan Christian Smuts: The Conscience of a South African*, p 210.
15 Hancock, *Smuts: The Fields of Force*, p 355.
16 JC Smuts, *Jan Christian Smuts*, pp 404–05.
17 Ibid, p 414.
18 Ibid, p 419.
19 Cameron, *Jan Smuts*, p 147.
20 Smuts, *Jan Christian Smuts*, p 403.
21 Koorts, *DF Malan*, p 346.
22 Crafford, *Jan Smuts*, p 321.
23 Smuts, *Jan Christian Smuts*, p 416.
24 Ibid.
25 Ibid, p 420.
26 Crafford, *Jan Smuts*, p 316.
27 Cameron, *Jan Smuts*, p 149.
28 Crafford, *Jan Smuts*, p 319.
29 Smuts, *Jan Christian Smuts*, p 426.
30 Crafford, *Jan Smuts*, p 322.
31 Hancock, *Smuts: The Fields of Force*, p 370.
32 Ibid, p 372.
33 Ibid, p 381.
34 Ibid, p 382.
35 Cameron, *Jan Smuts*, p 152.
36 Hancock, *Smuts: The Fields of Force*, p 384.
37 Ibid.
38 Ibid, p 385.

CHAPTER 16
'WE, THE UNITED NATIONS'

1 WK Hancock, *Smuts: The Fields of Force 1919–1950*, p 415.
2 David Reynolds, *In Command of History*, p 377.
3 JC Smuts, *Jan Christian Smuts*, p 439.
4 Trewhella Cameron, *Jan Smuts: An Illustrated Biography*, p 154.
5 Smuts, *Jan Christian Smuts*, p 442.
6 O Geyser, *Jan Smuts and his International Contemporaries*, p 185.
7 Smuts, *Jan Christian Smuts*, p 448.
8 Ibid, p 251.
9 Ibid, p 452.
10 Ibid, p 453.
11 Ibid, p 456.
12 Ibid.
13 Ibid, p 457.
14 Cameron, *Jan Smuts*, p 155.
15 Hancock, *Smuts: The Fields of Force*, p 422.
16 Cameron, *Jan Smuts*, p 156.
17 Kenneth Ingham, *Jan Christian Smuts: The Conscience of a South African*, p 231.
18 Cameron, *Jan Smuts*, p 157.
19 Smuts, *Jan Christian Smuts*, p 461.
20 Hancock, *Smuts: The Fields of Force*, 421.
21 Smuts, *Jan Christian Smuts*, p 462.
22 Mark Mazower, *No Enchanted Palace: The End of Empire and the Ideological Origins of the United Nations*, p 128.
23 Hancock, *Smuts: The Fields of Force*, p 432.
24 Ibid.
25 Mazower, *No Enchanted Palace*, p 29.
26 Ibid, p 433.
27 Smuts, *Jan Christian Smuts*, p 469.
28 Ibid, p 472.
29 Mazower, *No Enchanted Palace*, p 31.
30 Ibid.
31 Cameron, *Jan Smuts*, p 159.
32 Smuts, *Jan Christian Smuts*, p 475.
33 Cameron, *Jan Smuts*, p 158.
34 Ibid, p 159.
35 Mazower, *No Enchanted Palace*, p 65.
36 Ibid.
37 Smuts, *Jan Christian Smuts*, p 484.

CHAPTER 17
A YEAR OF SADNESS

1 WK Hancock, *Smuts: The Fields of Force 1919–1950*, p 444
2 Trewhella Cameron, *Jan Smuts: An Illustrated Biography*, p 163.
3 Ibid, p 169.
4 JC Smuts, *Jan Christian Smuts*, p 498.
5 Mark Mazower, *No Enchanted Palace: The End of Empire and the Ideological Origins of the United Nations*, p 189.
6 Ibid, p 28.
7 Ibid, p 29.
8 Kenneth Ingham, *Jan Christian Smuts: The Conscience of a South African*, p 237.
9 Smuts, *Jan Christian Smuts*, p 500.
10 Hancock, *Smuts: The Fields of Force*, p 470.
11 Ingham, *Jan Christian Smuts*, p 238.
12 Cameron, *Jan Smuts*, p 163.
13 Ibid, p 164.
14 TRH Davenport, *South Africa: A Modern History*, p 320.
15 Cameron, *Jan Smuts*, p 171.
16 Ibid.
17 Hancock, *Smuts: The Fields of Force*, p 497.
18 Ibid, p 500.
19 Smuts, *Jan Christian Smuts*, p 506.
20 Arthur Herman, *Gandhi & Churchill: The Epic Rivalry That Destroyed an Empire and Forged our Age*, p 601.
21 Hancock, *Smuts: The Fields of Force*, p 502.
22 Piet van der Byl, *The Shadows Lengthen*, p 63.
23 Ibid, p 60.
24 Ibid, p 63.
25 Cameron, *Jan Smuts*, p 175.
26 Ibid, p 175.

CHAPTER 18
LAST CLIMB

1 WK Hancock, *Smuts: The Fields of Force 1919–1950*, p 508.
2 Ibid, p 511.
3 JC Smuts, *Jan Christian Smuts*, p 513.
4 Hancock, *Smuts: The Fields of Force*, p 517.

5 Smuts, *Jan Christian Smuts*, p 513.
6 Hancock, *Smuts: The Fields of Force*, p 513.
7 Trewhella Cameron, *Jan Smuts: An Illustrated Biography*, p 180.
8 Ibid, p 180.
9 Ibid, p 179.
10 Smuts, *Jan Christian Smuts*, p 521.
11 Ibid, p 521.
12 Hancock, *Smuts: The Fields of Force*, p 522.
13 Ibid, p 525.
14 Cameron, *Jan Smuts*, p 186.
15 Ibid.
16 Smuts, *Jan Christian Smuts*, p 523.
17 Ibid, p 527.

CHAPTER 19
FORGED FROM STEEL

1 Leif Egeland, in Zelda Friedlander, *Jan Smuts Remembered*, p 28.
2 HC Armstrong, *Grey Steel: JC Smuts – A Study in Arrogance*, p 10.
3 'Smuts – The Man Behind the Legend', *Reader's Digest*, vol 123, October 1982, p 57.
4 Gail Nattrass and SB Spies, *Jan Christiaan Smuts: Memoirs of the Boer War*, p 19.
5 Edgar Brookes, in Zelda Friedlander, *Jan Smuts Remembered*, p 19.
6 Ibid.
7 WK Hancock, *Smuts, The Sanguine Years 1870–1919*, p 80.
8 Leslie Blackwell, *Blackwell Remembers*, p 97.
9 Harry Lawrence, in Zelda Friedlander, *Jan Smuts Remembered*, p 50.
10 JC Smuts, *Jan Christian Smuts*, p 26.
11 Ibid, p 241.
12 Kathleen Minscher, *I Lived in His Shadow*, p 34.
13 JC Smuts, *Jan Christian Smuts*, p 328.
14 Sarah Gertrude Millin, *General Smuts*, p 17.
15 Daphne Moore, in Zelda Friedlander, *Jan Smuts Remembered*, p 59.
16 Kenneth Ingham, *Jan Christian Smuts: The Conscience of a South African*, p 211.
17 JC Smuts, *Jan Christian Smuts*, xv-xvi.
18 Millin, *General Smuts*, p 19.
19 Minscher, *I Lived in His Shadow*, p 91.
20 Harry Lawrence, in Zelda Friedlander, *Jan Smuts Remembered*, p 51.
21 JC Smuts, *Jan Christian Smuts*, p 401.
22 Ibid, p 264.
23 Piet Beukes, *The Holistic Smuts: A Study in Personality*, p 38.
24 FS Crafford, *Jan Smuts: A Biography*, p 109.
25 Smuts, *Jan Christian Smuts*, p 236.
26 Crafford, *Jan Smuts: A Biography*, p 219.
27 Beukes, *The Holistic Smuts*, p 37.
28 Alan Paton, quoted by Beukes, Ibid, p 37.
29 Ingham, *Jan Christian Smuts*, p 7.
30 Ibid, p 23.
31 Piet Meiring, *Smuts the Patriot*, p 179.
32 Leif Egeland, in Zelda Friedlander, *Jan Smuts Remembered*, p 33.
33 Piet van der Byl, *The Shadows Lengthen*, p 63.
34 EG Malherbe, *Never a Dull Moment*, p 278.
35 Beukes, *The Holistic Smuts*, p 186.
36 Ibid, p 187.
37 Ibid, p 186.
38 Ibid, p 190.
39 Ibid, p 191.

CHAPTER 20
'A REFUGE FOR STOICS'

1 JC Smuts, *Jan Christian Smuts*, p 120.
2 Ibid, p 122.
3 Ibid, p 121.
4 Ibid.
5 Ibid, p 271.
6 Author's interviews with granddaughters Mary Hehir and Mary Smuts.
7 JC Smuts, *Jan Christian Smuts*, p 271.
8 FS Crafford, *Jan Smuts: A Biography*, p 246.
9 JC Smuts, *Jan Christian Smuts*, p 276.
10 Kathleen Minscher, *I Lived in His*

Shadow, p 33.

11 Sarah Gertrude Millin, *General Smuts*, p 265.

12 Ibid, p 266.

13 Ibid.

14 Minscher, *I Lived in His Shadow*, p 35.

15 Piet Beukes, *The Romantic Smuts*, p 126.

16 WK Hancock, *Smuts: The Fields of Force 1919–1950*, p 342.

17 Kenneth Ingham, *Jan Christian Smuts: The Conscience of a South African*, p 242.

18 T Cameron, *Jan Smuts: An Illustrated Biography*, p 141.

19 Crafford, *Jan Smuts*, p 250.

CHAPTER 21
AT EASE WITH WOMEN

1 Piet Beukes, *The Romantic Smuts*, p 7.

2 Ibid.

3 Basil Williams, *Botha, Smuts and South Africa*, p 126.

4 JC Smuts, *Jan Christian Smuts*, p 244.

5 Piet Beukes, *The Holistic Smuts: A Study in Personality*, p 67.

6 JC Smuts, *Jan Christian Smuts*, p 119.

7 FV Engelenburg, quoted in Beukes, *The Holistic Smuts*, p 71.

8 Beukes, *The Romantic Smuts*, p 16.

9 Ibid, p 24.

10 Ibid, p 9.

11 Ibid.

12 Ibid, p 15.

13 Ibid, p 30.

14 Ibid, p 18.

15 JC Smuts, *Jan Christian Smuts*, p 95.

16 Beukes, *The Romantic Smuts*, p 146.

17 WK Hancock, *Smuts: The Sanguine Years 1870–1919*, p 460.

18 Ibid, p 460. In September 1920, an unwell Olive returned suddenly to South Africa and only three months later died alone in Wynberg, Cape, at the age of 65, in severe pain from her chronic illness.

19 Beukes, *The Romantic Smuts*, p 55.

20 Ibid, p 56.

21 Kenneth Ingham, *Jan Christian Smuts: The Conscience of a South African*, p 51.

22 Beukes, *The Romantic Smuts*, p 65.

23 Ibid, p 50.

24 Hancock, *Smuts: The Sanguine Years*, p 44.

25 Ibid, p 443.

26 Ibid.

27 Ibid, p 403.

28 WK Hancock, *Smuts: The Fields of Force 1919–1950*, p 404.

29 Ibid, p 405.

30 Beukes, *The Romantic Smuts*, p 117.

31 Hancock, *Smuts: The Fields of Force*, p 405.

32 Ibid, p 406.

33 Beukes, *The Romantic Smuts*, p 119.

34 Hancock, *Smuts: The Fields of Force*, footnote, p 406.

35 Beukes, *The Romantic Smuts*, p 12.

36 Ibid, p 124.

37 Daphne Moore, quoted by Beukes, Ibid, p 126.

38 Beukes, Ibid, pp 127-8.

39 Ibid, p 128.

40 Ibid, p 139.

41 Ibid.

42 Ibid, p 140.

43 Ibid, p 142.

44 Ibid.

45 Ibid, p 158 et seq.

CHAPTER 22
FINDING ORDER IN COMPLEXITY

1 Piet Beukes, *The Holistic Smuts: A Study in Personality*, p 46.

2 Ibid, p 46.

3 WK Hancock, *Smuts: The Sanguine Years 1870–1919*, p 49.

4 Ibid, p 50.

5 Beukes, *The Holistic Smuts*, p 60.

6 Charles Darwin, quoted by Beukes, Ibid, p 62.

7 Ibid, p 62.

8 Ibid, p 84.

9 Ibid, p 73.

10 Ibid, p 87.

11 Ibid, p 88.

12 N Levi, *Jan Smuts*, quoted by Beukes, Ibid, p 89.

13 Alan Paton, *Hofmeyr*, p 92.

14 Hancock, *Smuts: The Sanguine Years*, p 170.

15 JC Smuts, *Jan Christian Smuts*, p 287.
16 Leslie Blackwell, *Blackwell Remembers*, p 98.
17 Beukes, *The Holistic Smuts*, p 115.
18 Smuts, *Jan Christian Smuts*, p 290.
19 Hancock, *Smuts: The Sanguine Years*, p 306.
20 Ibid, p 300.
21 Beukes, *The Holistic Smuts*, p 123.
22 WK Hancock, *Smuts: The Fields of Force 1919–1950*, p 170.
23 Hancock, *Smuts: The Sanguine Years*, p 307.
24 Beukes, The Holistic Smuts, p 128.
25 Ibid, p 133.
26 Ibid, p 209.
27 Smuts, *Jan Christian Smuts*, p 292.
28 Kenneth Ingham; *Jan Christian Smuts – The Conscience of a South African,* p 222.
29 Alan Paton, *Hofmeyr*, pp 64–65
30 Beukes, *The Holistic Smuts*, pp 198–9.
31 Ibid, p 202.
32 Ibid, p 37.
33 Ingham, *Jan Christian Smuts*, p 7.
34 Hancock, *Smuts: The Fields of Force*, p 509.
35 Ds Reyneke, in Zelda Friedlander, *Jan Smuts Remembered*, p 72.

CHAPTER 23
'OUR WISEST ECOLOGIST'

1 WK Hancock, *Smuts: The Fields of Force 1919–1950,* p 177.
2 JC Smuts, *Jan Christian Smuts*, p 331.
3 Hancock, *Smuts: The Fields of Force*, p 174.
4 Ibid, p 174.
5 Smuts, *Jan Christian Smuts*, p 333.
6 Trewhella Cameron, *Jan Smuts: An Illustrated Biography*, p 101.
7 Smuts, *Jan Christian Smuts*, pp 335–6.
8 Hancock, *Smuts: The Fields of Force*, p 222.
9 Ibid, pp 232–235.
10 Ibid, p 235.
11 Ibid, p 236.
12 Piet Beukes, *Smuts The Botanist,* p 101.
13 Ibid, p 84.
14 Smuts, *Jan Christian Smuts*, p 339.
15 Beukes, *Smuts The Botanist*, p 87.
16 Cameron, *Jan Smuts*, p 101.
17 Smuts, *Jan Christian Smuts*, p 335.
18 Beukes, *Smuts The Botanist*, p 83.
19 Ibid, p 83.
20 Dr IB Pole Evans, quoted in Cameron, *Jan Smuts*, p 103.
21 Prof JFV Phillips, in Zelda Friedlander, *Jan Smuts Remembered*, p 63.

CHAPTER 24
AN UNCERTAIN TRUMPET

1 Edgar Brookes, in Zelda Friedlander, *Jan Smuts Remembered*, p 20.
2 Bernard Friedman, *Smuts: A Reappraisal*, p 86.
3 WK Hancock, *Smuts: The Sanguine Years 1870–1919,* pp 311–12.
4 Piet Beukes, *The Holistic Smuts: A Study in Personality,* p 120.
5 Hancock, *Smuts: The Sanguine Years*, p 56.
6 Kenneth Ingham, *Jan Christian Smuts: The Conscience of a South African*, p 9.
7 Beukes, *The Holistic Smuts*, p 191.
8 Hancock, *Smuts: The Sanguine Years*, p 30.
9 Ibid, p 57.
10 Ingham, *Jan Christian Smuts*, p 14.
11 Hancock, Smuts: The Sanguine Years, p 55.
12 Lincoln-Douglas debate, Charleston, Illinois, 18 September 1858, http://en.wikipedia.org/wiki/Lincoln%E2%80%93Douglas_debates.
13 Hancock, *Smuts: The Sanguine Years*, p 317.
14 Ibid, p 316.
15 Beukes, *The Holistic Smuts*, p 192.
16 JC Smuts, *Jan Christian Smuts*, pp 192–196.
17 WK Hancock, *Smuts: The Fields of Force 1919–1950*, p 113.
18 Ibid, p 120.

19 Ibid, p 121.
20 Ibid, p 126.
21 Ingham, *Jan Christian Smuts*, p 154.
22 Hancock, *Smuts: The Fields of Force*, p 213.
23 Ingham, Jan Christian Smuts, p 160.
24 Trewhella Cameron, *Jan Smuts: An Illustrated Biography*, p 113.
25 Ibid, p 115.
26 Ibid.
27 Ibid,
28 Hancock, *Smuts: The Fields of Force*, p 259.
29 Cameron, Jan Smuts, p 131.
30 Ibid.
31 Friedman, *Smuts*, p 118.
32 Ibid, p 119.
33 TRH Davenport, *South Africa: A Modern History*, p 297.
34 Hancock, *Smuts: The Fields of Force*, p 475.
35 Ibid, p 476.
36 Saul Dubow, 'Smuts, the United Nations and the Rhetoric of Race and Rights', *Journal of Contemporary History*, vol 43 (1), pp 43–72.
37 Hancock, *Smuts: The Fields of Force*, p 476.
38 Ibid, p 485.
39 Ibid, p 486.
40 Ibid, p 487.
41 Ibid.
42 Christof Heyns and Willem Gravett, Faculty of Law, University of Pretoria, draft article submitted for publication, 2014.
43 Ibid.
44 Hancock, *Smuts: The Fields of Force*, p 489.
45 Enoch Powell, *Joseph Chamberlain*, p 151.

CHAPTER 25
COUNSELLOR TO KINGS

1 A Scott Berg, *Wilson*.
2 Ibid, p 11.
3 Another strange similarity between Smuts and Wilson was that they both enjoyed close but chaste relationships with married women who were not their wives. Wilson wrote regularly and prolifically to a Mary Hulbert Peck about sensitive matters he felt unable to discuss with his wife or other men.
4 Margaret MacMillan, *Peacemakers: Six Months that Changed the World*, p 97.
5 Mark Mazower, *No Enchanted Palace: The End of Empire and the Ideological Origins of the United Nations*, p 44.
6 Berg, Wilson, p 9.
7 From Alexander I George and Juliette L George, *Woodrow Wilson and Colonel House: A Personality Study*, p 120.
8 MacMillan, *Peacemakers*, pp 97–8.
9 Ibid, p 98.
10 Kenneth Ingham, *Jan Christian Smuts*, p 101.
11 MacMillan, *Peacemakers*, p 99.
12 Ingham, *Jan Christian Smuts*, p 161.
13 Hancock & Van der Poel, *Selections from the Smuts Papers*, Vol IV, p 42.
14 Wilson actually believed as strongly as Smuts that imposing crushing terms on Germany would result in another war, but was unable to overcome the resistance of Clemenceau & co and had to settle for what JM Keynes described as 'a Carthaginian peace' – that is, the ruin of the German economy.
15 Hancock & Van der Poel, *Selections from the Smuts Papers*, Vol IV, p 209.
16 Ingham, *Jan Christian Smuts*, p 109.
17 Ibid, p 115.
18 Scott Berg, *Wilson*, p 705.
19 Ibid, p 705.
20 WK Hancock, *Smuts: The Fields of Force 1919–1950*, p 128.
21 Henry Kissinger, *World Order*, p 256 et seq.
22 Trewhella Cameron, *Jan Smuts: An Illustrated Biography*, p 176.
23 WK Hancock, *Smuts: The Sanguine Years 1870–1919*, p 444.
24 Ibid, p 521.
25 Ibid.
26 Ibid, pp 539–48.
27 JC Smuts, *Jan Christian Smuts*, p 432.

28 O Geyser, *Jan Smuts and his International Contemporaries*, p 99.
29 Ibid.
30 Ibid, p 100.
31 Ibid, p 101.
32 Lawrence James, *Churchill and Empire: Portrait of an Imperialist*, p 217.
33 Geyser, *Jan Smuts and his International Contemporaries*, p 104. Today, on Churchill's desk in the study preserved at Chartwell, his country home, there are several family photographs. The only non-family photo is one of Smuts.
34 John Colville, quoted in Geyser, Ibid, p 194.
35 Lord Moran, quoted in Geyser, Ibid, p 107.
36 Harold Macmillan, quoted in Geyser, Ibid, p 108.
37 Lord Alanbrooke, *War Diaries 1939–45*, pp 493–95
38 Cameron, Jan Smuts, p 160.
39 Ibid, p 161.
40 Leif Egeland, in Zelda Friedlander, *Jan Smuts Remembered*, p 31.
41 Cameron, Jan Smuts, p 117.
42 Ibid, p 172.
43 Ibid.
44 Hancock, *Smuts: The Fields of Force*, p 520.
45 FS Crafford, *Jan Smuts: A Biography*, p 153.
46 Geyser, *Jan Smuts and his International Contemporaries*, p 185.
47 Hancock, *Smuts: The Fields of Force*, p 130.

48 Antony Lentin, *Jan Smuts: Man of Courage and Vision*, p 145.
49 Geyser, *Jan Smuts and his International Contemporaries*, p 193.
50 Ibid, pp 194–95.
51 Ibid, p 195.
52 Ibid, p 198.
53 Hancock, *Smuts: The Fields of Force*, p 407.
54 Geyser, *Jan Smuts and his International Contemporaries*, p 161.
55 Ibid, p 162.
56 Ibid, p 166.
57 Ibid, p 174.
58 Hancock, *Smuts: The Fields of Force*, p 407.
59 Ibid, p 408.

CHAPTER 26
ENVOI

1 Hermann Giliomee, *The Last Afrikaner Leaders: A Supreme Test of Power*, p 13.
2 Kenneth Ingham, *Jan Christian Smuts: The Conscience of a South African*, p xi.
3 Nelson Mandela, *Long Walk to Freedom*, p 47.
4 Lawrence James, *Churchill and Empire: Portrait of an Imperialist*, p 183.
5 EG Malherbe, *Never A Dull Moment*, p 283.
6 Piet Meiring, *Smuts the Patriot*, p 2.
7 Ibid, p 195.

Select Bibliography

Alanbrooke, Field Marshal Lord, *War Diaries 1939–1945* (London, 2001).

Armstrong, HC, *Grey Steel: JC Smuts – A Study in Arrogance* (London, 1937).

Barlow, Arthur G, *Almost in Confidence* (Cape Town and Johannesburg, 1952).

Bateman, Philip, *Smuts: The Man Behind the Legend* (Reader's Digest, vol 123, 1982).

Beukes, Piet, *The Holistic Smuts: A Study in Personality* (Cape Town, 1989).

Beukes, Piet, *The Romantic Smuts: Women and Love in his Life* (Cape Town, 1992).

Beukes, Piet, *Smuts the Botanist: The Cape Flora and the Grasses of Africa* (Cape Town, 1996).

Berg, A Scott, *Wilson* (Great Britain, 2013).

Blackwell, Leslie, *Blackwell Remembers* (Cape Town, 1971).

Blom-Cooper QC, Louis, 'Jan Christiaan Smuts (1870–1950): Middle Templar extraordinary', article in *Advocate* (London, 2013).

Crafford, FS, *Jan Smuts: A Biography* (London and Cape Town, 1945).

Cameron, Trewhella, *Jan Smuts: An Illustrated Biography* (Cape Town, 1994).

Colville, Sir John, *The Fringes of Power: Downing Street Diaries* vol 1 (Great Britain, 1985).

Davenport, TRH, *South Africa: A Modern History*, 4th edition (Great Britain, 1991).

Dubow, Saul, 'Smuts, the United Nations and the Rhetoric of Race and Rights', *Journal of Contemporary History*, vol 43 (1) (SAGE Publications, 2008).

Friedlander, Zelda, *Jan Smuts Remembered* (Cape Town, 1970).

Friedman, Bernard, *Smuts: A Reappraisal* (Johannesburg, 1975).

Geyser, Ockert, *Jan Smuts and his International Contemporaries* (Johannesburg and London, 2001).

Giliomee, Hermann, *The Afrikaners: Biography of a People* (Cape Town, 2003).

Giliomee, Hermann, *The Last Afrikaner Leaders: A Supreme Test of Power* (Cape Town, 2012).

Giliomee, Hermann & Mbenga, Bernard, *New History of South Africa* (Cape Town, 2007).

Hancock, WK, *Smuts: The Sanguine Years 1870–1919* (Cambridge, 1962).

Hancock, WK, *Smuts: The Fields of Force 1919–1950* (Cambridge, 1968).

Hancock, WK & Van der Poel, J, *Selections from the Smuts Papers,* vols 1–4 (Cambridge, 1966).

Herman, Arthur, *Gandhi & Churchill – The Epic Rivalry that Destroyed an Empire and Forged our Age* (London, 2008).

Heyns, Christof and Gravett, Willem, Faculty of Law, University of Pretoria, draft paper submitted for publication, 2014.

Ingham, Kenneth, *Jan Christian Smuts: The Conscience of a South African* (London, 1986).

James, Lawrence, *Churchill and Empire: Portrait of an Imperialist* (Great Britain, 2013).

Johnson, RW, *South Africa – The First Man, The Last Nation* (London & Johannesburg, 2004).

Johnson, Boris, *The Churchill Factor: How One Man Made History* (Great Britain, 2014).

Joseph, Joan, *South African Statesman Jan Christiaan Smuts* (Folkestone, UK, 1970).

Kissinger, Henry, *World Order: Reflections on the Character of Nations and the Course of History* (London, 2014).

Koorts, Lindi, *DF Malan and the Rise of Afrikaner Nationalism* (Cape Town, 2014).

L'Ange, Gerald, *Urgent Imperial Service: South African Forces in German South West Africa* 1914–1915 (Johannesburg, 1991).

Lawrence, Jeremy, *Harry Lawrence* (Cape Town, 1978).

Lean, Phyllis Scarnell, *One Man in His Time*, The General Smuts War Veterans Foundation (Johannesburg, 1964).

Lentin, Antony, *Jan Smuts: Man of Courage and Vision* (Johannesburg and Cape Town, 2010).

Levi, N, *Jan Smuts* (London, 1917).

Mandela, Nelson, *Long Walk to Freedom* (London, 1994).

Mazower, Mark, *No Enchanted Palace: The End of Empire and the Ideological Origins of the United Nations* (Princeton University, 2009).

MacMillan, Margaret, *Peacemakers – Six Months that Changed the World* (London, 2001).

Malherbe, EG, *Never A Dull Moment* (Cape Town, 1981).

Meiring, Piet, *Smuts the Patriot* (Cape Town, 1975).

Meredith, Martin, *Diamonds, Gold and War: The Making of South Africa* (London & Johannesburg, 2007).

Millin, Sarah Gertrude, *General Smuts,* vols 1& 2 (London, 1936).

Minscher, Kathleen, *I Lived In His Shadow* (Cape Town, 1965).

Nasson, Bill, *WWI and the People of South Africa* (Cape Town, 2014).

Nasson, Bill, *Jan Smuts, His Different Dominion, and the Great War*: Smuts Memorial Lecture (Cape Town, 2014).

Nattrass, Gail and Spies, SB, *Jan Smuts: Memoirs of the Boer War* (Johannesburg, 1994).

Nimocks, Walter, *Milner's Young Men: The 'Kindergarten' in Edwardian Imperial Affairs* (London, 1970).

Pakenham, Thomas, *The Boer War* (Cape Town, 1979).

Pakenham, Thomas, *The Boer War,* illustrated edition (Britain and Johannesburg, 1993).

Paton, Alan, *Hofmeyr,* abridged edition (Cape Town 1971).

Reitz, Deneys, *Commando: A Boer Journal of the Boer War* (London, 1929).

Reynolds, David, *In Command of History: Churchill Fighting and Writing the Second World War* (London, 2004).

Smuts JC, *Jan Christian Smuts* (SA edition, 1952).

Van der Byl, Piet, *The Shadows Lengthen* (Cape Town, 1973).

Van Onselen, Charles, *The Fox and The Flies* (London, 2008).

Van Wyk, At, *Vyf Dae: Oorlogskrisis van 1939* (Cape Town, 1985).

Welsh, Frank, *A History of South Africa* (London, 1998).

Williams, Basil, *Botha, Smuts and South Africa* (London, 1946).

Williams, David, *Springboks, Troepies and Cadres: Stories of the South African Army 1912–2012* (Cape Town, 2012).

Newspapers

Rand Daily Mail

The Star

Cape Argus

Cape Times

Die Burger

Die Transvaler

Wikipedia, the free encylopedia: https://en.wikipedia.org/wiki/Jan Smuts

Acknowledgements

Many people have helped me by way of encouragement or advice. James Clarke and Tim Couzens kept urging me to write this book, so I burdened them with drafts; David Williams read every word as I went along and gave me much useful feedback; Gordon Forbes suggested the title; while Derek du Plessis, Eugene Ashton, Alfred LeMaitre and Christof Heyns made helpful contributions to various parts of the final text. I am grateful to all of them.

Members of the wider Smuts family, Phillip Weyers (especially), Mary Hehir and Bob and Mary Tait gave generously of their time, which was highly appreciated.

My thanks also go to Jonathan Ball, doyen of South African publishers, and Jeremy Boraine, who gauged the time to be right for another study of Smuts and encouraged its writing. Frances Perryer's interest in the subject and meticulous editing were of great value to me and the book's designer, Kevin Shenton, Ceri Prenter, Rhianne van der Linde and proofreader Valda Strauss were a pleasure to work with.

I hope to have not committed too many errors in the text, but such mistakes as there are, are my responsibility alone.

Richard Steyn

Index